MATLAB Recipes

A Problem-Solution Approach

Michael Paluszek
Stephanie Thomas

Apress®

MATLAB Recipes: A Problem-Solution Approach

Michael Paluszek
Princeton, New Jersey, USA

Stephanie Thomas
Princeton Junction, New Jersey, USA

ISBN-13 (pbk): 978-1-4842-0560-0
DOI 10.1007/978-1-4842-0559-4

ISBN-13 (electronic): 978-1-4842-0559-4

Library of Congress Control Number: 2015955885

Managing Director: Welmoed Spahr
Lead Editor: Steve Anglin
Technical Reviewer: Jonah Lissner
Editorial Board: Steve Anglin, Louise Corrigan, Jonathan Gennick, Robert Hutchinson,
    Michelle Lowman, James Markham, Susan McDermott, Matthew Moodie, Jeffrey Pepper,
    Douglas Pundick, Ben Renow-Clarke, Gwenan Spearing, Steve Weiss
Coordinating Editor: Mark Powers
Copy Editor: Kim Burton-Weisman
Compositor: SPi Global
Indexer: SPi Global
Artist: SPi Global

Distributed to the book trade worldwide by Springer Science+Business Media New York, 233 Spring Street, 6th Floor, New York, NY 10013. Phone 1-800-SPRINGER, fax (201) 348-4505, e-mail orders-ny@springer-sbm.com, or visit www.springeronline.com. Apress Media, LLC is a California LLC and the sole member (owner) is Springer Science + Business Media Finance Inc (SSBM Finance Inc). SSBM Finance Inc is a Delaware corporation.

For information on translations, please e-mail rights@apress.com, or visit www.apress.com.

Apress and friends of ED books may be purchased in bulk for academic, corporate, or promotional use. eBook versions and licenses are also available for most titles. For more information, reference our Special Bulk Sales–eBook Licensing web page at www.apress.com/bulk-sales.

Any source code or other supplementary materials referenced by the author in this text is available to readers at www.apress.com/9781484205600. For detailed information about how to locate your book's source code, go to www.apress.com/source-code/. Readers can also access source code at SpringerLink in the Supplementary Material section for each chapter.

Printed on acid-free paper

For Marilyn and Matt

Contents at a Glance

Contents

About the Authors

Michael Paluszek is president of Princeton Satellite Systems, Inc. (PSS), in Plainsboro, New Jersey. Mr. Paluszek founded PSS in 1992 to provide aerospace consulting services. He used MATLAB to develop the control system and simulation for the Indostar-1 geosynchronous communications satellite, resulting in the launch of PSS's first commercial MATLAB toolbox, the Spacecraft Control Toolbox, in 1995. Since then he has developed toolboxes and software packages for aircraft, submarines, robotics, and fusion propulsion, resulting in PSS's current extensive product line. He is currently leading a US Army research contract for precision attitude control of small satellites and IS working with the Princeton Plasma Physics Laboratory on a compact nuclear fusion reactor for energy generation and propulsion.

Prior to founding PSS, Mr. Paluszek was an engineer at GE Astro Space in East Windsor, NJ. At GE, he designed the Global Geospace Science Polar despun platform control system and led the design of the GPS IIR attitude control system, the Inmarsat-3 attitude control systems, and the Mars Observer delta-V control system, leveraging MATLAB for control design. Mr. Paluszek also worked on the attitude determination system for the DMSP meteorological satellites. Mr. Paluszek flew communication satellites on more than 12 satellite launches, including the GSTAR III recovery, the first transfer of a satellite to an operational orbit using electric thrusters. At Draper Laboratory, Mr. Paluszek worked on the Space Shuttle program, the international space station, and submarine navigation. His space station work included the design of the control moment gyroscope, based control systems for attitude control.

Mr. Paluszek received his bachelor's degree in electrical engineering, and a master's and engineer's degree in aeronautics and astronautics from the Massachusetts Institute of Technology. He is author of numerous papers and has over a dozen US patents.

Stephanie Thomas is vice president of Princeton Satellite Systems, Inc., in Plainsboro, New Jersey. She received her bachelor's and master's degrees in aeronautics and astronautics from the Massachusetts Institute of Technology in 1999 and 2001. Ms. Thomas was introduced to PSS's Spacecraft Control Toolbox for MATLAB during a summer internship in 1996 and has been using MATLAB for aerospace analysis ever since. She built a simulation of a lunar transfer vehicle in C++, LunarPilot, during the same internship. In her nearly 20 years of MATLAB experience, she has developed many software tools, including the Solar Sail Module for the Spacecraft Control Toolbox; a proximity satellite operations toolbox for the Air Force; collision monitoring Simulink blocks for the Prisma satellite mission; and launch vehicle analysis tools in MATLAB and Java, to name a few. She has developed novel methods for space situation assessment, such as a numeric approach to assessing the general rendezvous problem between any two satellites implemented in both MATLAB and C++.

Ms. Thomas has contributed to PSS's Attitude and Orbit Control textbook, featuring examples using the Spacecraft Control Toolbox, and written many software users' guides. She has conducted SCT training for engineers from diverse locales, such as Australia, Canada, Brazil, and Thailand, and has performed MATLAB consulting for NASA, the US Air Force, and the European Space Agency.

About the Technical Reviewer

Jonah Lissner is a research scientist advancing PhD and DSc programs, scholarships, applied projects, and academic journal publications in theoretical physics, power engineering, complex systems, metamaterials, geophysics, and computation theory. He has strong cognitive ability in empiricism and scientific reason for hypothesis building, theory learning, mathematical and axiomatic modeling, and testing for abstract problem solving. His dissertations, research publications and projects, CV, journals, blog, novels, and system are listed at http://Lissnerresearch.weebly.com.

Acknowledgments

We don't have any acknowledgements now but may want to add some to thank those who review the book before it is published.

Introduction

Writing software has become part of the job description for nearly every professional engineer and engineering student. While there are many excellent prebuilt software applications for engineers, almost everyone can benefit from writing custom software for their own problems.

MATLAB® has origins for that very reason. Scientists that needed to do operations on matrices used numerical software written in FORTRAN. At the time, using computer languages required the user to go through the write-compile-link-execute process that was time-consuming and error-prone. MATLAB presented a scripting language that allowed the user to solve many problems with a few lines of a script that executed instantaneously. MATLAB had built-in visualization tools that helped the user better understand the results. Writing MATLAB was a lot more productive and fun than writing FORTRAN.

MATLAB has grown greatly since its origins. The power of the basic MATLAB software has grown dramatically, and hundreds of MATLAB libraries are now available, both commercially and as open source. MATLAB is so sophisticated that most new users only use a fraction of its power.

The goal of *MATLAB Recipes* is to help all users harness the power of MATLAB. This book has two parts. The first part, Chapters 1 through 5, gives a framework that you can use to write high-quality MATLAB code that you, your colleagues, and possibly your customers, can utilize. We cover coding practices, graphics, debugging and other topics in a problem-solution format. You can read these sections from cover to cover or just look at the recipes that interest you and use them in your latest MATLAB code.

The second part of the book, Chapters 6 through 12, shows complete MATLAB applications revolving around the control and simulation of dynamical systems. Each chapter provides the technical background for the topic, ideas on how you can write a simple control system, and an example of how you might simulate the system. Each system is implemented in a MATLAB script supported by a number of MATLAB functions. Each chapter also highlights a general MATLAB topic, like graphics or writing graphical user interfaces (GUIs). We have deliberately made the control systems simple so that the reader won't need a course in control theory to get results. Control experts can easily take the script and implement their own ideas. We cover a number of areas, ranging from chemical processes to satellites—and we apologize if we didn't write an example for your area of interest!

The book has something for everyone—from the MATLAB novice to the authors of commercial MATLAB packages. We learned new things writing this book! We hope that you enjoy the book and look forward to seeing your software that it inspires.

PART I

Coding in MATLAB

CHAPTER 1

■ ■ ■

Coding Handbook

The purpose of this chapter is to provide an overview of MATLAB syntax and programming, highlighting features that may be underutilized by many users and noting important differences between MATLAB and other programming languages and integrated development environments (IDEs). You should also become familiar with the very detailed documentation that is available from MathWorks in the help browser. The "Language Fundamentals" section of the MathWorks web site describes entering commands, operators, and data types.

Over the last two decades, MATLAB has matured a lot from its origins as a linear algebra package. Originally, all variables were double-precision matrices. Today, MATLAB provides different variable types, such as integers, data structures, object-oriented programming and classes, and integration with Java. The MATLAB application is a full IDE with an integrated editor, debugger, command history, and code analyzer, and offering report capabilities. Engineers who have worked with MATLAB for many years may find that they are not taking advantage of the full range of capabilities now offered. In this text, we hope to highlight the more useful new features.

The first part of this chapter provides an overview of the most commonly used MATLAB types and constructs. We'll then provide some recipes that make use of these constructs to show you some practical applications of modern MATLAB.

MATLAB Language Primer

A Brief Introduction to MATLAB

MATLAB is both an application and a programming language. It was developed primarily for numerical computing and it is widely used in academia and industry. MATLAB was originally developed by a college professor in the 1970s to provide easy access to linear algebra libraries. MathWorks was founded in 1984 to continue the development of the product. The name is derived from **MAT**rix **LAB**oratory. Today, MATLAB uses the LAPACK (**Linear Algebra Pack**age) libraries for the underlying matrix manipulations. Many toolboxes are available for different engineering disciplines; this book focuses on features available only in the base MATLAB application.

The MATLAB application is a rich development environment for the MATLAB language. It provides an editor, command terminal, debugger, plotting capabilities, creation of graphical user interfaces, and more recently, the ability to install third-party apps. MATLAB can interface with other languages, including Fortran, C, C++, Java, and Python. A code analyzer and profiler are built in. Extensive online communities provide forums for sharing code and asking questions.

Electronic supplementary material The online version of this chapter (doi:10.1007/978-1-4842-0559-4_1) contains supplementary material, which is available to authorized users.

S. Thomas and M. Paluszek, *MATLAB Recipes*, DOI 10.1007/978-1-4842-0559-4_1

3

The following are the main components of the MATLAB application:

Command Window The terminal for entering commands and operating on variables in the base workspace. The MATLAB prompt is > >.

Command History A list of previously executed commands.

Workspace display Lists the variables and their values in the current workspace (application memory). Variables remain in memory once created until you explicitly clear them or close MATLAB.

Current Folder The file browser displaying the contents of the current folder and providing file system navigation. Recent versions of MATLAB can also display the SVN status on configuration managed files.

File Details A panel displaying information on the file selected in the Current Folder panel.

Editor The editor for m-files with syntax coloring and a built-in debugger. It can also display any type of text file, and recognizes and appropriately colors other languages, including Java, C/C++, and XML/HTML.

Variables editor A spreadsheet-like graphical editor for variables in the workspace.

GUIDE The graphical interface development window.

Help browser A searchable help documentation on all MATLAB products and third-party products you have installed.

Profiler A tool for timing code as it runs.

These components can be docked in various configurations. The default layout of the main application window or *desktop* contains the first five components listed and is shown in Figure 1-1. The Command Window is in the center. The upper-left panel shows a file browser with the contents of the Current Folder. Under this is a file information display. On the right-hand side are the workspace display and the Command History panel. The *base workspace* is all the variables currently in application memory. Commands from the history can be double-clicked or dragged onto the command line to be executed. The extensive toolbar includes buttons for running the code analyzer, opening the code profiler, and the Help window, as well as typical file and data operations. Note the PLOTS and APPS tabs above the toolbar. The PLOTS tab allows the graphical creation and management of plots from data selected in the workspace browser. The APPS tab allows you to access and manage the third-party apps that you install.

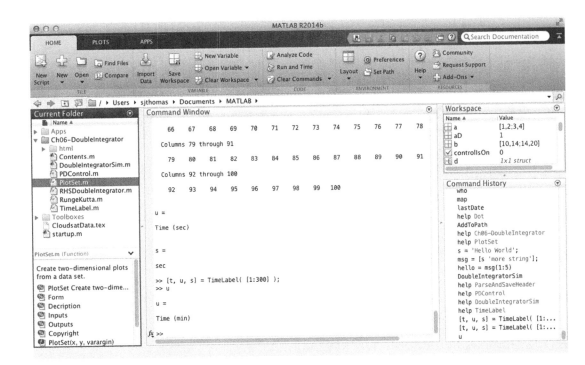

Figure 1-1. *MATLAB desktop with the Command Window*

The Editor with the default syntax coloring is shown in Figure 1-2 (you can see a file from this chapter). The horizontal lines show the division of the code into "cells" using a double-percent sign, which can be used for sequential execution of code and for creating sections of text when publishing. The cell titles are bolded in the editor. MATLAB keywords are highlighted in blue, comments in green, and strings in pink. The toolbar includes buttons for commenting code, indenting, and running or debugging the code. The Go To pop-up menu gives access to subfunctions within a large file. Note the PUBLISH and VIEW tabs with additional features on publishing (covered in the next chapter) and options for the editor view.

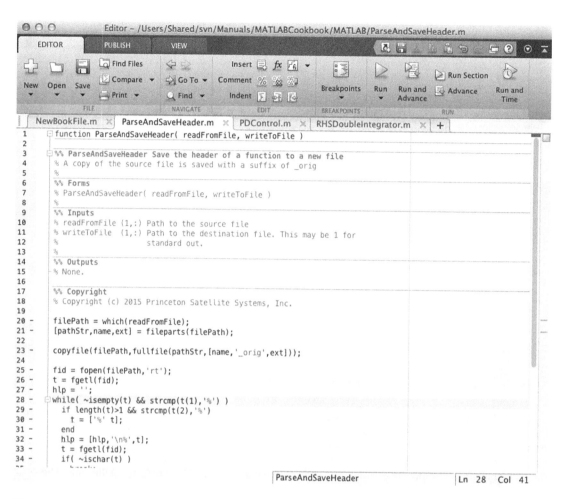

Figure 1-2. *MATLAB File Editor*

The Help browser is shown in Figure 1-3. MATLAB offers extensive help, including examples and links to online videos and tutorials. Third-party toolboxes can also install help in this browser. Like any browser, you can open multiple tabs; there is a search utility; and you can mark favorite topics. Topics available in the help browser are referred to throughout this book.

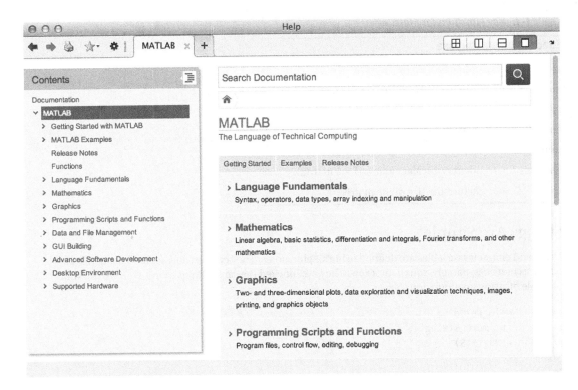

Figure 1-3. *MATLAB Help Window*

Everything Is a Matrix

By default, all variables in MATLAB are double-precision matrices. You do not need to declare a type for these variables. Matrices can be multidimensional and are accessed using 1-based indices via parentheses. You can address elements of a matrix using a single index, taken columnwise, or one index per dimension. To create a matrix variable, simply assign a value to it, like this 2 × 2 matrix a:

```
>> a = [1 2; 3 4];
>> a(1,1)
    1

>> a(3)
     2
```

You can simply add, subtract, multiply, and divide matrices with no special syntax. The matrices must be the correct size for the linear algebra operation requested. A transpose is indicated using a single quote suffix, ', and the matrix power uses the operator ^.

```
>> b = a'*a;
>> c = a^2;
>> d = b + c;
```

By default, every variable is a numerical variable. You can initialize matrices to a given size using the zeros, ones, eye, or rand functions, which produce zeros, ones, identity matrices (ones on the diagonal), and random numbers, respectively. Use isnumeric to identify numeric variables. Table 1-1 shows a selection of key matrix functions.

Table 1-1. *Key Functions for Matrices*

Function	Purpose
zeros	Initialize a matrix to zeros
ones	Initialize a matrix to ones
eye	Initialize an identity matrix
rand, randn	Initialize a matrix of random numbers
isnumeric	Identify a matrix or scalar numeric value
isscalar	Identify a scalar value (a 1 × 1 matrix)
size	Return the size of the matrix

Strings Are Simple

String and character variables are defined using single quotes. They can be concatenated using the same syntax as matrices, namely, square brackets. They are indexed the same way as matrices. Here is a short example of string manipulation:

```
>> s = 'Hello_World' ;
>> msg = [s 'more_string'];
>> hello = msg(1:5)

hello =

Hello
```

Use ischar to identify string variables. Also note that isempty returns true for an empty string; that is, ' '. For a description of string syntax, type **help strings** at the MATLAB command line, and for a comprehensive list of string functions, type **help strfun**. Table 1-2 shows a selection of key string functions.

Table 1-2. *Key Functions for Strings*

Function	Purpose
ischar	Identify a character string
char	Convert integer codes or cell array to character string
sprintf	Write formatted data to a string
strcmp, strncmp	Compare strings
strfind	Find one string within another
num2str, mat2str	Convert a number or matrix to a string
lower	Convert a string to lowercase

Use Strict Data Structures

Data structures in MATLAB are highly flexible, leaving it up to the user to enforce consistency in fields and types. You are not required to initialize a data structure before assigning fields to it, but it is a good idea to do so, especially in scripts, to avoid variable conflicts.

Replace

```
d.fieldName = 0;
```

with

```
d = struct;
d.fieldName = 0;
```

In fact, we have found that it is generally a good idea to create a special function to initialize larger structures that are used throughout a set of functions. This is similar to creating a class definition. Generating your data structure from a function, instead of typing out the fields in a script, means that you always start with the correct fields. Having an initialization function also allows you to specify the types of variables and provide sample or default data. Remember, since MATLAB does not require you to declare variable types, doing so yourself with default data makes your code that much clearer.

■ **Tip**   Create an initialization function for data structures.

You make a data structure into an array simply by assigning an additional copy. The fields must be in the same order, which is yet another reason to use a function to initialize your structure. You can nest data structures with no limit on depth.

```
d = MyStruct;
d(2) = MyStruct;

function d = MyStruct

d = struct;
d.a = 1.0;
d.b = 'string';
```

MATLAB now allows *dynamic field names* using variables; for example, structName.(dynamicExpression). This provides improved performance over getfield, where the field name is passed as a string. This allows all sorts of inventive structure programming. Take our data structure array in the previous code snippet to get the values of field a using a dynamic field name; the values are returned in a cell array.

```
>> field = 'a';
>> values = {d.(field)}

values =

    [1]    [1]
```

Use isstruct to identify structure variables and isfield to check for the existence of fields. Note that isempty will return *false* for a struct initialized with struct, even if it has no fields. Table 1-3 shows a selection of key struct functions.

Table 1-3. *Key Functions for Structs*

Function	Purpose
struct	Initialize a structure with or without fields
isstruct	Identify a structure
isfield	Determine if a field exists in a structure
fieldnames	Get the fields of a structure in a cell array
rmfield	Remove a field from a structure
deal	Set fields in a structure to a value

Cell Arrays Hold Anything and Everything

One variable type unique to MATLAB is cell arrays. This is really a list container, and you can store variables of any type in elements of a cell array. Cell arrays can be multidimensional, just like matrices, and are useful in many contexts.

Cell arrays are indicated by curly braces, {}. They can be of any dimension and contain any data, including string, structures, and objects. You can initialize them using the cell function, recursively display the contents using celldisp, and access subsets using parentheses, just like with a matrix. The following is a short example.

```
>> c = cell(3,1);
>> c{1} = 'string';
>> c{2} = false;
>> c{3} = [1 2; 3 4];
>> b = c(1:2);
>> celldisp(b)
b{1} =
string

b{2} =
     0
```

Using curly braces for access gives you the element data as the underlying type. When you access elements of a cell array using parentheses, the contents are returned as another cell array, rather than the cell contents. MATLAB help has a special "Comma-Separated Lists" section, which highlights the use of cell arrays as lists. The code analyzer also suggests efficient ways to use cell arrays. Take the following, for instance.

Replace

```
a = {b{:} c};
```

with

```
a = [b {c}];
```

Cell arrays are especially useful for sets of strings, with many of MATLAB's string search functions optimized for cell arrays, such as strcmp.

Use iscell to identify cell array variables. Use deal to manipulate structure array and cell array contents. Table 1-4 shows a selection of key cell array functions.

Table 1-4. *Key Functions for Cell Arrays*

Function	Purpose
cell	Initialize a cell array
cellstr	Create cell array from a character array
iscell	Identify a cell array
iscellstr	Identify a cell array containing only strings
celldisp	Recursively display the contents of a cell array

Optimize Your Code with Logical Arrays

A *logical array* is composed of only ones and zeros. You can initialize logical matrices using the true and false functions, and there is an islogical function to test if a matrix is logical. Logical arrays are outputs of numerous built-in functions, like isnan, and are often recommended by the code analyzer as a faster alternative to manipulating array indices. For example, you may need to set any negative values in your array to zero.

Replace

```
k = find(x<0);
x(k) = 0;
```

with

```
x(x<0) = 0;
```

where x<0 produces a logical array with 1, where the values of *x* are negative and 0 elsewhere.

MATLAB provides both traditional relational operators, such as && for AND and || for OR, as well as unique element-wise operators. These element-wise operators, such as single & and |, compare matrices of the same size and return logical arrays.

Use Persistent and Global Scope to Minimize Data Passing

In general, variables defined in a function have a local scope and are only available within that function. Variables defined in a script are available in the workspace and, therefore, from the command line.

MATLAB has a *global* scope, which is the same as any other language, applying to the base workspace and maintaining the variable's value throughout the MATLAB session. Global variables are empty once declared, until initialized. The clear and clearvars functions each have flags for removing only the global variables.

```
>> global MY_GLOBAL_VAR; % variable is empty
>> MY_GLOBAL_VAR = 1.0;
>> whos
  Name              Size    Bytes   Class     Attributes
  MY_GLOBAL_VAR     1x1         8   double    global

>> clearvars -GLOBAL
```

Table 1-5 shows some key functions for logical operations.

Table 1-5. *Key Functions for Logical Operations*

Function	Purpose
logical	Convert numeric values to logical
islogical	Identify a logical array (composed of 1 s and 0 s)
true	Return a true value (1) or array (M,N)
false	Return a false value (0) or array (M,N)
any	Return true if any value in the array is a nonzero number
all	Return true if none of the values in the array is 0
and, or	Functional forms of element-wise operators & and │
isnan, isinf, isfinite	Values testing functions returning logical arrays

MATLAB has a unique scope that pertains to a single function, `persistent`. This is useful for initializing a function that requires a lot of data or computation, and then saving that data for use in later calls. The variable can be reset using the `clear` command on the function, such as `clear functionName`. This can also be a source of bugs, thus it is important to note the use of persistent variables in a function's help comments so that you don't get unexpected results when you switch models.

■ **Tip**   Use a persistent variable to store initialization data for subsequent function calls.

Variables can also be in scope for multiple functions defined in a single file, if the end keyword is used appropriately. In general, you can omit a final end for functions, but if you use it to wrap the inner functions, the functions become *nested* and can access variables defined in the parent function. This allows subroutines to share data without passing large numbers of arguments. The editor highlights the variables that are so defined.

In the following example, the `constant` variable is available to the nested function inside the parent function.

```
                        NESTED FUNCTION

function y = parentFunction( x )
constant = 3.0;
y = nestedFunction( x );

    function z = nestedFunction( x )

    z = constant*x;

    end
end
```

Table 1-6 shows a selection of scope functions.

Table 1-6. *Key Functions for Scope Operations*

Function	Purpose
persistent	Specify the persistent scope for a variable in a function
global	Specify the global scope for a variable
clear	Clear a function or variable
who, whos	List the variables in a workspace
mlock, munlock	Lock (and unlock) a function or MEX file that prevents it from being cleared

Understanding Unique MATLAB Operators and Keywords

Some common operators have special features in MATLAB, which we call attention to here.

Colon

The colon operator for creating a list of indices in an array is unique to MATLAB. A single colon used by itself addresses all elements in that given dimension; a colon used between a pair of integers creates a list.

```
>> a(1,1:2)
ans =
     1 2
>> a(:,1)
ans =
     1
     3
```

The colon operator applies to all variable types when accessing elements of an array: cell arrays, strings, and data structure arrays.

The colon operator can also be used to create an array using an interval, as a shorthand for linspace. The interval and the endpoints can be doubles. Using it for matrix indices is really an edge case using a default interval of 1. For example, 0.1:0.2:0.5 produces 0.1 0.3 0.5.

```
>> a = 0.1:0.2:0.5
a =
        0.1     0.3     0.5
```

13

Tilde

The tilde (~) is the logical NOT operator in MATLAB. The output is a logical matrix of the same size as the input, with values of 1 if the input value is zero and a value of 0 otherwise.

```
>> a = [0 -1; 1 0];
>> ~a
ans =
     1   0
     0   1
```

In newer versions, it also can be used to ignore an input or output to a function; this is suggested often in the code analyzer as preferable to the use of a dummy variable.

```
[~,b] = MyFunction(x,y);
```

Dot

By *dot*, we mean using a period with standard arithmetic operators, like .* or .\ or .^. This is special syntax in MATLAB used to apply an operator on an element per element basis over the matrices, instead of performing the linear algebra operation otherwise implied. This is also termed an *array operation* as opposed to a *matrix operation*. Since the matrix and array operations are the same for addition and subtraction, the dot is not required.

```
y = a.*b;
```

MATLAB is optimized for array operations. Using this syntax is a key way to reduce for loops in your MATLAB code and make it run faster. Consider the traditional alternative code.

```
a = rand(1,1000);
b = rand(1,1000);
y = zeros(1,1000);
for k = 1:1000
  y(k) = a(k)*b(k);
end
```

Even this simple example takes two to three times as long to run as the vectorized version shown.

end

The end keyword serves multiple purposes in MATLAB. It is used to terminate for, while, switch, try, and if statements, rather than using braces, as in other languages. It is also used to serve as the last index of a variable in a given dimension. Using end appropriately can make your code more robust to future changes in the size of your data.

```
>> a = [1 2 3; 4 5 6; 7 8 9];
>> b = a(1:end-1,2:end)
b =
     2   3
     5   6
```

Harnessing the Power of Multiple Inputs and Outputs

Uniquely, MATLAB functions can have multiple outputs. They are specified in a comma-separated list, just like the inputs. Additionally, you do not need to specify the data types of the inputs or outputs, and you can silently override the output types by assigning any data you want to the variables. Thus, a function can have an infinite number of syntaxes defined within a single file. Outputs must be assigned the names given in the signature; you cannot pass a variable to the return keyword.

MATLAB provides helper functions for specifying a variable number of inputs or outputs, namely, varargin and varargout. These variables are cell arrays, and you access and assign elements using curly braces. Here is an example function definition:

```
function [y,varargout] = varargFunction(x,varargin)

y = varargin{1};
varargout{1} = size(x,1);
varargout{2} = size(x,2);
```

The following example demonstrates that the outputs were correctly assigned.

USING VARARGOUT AND VARARGIN

```
>> [y,a,b] = varargFunction(rand(3,2),1.0)

y =
     1

a =
     3

b =
     2
```

This allows you to accept unlimited arguments or parameter pairs in your function. It is up to you to create consistent forms for your function and document them clearly in the help comments.

You can also count the input and output arguments for a given call to your function using nargin and nargout, and use this with logical statements or a switch statement to handle multiple cases.

If you need very complex input handling, MATLAB now provides an inputParser class, which allows you to parse and validate an input scheme. You can define functions to validate the inputs, optional arguments, and predefine parameter pairs.

Use Function Handles for Efficiency

Function handles are pointers to functions. They are closely related to anonymous functions, which allow you to define a short function inline, and return the function handle. When you create a handle, you can change the input scheme and give values for certain inputs, such as parameters. Using handles as inputs to integrators and similar routines is much faster than passing in a string variable of the function name.

In the following snippet, we created an anonymous function handle to myFunction with a different signature and a specific value for *a*. Note the use of the ampersand, which designates a function handle. The handle can be evaluated with inputs, just like a regular function.

```
function y = myFunction(a, b, c)
...

a = 2;
h = @(c,b) myFunction(a,b,c);
y = h(c,b);
```

The handle h can be passed to a function such as an integrator that is expecting a signature with only two variables. You will also commonly use function handles to specify an events function for integrators or similar tools, as well as output functions that are called between major steps. Output functions can print information to the screen or a figure; for example, odeplot and odeprint.

In order to test if a variable is a function handle, you need to use the function handle class name with isa, for example:

```
isa(f,'function_handle')
```

ishandle works only for graphics handles. For more information, see the help documentation for function_handle. Table 1-7 provides the few key functions for dealing with function handles.

Table 1-7. *Key Functions for Handles*

Function	Purpose
feval	Execute a function from a handle or string
func2str	Construct a string from a function handle
str2func	Construct a handle from a function name string
isa	Test for a function handle

Advanced Data Types

The data types discussed so far are all that are needed for most engineering programming. However, for specialized applications, there are additional options for data types, including the following.

> **Classes** Classes, with properties and methods, can be defined using the classdef keyword in an m-file similar to writing a function. See also the properties, methods, and events keywords.

> **Tables** Tables are new to release R2013 of MATLAB and allow tabular data to be stored with metadata in one variable. It is an effective way to store and interact with data that one might put in a spreadsheet. The table columns can be named, assigned units and descriptions, and accessed as one would fields in a data structure, such as T.DataName. See the function readtable on creating a table from a file.

> **Categorical Arrays** Arrays of data from a discrete set of categories (an enumeration) can be stored in this special type, which provides more efficient searching than elements of a cell array. See categorical and categories.

Time Series The timeseries object and the related tscollection object provide methods for associating data samples with timestamps. Plotting a timeseries object uses the stored time vector automatically.

Map Containers The map container allows you to store and look up data using a key that may be nonnumeric. This is an object instantiated via containers.Map.

The MATLAB documentation is thorough, should you find these data types advantageous to your application.

Primer Recipes

The next part of this chapter provides recipes for some common tasks in modern MATLAB, like adding help to your functions, loading binary data, writing to a text file, creating a MEX file, and parsing functions into "pcode."

1-1. Creating Function Help

Problem

You need to document your functions so that others may use them and so that you remember how they work.

Solution

MATLAB provides a mechanism for providing command-line access to documentation about your function or script using the help command, if you put the documentation in the right place.

How It Works

The comments you provide at the top of your function file, called a *header*, become the function help. The help can be printed at the command line by typing **help MyFunction**. Whereas the style and format of these comments are covered in the next chapter, your attention is drawn to the functionality here.

The help comments can go either above or below the declarative line of your function. If you include the words "see also" in your comments, followed by the names of additional functions, MATLAB helpfully supplies links to those functions' help. All comments are printed until the first blank line is reached.

Consider the help for a function that calculates a dot product. The first line should be a single sentence description of the function, which is utilized by lookfor. If you insert your function name in all capital letters, MATLAB automatically replaces it with the true case version when printing the help. Your comments might look like this:

```
function d = Dot( w, y )
%% DOT Dot product of two arrays.
%% Forms
%   d = Dot( w, y )
%   d = Dot( w )
%
%% Description
% Dot product with support for arrays. The number of columns of w and y can be:
%
```

```
% * Both > 1 and equal
% * One can have one column and the other any number of columns
%
% If there is only one input the dot product will be taken with itself.
%
%% See also
% Cross
```

When printed to the command line, MATLAB removes the percent signs and just displays the text, like this:

```
>> help Dot
  Dot Dot product of two arrays.
 % Forms
    d = Dot( w, y )
    d = Dot( w )

 % Description
  Dot product with support for arrays. The number of columns of w and y can be:

  * Both > 1 and equal
  * One can have one column and the other any number of columns

  If there is only one input the dot product will be taken with itself.
 % See also
Cross
```

You can link to additional help documentation attached to subfunctions in your file. This can be handy for providing more detailed examples or descriptions of algorithms. In order to do so, you have to embed an HTML link in your help comments. For example:

```
% More detailed help is in the <a href="matlab: help foo>extended_help">extended help
    </a>.

function extended_help
%EXTENDED_HELP Additional technical details and examples
%
% Describe additional details of your algorithms or provide examples.

error('This_is_a_placeholder_function_just_for_helptext');
```

This type sets in the Command Window as

```
More detailed information is in the extended help.
```

MATLAB also provides the capability for you to create HTML help for your functions that will appear in the help browser. This requires the creation of XML files to provide the contents hierarchy. See the MATLAB help topic "Display Custom Documentation" and the related recipe in the next chapter.

You can also run help reports to identify functions that are missing help or missing certain sections of help, such as a copyright notice. To learn how to launch this report on your operating system, see the MathWorks "Check Which Programs Have Help" help topic.

1-2. Locating Directories for Data Storage

Problem

A variety of demos and functions in your toolbox generate data files and they end up all over your file system. You can't use an absolute path on your computer because the code is shared among multiple engineers.

Solution

Use mfilename to save files in the same location as the generating file or to locate a dedicated data directory that is relative to your file location.

How It Works

It's easy to sprinkle save commands throughout your scripts, or print figures to image files, and end up with files spread all over your file system. MATLAB provides a handy function, mfilename, which can provide the path to the folder of the executing m-file. You can use this to locate a data folder dedicated to either input files or output files for your routine. This uses the MATLAB functions fileparts and fullfile.

For example, to save an output mat-file in the same location as your function or script:

```
thisPath = mfilename('fullpath');
thisDir = fileparts(thisPath);
save(fullfile(thisDir,'fileName'),x,y);
```

To save output to a dedicated directory, you only need an additional call to fileparts. In this case, the directory is called DataDir.

```
thisPath = mfilename('fullpath');
prevDir = fileparts(fileparts(thisPath));
dataDir = fullfile(prevDir,'DataDir','fileName');
save(fullfile(dataDir,'fileName'),x,y);
```

If you are printing images, you can either use the functional form of print, as with save, or change the path to the directory you want. You should save the current directory and return there when your script is complete.

```
thisPath = mfilename('fullpath');
cd0 = cd;
cd(fileparts(thisPath));
print -dpng MyFigure
cd(cd0)
```

Table 1-8 shows key functions for path operations.

Table 1-8. *Key Functions for Path Operations*

Function	Purpose
mfilename	The name, and optionally, the full path to the currently executing m-file
fileparts	Divide a path into parts (directory, file name, extension)
fullfile	Create a system-dependent file name from parts
cd	The current directory
path	The current MATLAB path

1-3. Loading Binary Data from a File

Problem

You need to store data in a binary file, perhaps for input to another software program.

Solution

MATLAB provides low-level utilities for creating and writing to binary files, including specifying the endianness.

How It Works

Reading and writing binary data introduces some complexities beyond text files. Let's start with MATLAB's example of creating a binary file of a magic square. This demonstrates fopen, fwrite, and fread. The options for precision are specified in the help for fread. For example, a 32-bit integer can be specified with the MATLAB-style string 'int32' or the C-style string 'integer*4'.

```
>> magic(4)

ans =

    16     2     3    13
     5    11    10     8
     9     7     6    12
     4    14    15     1

>> fid = fopen('magic4.bin','wb');
>> fwrite(fid,magic(4),'integer*4');
>> fclose(fid);
```

Now, let's try to read this data file back in. Since the data was stored as 32-bit integers, you have to specify this precision to get the data back.

```
>> fid = fopen('magic4.bin','rb');
>> c = fread(fid,inf,'integer*4')

c =

    16
     5
     9
     4
     2
    11
     7
    14
     3
    10
     6
    15
    13
     8
    12
     1
```

The shape of the matrix was not preserved, but you can see that the data was printed to the file in columnwise order. To fully re-create the data, you need to reshape the matrix.

```
>> data = reshape(c,5,5)

data =
    16     2     3    13
     5    11    10     8
     9     7     6    12
     4    14    15     1
```

If you need to specify the endianness of the data, you can so do in both fopen and fread. The local machine format is used by default, but you can specify the IEEE floating point with a little endian byte ordering, the same with big ending ordering, and both with 64-bit long data type. This may be important if you are using binary data from an online source or using data on embedded processors.

For example, to write the same data in a big endian format, simply add the 'ieee-be' parameter.

```
>> fid = fopen('magic5.bin','wb','ieee-be');
>> fwrite(fid,magic(5),'integer*4');
>> fclose(fid);
```

Table 1-9 lists key functions for interacting with binary data.

Table 1-9. *Key Functions for Binary Data*

Function	Purpose
fopen	Open a file in text or binary mode
fwrite	Write to a file
fread	Read the contents of a file
fclose	Close the file

21

1-4. Command-Line File Interaction

Problem

You have some unexpected behavior when you try to run a MATLAB script and you suspect a function conflict among different toolboxes.

Solution

MATLAB provides functions for locating and managing files and paths from the command line.

How It Works

MATLAB has a file browser built in to the command window, but it is still helpful to be familiar with the commands for locating and managing files from the command line. In particular, if you have a lot of toolboxes and files in your path, you may need to identify name conflicts.

For example, if you get the wrong behavior or a strange error from a function and you recently changed your path, you may have a file shadowing it in your path. To check for duplicate copies of a function name, use which with the -all switch. Shadowed versions of the function are marked. which can take a partial pathname.

```
>> which DemoPSS -all
/Users/.../Toolboxes/Missions/Demos/DemoPSS.m
/Users/.../Toolboxes/Math/Demos/DemoPSS.m     % Shadowed
/Users/.../Toolboxes/Imaging/Demos/DemoPSS.m  % Shadowed
/Users/.../Toolboxes/Common/Demos/DemoPSS.m   % Shadowed
```

To display the contents of a file at the command line, which is helpful if you need to see something in the file but don't need to open the file for editing, use type, as in Unix.

To list the contents of a directory, use what. A partial path can be used if there are multiple directories with the same name on your path. Specifying an output returns the results in a data structure array. MATLAB identifies which files are code, mat-files, p-files, and so forth. what is recursive and returns all directories with the given name anywhere in the path—useful if you use the same name of a directory for functions and demos, as follows.

```
>> what Database

MATLAB Code files in folder /Users/Shared/svn/Toolboxes/SourceCode/Core/Common/Demos/
    Database

Contents    TConstant

MATLAB Code files in folder /Users/Shared/svn/Toolboxes/SourceCode/Core/Common/
    Database

BuildConstant    Contents     MergeConstantDB
Constant         Database
```

Use exist to determine if a function or variable exists in the path or workspace. The code analyzer will prompt you to use the syntax with a second argument specifying the desired type, such as 'var', 'file', or 'dir'. The output is a numerical code indicating the type of file or variable found.

Open a file in the editor from the command line using edit.

Load a mat-file or ASCII file using load. Give an output to store the data in a variable, or else it will be loaded directly into the workspace. For mat-files, you can also specify particular variables to load.

```
d = load('MyMatFile','var1','var2');
```

The final command-line function introduced is lookfor. This function searches for a keyword through all help available on the MATLAB path. The keyword must appear in the first line of the help, such as the one-line help comment or H1 line. The printed result looks like a Contents file and includes links to the help for the found functions. Here is an example for the keyword integration.

```
>> lookfor integration
IntegrationAccuracyDemo        - Integration Accuracy for PropagateOrbitPlugin.
PropagatorComparison           - Integration accuracy study comparing RK4, RK45, and ode113.
lotkademo                      - Numerical Integration of Differential Equations
cumtrapz                       - Cumulative trapezoidal numerical integration.
trapz                          - Trapezoidal numerical integration.
```

Table 1-10 lists key functions to use at the command line.

Table 1-10. Key Functions for Command-Line Interaction

Function	Purpose
which	The location of a function in the path
what	List the MATLAB-specific files in directory
type	Display the contents of a file
dbtype	Display the contents of a file with line numbers
exist	Determine if a function or variable exists
edit	Open a file in the editor
load	Load a mat-file into the workspace
lookfor	Search help comments in the path for a keyword

1-5. Using a MEX File to Link to an External Library

Problem

There is an external C++ library that you need to use for an application. You would like to perform the analysis in MATLAB.

Solution

You can write and compile a special function in MATLAB using the C/C++ matrix API that allows you to call the external library functions via a MATLAB function. This is called a *MEX file*.

How It Works

A mex function is actually a shared library compiled from C/C++ or Fortran source code, and is callable from MATLAB. It can be used to link to external libraries such as GLPK, BLAS, and LAPACK. When writing a mex function, you provide a gateway routine mexFunction in your code, and use MATLAB's C/C++ Matrix Library API. You must have a MATLAB-supported compiler installed on your machine.

```
#include "mex.h"

void mexFunction( int nlhs, mxArray *plhs[], int nrhs, const mxArray *prhs[])
```

You can see that, as with regular MATLAB functions, you can provide multiple inputs and multiple outputs. mxArray is a C language type, actually the fundamental data type for all matrices in MATLAB, provided by the MATLAB API.

You use the mex function to compile your C, C++, for Fortran function into a binary. Passing the verbose flag, -v, provides verbose output familiar to C programmers. An extension such as 'mexmaci64', as determined on your system by mexext, is appended and you can then call the function from MATLAB like any other m-file. For example, on the Mac, MATLAB detects and uses Xcode automatically when compiling one of the built-in examples, yprime.c. This function solves simple three-body orbit problems. First, you need to copy the example into a local working directory.

```
>> copyfile(fullfile(matlabroot,'extern','examples','mex','yprime.c'),'.','f');
```

The following are excerpts from the verbose compile.

```
>> mex -v -compatibleArrayDims yprime.c
Verbose mode is on.
No MEX options file identified; looking for an implicit selection.
... Looking for compiler 'Xcode_with_Clang' ...
... Looking for environment variable 'DEVELOPER_DIR' ...No.
... Executing command 'xcode-select_-print-path' ...Yes ('/Applications/Xcode.app/
    Contents/Developer').
... Looking for folder '/Applications/Xcode.app/Contents/Developer' ...Yes.
... Executing command 'which_xcrun' ...Yes ('/usr/bin/xcrun').
... Looking for folder '/usr/bin' ...Yes.
...
Found installed compiler 'Xcode with_Clang'.
------------------------------------------------------------
        Compiler location: /Applications/Xcode.app/Contents/Developer
        Options file: /Applications/MATLAB_R2014b.app/bin/maci64/mexopts/clang_maci64.xml
        CC : /usr/bin/xcrun -sdk macosx10.9 clang
        DEFINES : -DMX_COMPAT_32 -DMATLAB_MEX_FILE
        MATLABMEX : -DMATLAB_MEX_FILE
        CFLAGS : -fno-common -arch x86_64 -mmacosx-version-min=10.9 -fexceptions -
            isysroot /Applications/Xcode.app/Contents/Developer/Platforms/MacOSX.
            platform/Developer/SDKs/MacOSX10.9.sdk
        INCLUDE : -I"/Applications/MATLAB_R2014b.app/extern/include" -I"/Applications/
            MATLAB_R2014b.app/simulink/include"
        COPTIMFLAGS : -O2 -DNDEBUG
        LD : /usr/bin/xcrun -sdk macosx10.9 clang
```

```
      LDFLAGS : -Wl,-twolevel_namespace -undefined error -arch x86_64 -mmacosx-
          version-min=10.9 -Wl,-syslibroot,/Applications/Xcode.app/Contents/Developer
          /Platforms/MacOSX.platform/Developer/SDKs/MacOSX10.9.sdk -bundle -Wl,-
          exported_symbols_list,"/Applications/MATLAB_R2014b.app/extern/lib/maci64/
          mexFunction.map"
      LDBUNDLE : -bundle
      LINKEXPORT : -Wl,-exported_symbols_list,"/Applications/MATLAB_R2014b.app/
          extern/lib/maci64/mexFunction.map"
      LINKLIBS : -L"/Applications/MATLAB_R2014b.app/bin/maci64" -lmx -lmex -lmat -
          lstdc++
      OBJEXT : .o
      LDEXT : .mexmaci64
--------------------------------------------------------
Building with 'Xcode_with_Clang'.
/usr/bin/xcrun -sdk macosx10.9 clang -c -DMX_COMPAT_32 -DMATLAB_MEX_FILE -I"/
    Applications/MATLAB_R2014b.app/extern/include" -I"/Applications/MATLAB_R2014b.app/
    simulink/include" -fno-common -arch x86_64 -mmacosx-version-min=10.9 -fexceptions -
    isysroot /Applications/Xcode.app/Contents/Developer/Platforms/MacOSX.platform/
    Developer/SDKs/MacOSX10.9.sdk -O2 -DNDEBUG /Users/Shared/svn/Manuals/
    MATLABCookbook/MATLAB/yprime.c -o /var/folders/22/l715021s5rnghdtkxsy_cbk40000gp/T//
    mex_47653762085718_983/yprime.o
/usr/bin/xcrun -sdk macosx10.9 clang -Wl,-twolevel_namespace -undefined error -arch
    x86_64 -mmacosx-version-min=10.9 -Wl,-syslibroot,/Applications/Xcode.app/Contents/
    Developer/Platforms/MacOSX.platform/Developer/SDKs/MacOSX10.9.sdk -bundle -Wl,-
    exported_symbols_list,"/Applications/MATLAB_R2014b.app/extern/lib/maci64/
    mexFunction.map" /var/folders/22/l715021s5rnghdtkxsy_cbk40000gp/T//
    mex_47653762085718_983/yprime.o -O -Wl,-exported_symbols_list,"/Applications/
    MATLAB_R2014b.app/extern/lib/maci64/mexFunction.map" -L"/Applications/
    MATLAB_R2014b.app/bin/maci64" -lmx -lmex -lmat -lstdc++ -o yprime.mexmaci64
rm -f /var/folders/22/l715021s5rnghdtkxsy_cbk40000gp/T//mex_47653762085718_983/yprime.o
MEX completed successfully.
```

Now, assuming that you copied the source into an empty directory, if you now print the contents, you will see something like the following:

```
>> dir
.          ..          yprime.c          yprime.mexmaci64
```

And you can run a test of the compiled library.

```
>> T = 0;
>> Y = rand(1,4);
>> yprime(T,Y)
```

Writing MEX files is not for the faint of heart and requires substantial programming knowledge in the base language. In the preceding printout, you can see that the standard C++ library is included, but you need to provide links and includes explicitly to other libraries that you want to use. Note that your MEX file will not have any function help, so it is a good idea to provide a companion m-file that supplies the help comments and calls your mex function internally.

■ **Tip** Provide a separate m-file with your MEX file that contains help comments, and optionally, calls the MEX file.

See the help articles, including "Components of MEX File" in MATLAB, as well as the many examples for help writing MEX files. In the case of GLPK (GNU Linear Programming Kit), an excellent MEX file is available under the GNU public license. It was written by Nicolo Giorgetti and is maintained by Niels Klitgord. It is now available on SourceForge at `http://glpkmex.sourceforge.net`.

1-6. Protect Your IP with Parsed Files

Problem

You want to share files with customers or collaborators without compromising your intellectual property in the source code.

Solution

Create protected versions of your functions using MATLAB's pcode function. Create a separate file with the help comments so that users have access to the documentation.

How It Works

The pcode function provides a capability to parse m-files into executable files with the content obscured. This can be used to distribute your software while protecting your intellectual property. A pcoded file on your path with a "p" extension, takes precedence over an m-file of the same name. Parsing an m-file is simple:

```
>> pcode Dot
```

The only argument available is the -INPLACE flag to store the p-file in the same directory as the source m-file; otherwise, it is saved to the current directory.

One difficulty you may encounter is that once you have parsed your functions and moved them into a new folder, you no longer have access to the function help you created. The command-line help is not implemented for pcoded files and typing "help MyFunction" no longer works. You have to create a separate m-file with the help comments, as with MEX files. You can write a function to extract the header from an m-file and save it. You will use fprintf for this, so it's important that the header not contain any special characters like backslashes.

```
function ParseAndSaveHeader( readFromFile, writeToFile )

filePath = which(readFromFile);
[pathStr,name,ext] = fileparts(filePath);

copyfile(filePath,fullfile(pathStr,[name,'_orig',ext]));

fid = fopen(filePath,'rt');
t = fgetl(fid);
hlp = '';
```

```
while( ~isempty(t) && strcmp(t(1),'%') )
  if length(t)>1 && strcmp(t(2),'%')
    t = ['%' t];
  end
  hlp = [hlp,'\n%',t];
  t = fgetl(fid);
  if( ~ischar(t) )
    break;
  end
end
hlp = [hlp,'\n%%\n%%_This_function_was_parsed_on_',date,'\n\n'];
fclose(fid);
if ischar(writeToFile)
  fid = fopen(writeToFile,'wt');
else
  fid = writeToFile;
end
fprintf(fid,hlp);
if ischar(writeToFile)
  fclose(fid);
end

pcode(filePath);
```

You save a copy of the m-file with the _orig suffix to prevent unpleasant mistakes with deleted files. Note that you add a final comment at the end with the date that the function was parsed.

1-7. Writing to a Text File

Problem

You need to write some information from MATLAB to a text file. One example is creating a template for new functions following a preferred format.

Solution

You use fopen, fprintf, and fclose to open a new text file, print desired lines to it, and then close it. The input function is used to allow the user to enter a one-line summary of the function.

How It Works

MATLAB has a full set of functions for input and output, including writing to files. See help iofun for a detailed listing. You can write to text files, spreadsheets, binary files, XML, images, or zip files.

One useful example is creating a template for new functions for your company, following your preferred header format. This requires using fopen and fclose, and fprintf to print the lines to the file. The first input is the desired name of the new function. Note that fprintf prints to the command line if given a file ID of 1. You are provided an option to do so with the second input, which is a boolean flag. You use the date function to get the current year for the copyright notice, which returns a string in the format 'dd-mmm-yyyy'; you use the string function strsplit to break the string into tokens. Using string indices would be an alternative. In addition, this demonstrates using input to prompt the user for a string, namely, a one-line description of the new function.

```
%% NEWBOOKFILE Create a new function with the default header style.
%  Pass in a file name and the header template will be printed to that file
%  in the current directory. You will be asked to enter a one-line summary.
%% Forms:
%  NewBookFile( fName, outputIsFile )
%% Input
%  fName           (1,1)    File name
%  outputIsFile    (1,1)    True if a file is created, otherwise header is
%                           printed to the command line.
%% Output
%  None.

function NewBookFile( fName, outputIsFile )

if (nargin < 2)
  outputIsFile = false;
end

if (nargin == 0 || isempty(fName))
  fName = input('Function_name:_','s');
end

% Check if the filename is valid and if such a function already exists.
if (~isvarname(fName))
  error('Book:error','invalid name');
end
if (outputIsFile && exist(fName,'file'))
  error('Book:error','file_%s_already_exists',fName);
end

% Get a one-line description (H1 line) from the user.
comment = input('One-line_description:_','s');

% Open the file or specify command line output.
if (outputIsFile)
  fid = fopen([fName '.m'],'wt');
  c = onCleanup(@() fclose(fid));
else
  fid = 1;
  fprintf(fid,'\n');
end

% Write the header to the file. Use the current year for the copyright
% notice.
fprintf(fid,'%%%%_%s_%s\n',upper(fName),comment);
fprintf(fid,'%%_Description.\n');
fprintf(fid,'%%%%_Forms\n');
fprintf(fid,'%%__y_=_%s(_x_)\n',fName);
fprintf(fid,'%%%%_Input\n');
fprintf(fid,'%%___x___(1,1)____Description\n%%\n');
fprintf(fid,'%%%%_Output\n');
```

```
fprintf(fid,'%%␣␣␣y␣␣␣(1,1)␣␣␣␣Description\n%%\n');
fprintf(fid,'%%%%␣Reference\n');
fprintf(fid,'%%␣Insert␣the␣reference.\n');
fprintf(fid,'%%%%␣See␣also\n');
fprintf(fid,'%%␣List␣pertinent␣functions.\n\n');

today = strsplit(date,'-');
year = today{end};

fprintf(fid,'%%%% Copyright\n');
fprintf(fid,'%%␣Copyright␣␣(c)␣%s Princeton␣Satellite␣Systems,␣Inc.\n%%␣All␣rights␣
    reserved.\n',year);
fprintf(fid,'\nfunction␣y␣=␣%s(x)\n',fName);

if outputIsFile
  edit(fName);
end
```

Note that this function checks for two errors: a bad function name and a function with the same name already exists on the path. You use the two-input form of error where the first input is a message identifier. The message identifier is useful if an error is returned from a catch block. The message identifier can be verified using lasterr. For instance, if you fail to enter a valid function name when prompted, you can see the results of the first error.

```
>> NewBookFile([])
Function name:
Error using NewBookFile (line 29)
invalid name

>> [LASTMSG, LASTID] = lasterr

LASTMSG =

Error using NewBookFile (line 29)
invalid name

LASTID =

Book:error
```

The function includes the ability to print the header to the command window, instead of creating a file, which is useful for testing, or if you went ahead and started with a blank file and need to add a header after the fact. This is accomplished by using 1 for the file identifier. This is what the header looks like:

```
>> NewBookFile('Test')
One-line description: This is a test function.

%% TEST This is a test function.
% Description.
%% Forms
```

```
%  y = Test( x )
%% Input
%   x  (1,1)   Description
%
%% Output
%   y    (1,1)  Description
%
%% Reference
% Insert the reference.
%% See also
% List pertinent functions.

%% Copyright
% Copyright (c) 2015 Princeton Satellite Systems, Inc.
% All rights reserved.

function y = Test(x)
```

Table 1-11 summarizes some key functions for interacting with text files.

Table 1-11. *Key Functions for Interacting with Text Files*

Function	Purpose
fprintf	Print formatted text to a file
strsplit	Split a string into tokens using a delimited
fgetl	Get one line of a file (until a newline character)
input	Get string input from the user via the command line

Summary

This chapter reviewed basic syntax for MATLAB programming. It highlighted differences between MATLAB and similar languages, like C and C++, in the language primer. Recipes give tips for efficient usage of key features, including writing to binary and text files. Tables at the end of each section highlight key functions you should have at your fingertips.

This chapter did not provide any information on using MATLAB's computational tools, like integration and numerical search, as those are covered in the applications chapter. Interacting with MATLAB graphics is also covered a later chapter.

CHAPTER 2

MATLAB Style

This chapter provides guidelines and recipes for suggested style elements to make your code and tools more understandable and easier to use.

When structuring a function, we have specific guidelines. The comments should be clear and descriptive, and follow the formatting guidelines set by your institution. The same goes for naming conventions. In addition, we recommend supplying "built-in" inputs and outputs; that is, example parameters so the function can be completely executed without any input from the user. These additional demo forms should be listed with the different syntaxes that you create for the function.

Documenting your code goes beyond adding a header and some comments to your code. MATLAB now allows you to integrate HTML help into your toolboxes that displays in the browser along with MATLAB's documentation. You can also use the publishing utility to create comprehensive technical reports. Incorporating these features into your style guidelines from the beginning will save you a lot of work when you want to release your toolbox to others.

2-1. Developing Your Own MATLAB Style Guidelines

Problem

Each engineer in your group has her own favorite naming and whitespace styles. When people work on each other's code, you end up with a mishmash that makes the code more difficult to read.

Solution

Develop and publish your own style guidelines. MATLAB can help enforce some guidelines, such as tab sizes, in the preferences.

How It Works

We recommend the classic book, *The Elements of MATLAB Style* by Richard K. Johnson (Cambridge University Press, 2010), as a starting point for developing your own style guidelines. Many of the recommendations are generic to good coding practice across programming languages, and others are specific to MATLAB, such as using publishing markup syntax in your comments. The book addresses formatting, naming, documentation, and programming.

We deviate from the book's recommendations in a few ways. For one, we prefer to capitalize the names of functions. This distinguishes your custom functions from built-in MATLAB functions in scripts. We also prefer to use single letter variables for structures, rather than long camel-case names. However, the key to

Electronic supplementary material The online version of this chapter (doi:10.1007/978-1-4842-0559-4_2) contains supplementary material, which is available to authorized users.

clear MATLAB code, which is also emphasized in Johnson's text, is to treat MATLAB code like compiled code. Be mindful of variable types, use parentheses even when MATLAB doesn't explicitly require them, and write plentiful comments.

For instance, when a variable value is a double, indicate this with a decimal point. This avoids confusion that the parameter may be an integer.

Replace

```
length = 1;
```

with

```
length = 1.0;
```

In if statements, always use parentheses. If you ever want to port the code to another language in the future, this saves you time, and it makes the code clearer and easier to read for programmers versed in multiple languages.

Replace

```
if thisIsTrue && thatIsTrue
```

with

```
if (thisIsTrue && thatIsTrue)
```

You should always avoid "magic numbers" in your code, which are easy to use when quickly typing out a function to test a concept. This is a number value that is typed in, such as to a logical statement, instead of assigned to a variable. Take the time to define a properly named variable and add a comment with the source of the number.

Replace

```
if (value > 2.0 || value < 0.0)
```

with

```
if (value > minValue || value < maxValue)
```

With the advent of color-coding IDEs, such as MATLAB's editor, adding a lot of whitespace to delineate code sections has fallen out of favor in style guidelines. Generally, one line of blank space is enough between blocks of code. We suggest adding an additional line of whitespace between the end of a function and the start of a subfunction. You shouldn't put whitespace between lines of code that are closely related.

Some programmers prefer to align blocks of code on their equal signs. This can be helpful, especially when coding sets of equations from references. However, it can also be tedious to maintain when code is under active development. If you like this style, you may prefer to wait on adding the aligning space until the function has passed internal code review and is ready for release. In our code, we generally align on equals signs only within smaller blocks as delineated by comments or whitespace.

Consider the following:

```
% Initialization
myVar1 = linspace(0,1);
b = 1.0;

% Calculation
[result1, result2] = MyFunction(myVar1,b);
plotH = plot(myVar1,result2);
```

This could be aligned in multiple ways, such as:

```
% Initialization
myVar1 = linspace(0,1);
b      = 1.0;

% Calculation
[result1, result2] = MyFunction(myVar1,b);
plotH              = plot(myVar1,result2);
```

Or, if aligning across the blocks, as:

```
% Initialization
myVar1             = linspace(0,1);
b                  = 1.0;

% Calculation
[result1, result2] = MyFunction(myVar1,b);
plotH              = plot(myVar1,result2);
```

In the code for this book, you will see the former, per-block style of alignment.

Another consideration with whitespace is tab sizes. Some guidelines recommend larger tabs of four or eight spaces, arguing that MATLAB code is rarely deeply nested. We routinely write a lot of deeply nested code, so our internal guideline is for two spaces. When you set the tab size in the MATLAB preferences and set it to insert spaces for tabs, you can use the Smart Indent features to easily highlight and update code blocks. Figure 2-1 shows the tab preferences pane in MATLAB R2014b, on a Mac.

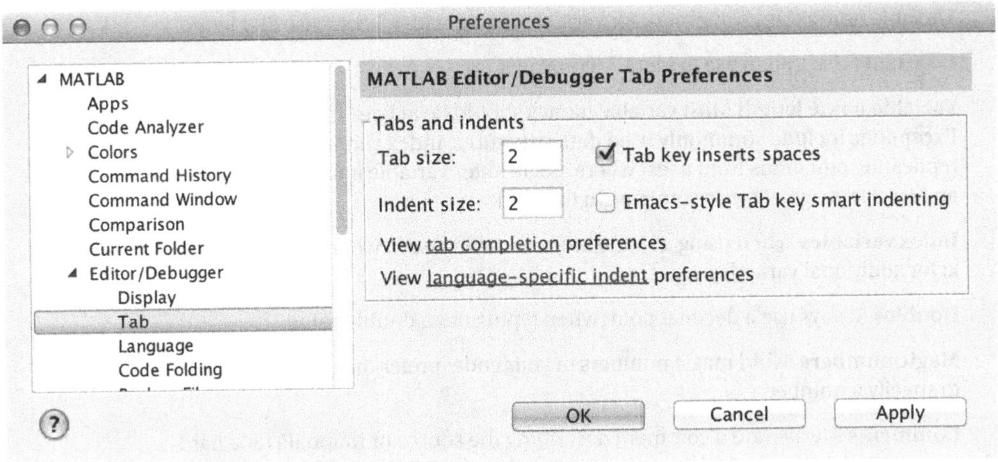

Figure 2-1. Tab preferences with size of 2 and spaces option checked

We prefer to use uppercase for function names (MyFunction), specifically to distinguish them from the lowercase function names of the built-in MATLAB functions. Otherwise, we use camel case (myVariableName) for variables; we often use a single letter or very short names for structures. For index variables, we tend to use k to avoid confusion with the variables i and j and their association with imaginary numbers. We follow the standard convention of capitalizing constant names; for example, for the Earth's gravitational constant, MU_EARTH.

In other words, you need to establish naming conventions for the following:

- Function names
- Variable names
- Structure names
- Index variables
- Constants

Additional naming conventions might include standard prefixes or suffixes for certain types of files or variables. One example is using the letters "RHS" in the name of a function that provides dynamics for integration; that is, the right-hand side of the equations when the derivatives are on the left. The word "Demo" is helpful in the name of a script that demonstrates a particular function or feature. You should be consistent about the order of variable name elements. For example, if r means radius and the second element is the name of the planet, then use R_EARTH and R_MOON. Don't make the second MOON_R. The order should be consistent throughout your code base.

Further rules could address the names of boolean variables or the use of verbs in function names. The most important step is to create and write down a set of conventions for your organization, or create some function templates so that your engineers write consistent code.

The following guidelines are used throughout this book:

> **Naming** Naming guidelines.
>
> **Function names** Use camel case for function names with the first letter capitalized. The first word is ideally an action verb or "RHS".
>
> **Script names** If the script is a demo of a particular function or set of functions, append "Demo" to the name.
>
> **Variable names** Use camel case for variable names with a lowercase first letter.
>
> **Constants** Use uppercase to identify constants.
>
> **Variable name length** Most variable names should be at least three characters. Exceptions include commonly used data structures, index variables, and when replicating equations from a text where single letter variable names are standard and easily recognizable to someone in the field.
>
> **Index variables** When using a single index variable, use k; when using two, j and k; for additional variables, use l, m.
>
> **Doubles** Always use a decimal point when typing out a double value.
>
> **Magic numbers** Avoid magic numbers in your code; prefer the use of a variable to specify a number.
>
> **Comments** Always add a comment describing the source or rationale for a hard-coded number in your code.
>
> **If statements** Always use parentheses around the conditional portion of IF statements.
>
> **Tabs** Use a tab size of two spaces and set MATLAB to insert spaces for tabs. Use Smart Indent to enforce consistent tabs before committing files.

Blank lines Use one blank line between most code sections and two blank lines between subfunctions.

Alignment Align code on the equal sign only within the code block (as separated by blank lines).

Guidelines for function headers are addressed in the next recipe.

2-2. Writing Good Function Help

Problem

You look at a function a couple months (or years) after you wrote it, or a colleague wrote it, and find it has only one cryptic comment at the top. You no longer remember how the function works, what it was supposed to do, or exactly what your comment means.

Solution

Establish a format for your function headers and stick to it. Use the publishing markup to enable you to generate good-looking documentation from the m-file.

How It Works

Write the header for your function at the top, using the publishing markup. This means that the very first line should start with a section break, %%, and include the name of your function, as that will be the title of the published page. This line should also include a one-sentence summary of the function; this must be in the first non-empty comment line of the file, which is also termed the H1 line. This summary can be used automatically by MATLAB when generating Contents.m files for your folders and by the lookfor function, which searches files on the path for keywords.

Document inputs and outputs separately using section titles. Indicate the type or size of the variable and provide a description. Use two spaces between the comment sign % and the line to generate monospaced text for the input and output lists. Use the following keys to indicate variable type and size:

- {} Cell array
- (1,1) Scalar value
- (:) String
- (:,:) Matrix of variable size
- (1,:) Row of variable length
- (:,1) Column of variable length
- (m,n) Matrix with row and column sizes (m,n) that must match other inputs or outputs
- (.) Data structure
- (:) Data structure array
- (*) Function handle

Always include a copyright notice. Take credit for authoring your code! The standard is to start with the initial year that the function is created, and then add a range of years when you update the function, for instance, Copyright (c) 2012, 2014–2015. The "c" in parenthesis approximates the actual copyright symbol. After the copyright, the next line should state "All Rights Reserved". Add a blank line between the main header and the copyright notice to suppress it from the command-line help display.

The following example shows a function that computes a dot product columnwise for two matrices. Note that this is still legible in the Command Window output of help Dot, with the first % of the cell breaks suppressed. Use the * markup for a bulleted list. The output is always one row, which is indicated in the size key.

FUNCTION HEADER EXAMPLE

```
%% DOT Dot product of two arrays.
%% Forms
%   d = Dot ( w, y )
%   d = Dot ( w )
%% Description
% Dot product with support for arrays. The number of columns of w and y can be:
%
% * Both > 1 and equal
% * One can have one column and the other any number of columns
%
% If there is only one input the dot product will be taken with itself.
%% Inputs
%   w  (:,:)  Array of vectors
%   y  (:,:)  Array of vectors
%% Outputs
%   d  (1,:)  Dot product of w and y
%% See also
% Cross

%% Copyright
% Copyright (c) 2015 Princeton Satellite Systems, Inc.
% All Rights Reserved.
```

When published to HTML, this will appear as follows, ignoring the generated Contents section:

DOT Dot product of two arrays.

Forms

```
d = Dot( w, y )
d = Dot( w )
```

Description

Dot product with support for arrays. The number of columns of w and y can be

- Both > 1 and equal

- One can be a single column and the other any number of columns

If there is only one input, the dot product will be taken with itself.

Inputs

```
w  (:,:)  vector
y  (:,:)  vector
```

Outputs

```
d  (1,:)  Dot product of w and y
```

See also

```
Cross
```

Finally, remember to describe any plots created or files generated; i.e. "side effects." It's also a good idea to identify whether a function uses persistent or global variables, which may require a `clear` command to reset. The following list summarizes the parts of the header, in order.

1. **H1 line** Start with a single line description of the function.

2. **Syntax** List the syntaxes supporter.

3. **Description** Provide a more detailed description. Describe any built-in demos, default values for parameters, persistent or global variables that users need to be aware of, and any "side effects," including plots or files saved. Indicate whether a function will request input from the user.

4. **Inputs** List the inputs with a size/format key. Include units, if applicable.

5. **Outputs** List the outputs as is done with inputs.

6. **See also** List any related functions.

7. **Reference** If applicable, list any references.

8. **Copyright** Include a copyright notice. There should be a blank line between the rest of the header and the copyright notice.

2-3. Overloading Functions and Utilizing varargin

Problem

You want to reuse a section of code that you have written, but you may use it in different situations or extract additional data for it in some circumstances but not others.

Solution

You can overload functions in MATLAB easily and implicitly. `varargin` and `varargout` make it simple to manage variable length input and output lists.

How It Works

MATLAB allows you to overload a function in any way you would like inside the file that defines it. This applies to the inputs and the outputs. There is generally a trade-off between writing the clearest code you can, with a single calling syntax, and avoiding duplication of code. Perhaps there are intermediate variables that may be useful as outputs in some cases, or you want to provide backward compatibility with an older syntax. When creating libraries for numerical computations, there always seem to be additional syntaxes that are useful. We recommend the following when overloading functions:

- Use varargin and varargout when possible and rename the variables with descriptive names as close to the top of the function as you can.

- Be sure to clearly document all input and output variants in the header. Adding another optional input or output and neglecting to document it is the number-one reason for out-of-date headers.

- Use comments to clearly identify what the outputs are when you are renaming them to match the function's syntax, or use varargout.

- Clear the function outputs if you are creating a plot and they are not needed, to avoid unnecessary printing to the command line.

The following example highlights use of these guidelines. We often use functions with a string "action" defining multiple input variations by name. This provides additional clarity beyond depending on input number or type to select an overloaded method.

FUNCTION OVERLOADING

```matlab
% d = OverloadedFunction('default data');
% OverloadedFunction('demo');
% [y,d] = OverloadedFunction('update',x,d);

function varargout = OverloadedFunction ( action, varargin )

switch action
  case 'default_data'
    d = DefaultData;
    varargout{1} = d;

  case 'demo'
    d = DefaultData;
    x = linspace(0,1);
    y = OverloadedFunction('update',x,d);
    figure('name', 'OverloadedFunction_Demo');
    plot(x,y);

  case 'update'
    x = varargin{1};
    d = varargin{2};
    y = Update(x,d);
    varargout{1} = y;
    varargout{2} = d;

end
```

2-4. Adding Built-in Inputs and Outputs to Functions

Problem

You would like to provide default values for some optional inputs or provide a short demonstration of how a function works.

Solution

Add built-in inputs and outputs to your function using an action input or nargin. This can include a full demo that calls the function and generates plots, as appropriate.

How It Works

Built-in inputs provide an example set of parameters that produce output. In many cases, we provide an input range that can create a plot demonstrating the computation performed in the function. In MATLAB, you must explicitly handle input options in the code, as you can't add a default value in the function definition itself.

One convention that we find useful is to allow an empty matrix, [ ], to be entered for an input to use its default value. This allows you to request a default for one input, but provide values for subsequent inputs. The following example shows both a demo that creates a plot and a default value for a constant.

```
function output = MyFunction( variable, constant )

if (nargin == 0)
  % perform demo
  variable = linspace(0,100);
  MyFunction( variable );
  return;
end
if (nargin < 2 || isempty (constant))
  % default value of constant
  constant = VALUE;
end
```

Notice that the built-in demo, which is performed when there are no inputs at all, calls the function itself and then returns. This makes the demo also a built-in test. The code to generate the built-in outputs, which could be a text report to the command line or a plot, generally comes at the end of the function. This enables you to create the built-in outputs with inputs that the user specifies, and not just the built-in inputs. For instance, there might be alternative values of the constant. Note that in the following output generation example, the name of the figure is specified, including the name of the function, which is exceedingly helpful if you routinely generate dozens of plots during your work.

```
... body of function with calculations ...

if (nargout==0)
  % Default output is a plot
  figure('Name', 'Demo of MyFunction')
  plot(variable, output)
  clear output
end
```

■ **Tip** Assign a name to figures that you create. Include the name of the function or demo for clarity. The name will be displayed in the title bar of the figure and in MATLAB's Windows menu.

Writing all of your functions this way has several advantages. For one, you are showing valid ranges of the variables up front, without requiring a reader to refer to a separate test function or demo in another folder. Having this hard data available every time you open the function helps keep your code and your comments consistent. Also, you have a test of the function, which you can easily rerun at any time right from the editor. You can publish the function with execution turned on, which performs the demo and includes the command-line output and plots right in the HTML file (or LaTeX or Word, if you so choose.) All of this helps reduce bugs and documents your function for other readers or yourself in the future.

Following this guideline, here is the general format followed for all functions in this book:

1. Detailed header

2. Copyright

3. Function definition

4. Default inputs

5. Function demo—that calls itself

6. Code body with calculations

7. Default output

Note that no final `return` statement is necessary.

In summary, the following usages of this function have been enabled by adding default inputs and outputs:

```
output = MyFunction( variable, constant );
output = MyFunction( variable );    % uses default value of constant
MyFunction;                         % performs built-in demo
MyFunction(variable, constant);     % creates a plot for the given input
```

2-5. Smart Structuring of Scripts

Problem

You write a few lines of code in a script to test some idea. Can you figure out what it does a year later?

Solution

Treat your scripts like functions, and structure them well. Take the time to follow a template.

How It Works

A script is any collection of commands that you put in a file and execute together. In our toolboxes, we treat scripts as demos of our toolbox functions, and therefore as instructional. Here are some guidelines we recommend when creating scripts:

Create help Help headers are not just for functions; write them for your scripts too. In a year from now, will you remember what this script does? Will someone else in your company be able to understand it? Write a detailed description including a list of any files required or generated.

Use publishing markup Create cells in your scripts (using %%) to delineate sections. Write detailed comments after the section headings. Publish your script to HTML and see how it looks. You can even add equations using LaTeX markup or by inserting images.

Initialize your variables Take care to fully initialize your variables or you could have conflicts when you run multiple scripts in a row. This especially applies to data structures and cell arrays. See the recipes for data types in Chapter 1 for the correct way to initialize different variables.

Specify a directory for saved files Make sure that you are saving any data into a particular location and not just wherever the current directory happens to be.

Our scripts use the following pattern. Cell breaks are used between the sections.

1. Detailed header using publishing markup

2. Copyright notice

3. User parameters (meant to be changed between runs) are grouped at the top

4. Constants are defined

5. Initialize plotting arrays before loops

6. Perform calculations

7. Create plots

8. Store outputs in files, if desired

The following is a complete example, which can be executed.

```
%% DEMO This is a template for a script layout.
% A detailed description of the script includes and files loaded or
% generated and an idea of what data and plots will be created.
% We will calculate a sine or cosine with or without scaling of the input.
% The script creates one plot and saves the workspace to a file called
% Demo.mat.
%% See also
% sin, cos
```

```matlab
%% User parameters
param1 = 0.5;
nPoints = 50;
useSine = false;

%% Constants
MY_CONSTANT = 0.25;

%% Calculation loop
yPlot = zeros(2,nPoints);
x     = linspace(0,4*pi,nPoints);
for k = 1:nPoints
  if (useSine)
    y = sin( [1.0;param1]*x(k) + MY_CONSTANT );
  else
    y = cos( [1.0;param1]*x(k) + MY_CONSTANT );
  end
  yPlot (:,k) = y;
end

%% Plotting
figure('Name', 'DEMO');
plot(x,yPlot);

%% Save workspace to a file
saveDir = fileparts(mfilename('fullpath'));
save(fullfile(saveDir, 'Demo'))
```

You can verify that the data is stored by clearing the workspace and loading the mat-file after the demo has run.

```matlab
>> clear all
>> ScriptDemo
>> clear all
>> load Demo.mat
>> who
```

Your variables are:

```
MY_CONSTANT  nPoints     useSine     y
k            param1      x           yPlot
```

2-6. Implementing MATLAB Command-Line Help for Folders

Problem

You have a set of folders in your code base and you would like users to easily navigate them as they can the built-in MATLAB library.

Solution

Placing Contents.m files in each folder can provide metadata for the contents of the folders, and this can be displayed on the command line.

How It Works

Command-line help isn't just for functions and scripts. Folders can also have help in the form of a contents listing, which includes the function names and a single-line description of each. Toolboxes can also provide documentation in response to a ver command with a toolbox-level contents listing. This information is provided in a Contents.m file that consists entirely of comments.

The Contents Report can generate Contents.m files for you. It can also check and fix existing Contents.m files. It automatically uses the H1 line, or the first line of the header, in the function or script. Recipe 2-2 provided an example of a function header that includes this line. To read more and learn how to run the report on your operating system, see the MATLAB help topic "Create Help Summary Files."

Version information isn't limited to a single Contents file per toolbox; it is generated by a special line inserted into the top of any Contents.m file:

```
% Version xxx dd-mmm-yyyy
```

You can also add a descriptive line above the Version information and add subheadings to groups of files. For example, consider the output from the codetools directory included in MATLAB:

```
>> help codetools
  Commands for creating and debugging code
  MATLAB Version 8.4 (R2014b) 08-Sep-2014

  Editing and publishing
    edit              - Edit or create a file
    grabcode          - Copy MATLAB code from published HTML
    mlint             - Check files for possible problems
    notebook          - Open MATLAB Notebook in Microsoft Word (on Microsoft
                        Windows platforms)
    publish           - Publish file containing cells to output file
    snapnow           - Force snapshot of image for published document

  Directory tools
    mlintrpt          - Run mlint for file or folder, reporting results in browser
    visdiff           - Compare two files (text, MAT, or binary) or folders
```

As with the header of a function, there can be no blank lines in the Contents file, only comments. This is shown in an example in Chapter 6 of this book, the Double Integrator, where we added letters of the alphabet as section breaks.

```
% MATLAB/Ch06-DoubleIntegrator
%
% D
%   DoubleIntegratorSim - Double Integrator Demo
%
```

```
% P
%     PDControl            - Design and implement a PD Controller in sampled time.
%     PlotSet             - Create two-dimensional plots from a data set.
%
% R
%     RHSDoubleIntegrator - Right hand side of a double integrator.
%     RungeKutta          - Fourth order Runge-Kutta numerical integrator.
%
% T
%     TimeLabel           - Produce time labels and scaled time vectors
```

Figure 2-2 shows how to access the Contents Report for this folder from the Command Window.

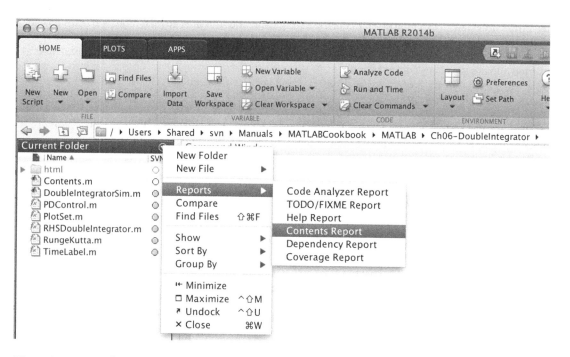

Figure 2-2. *Access the Contents Report on Double Integrator*

The actual report is shown in Figure 2-3. You can see that there are links to edit the Contents.m file, such as for adding version information; fixing the spacing; or fixing all problems. The report detects if you have changed the H1 description line of the function and it conflicts with the text in the Contents file.

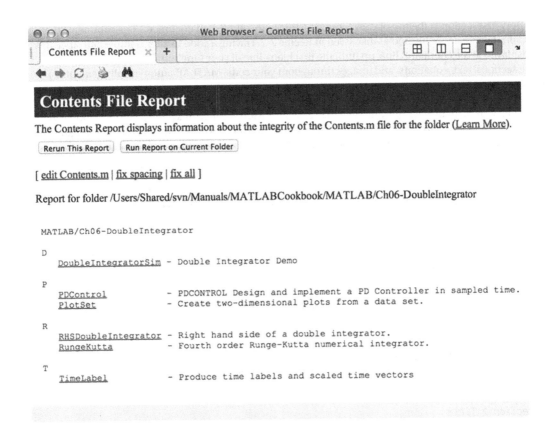

Figure 2-3. *Completed Double Integrator contents report*

2-7. Publishing Code into Technical Reports

Problem

You are creating a report based on some analysis you are doing in MATLAB. You are laboriously copying and pasting code snippets and figures into your report document. You discover a bug in your code, and you have to do it all over again...

Solution

The publishing feature in MATLAB allows you to run a script and automatically generate a document containing the results, including images of each figure generated and the code itself, with text and equations that you insert. These reports can be easily regenerated when you change your code.

How It Works

The publishing features allow you to generate HTML, LaTeX, Word, and PowerPoint documents from your code. These documents can display the code itself, as well as command-line output and plots. You can even capture snapshots of your figures during loops and include equations using LaTeX markup. Every programmer should become familiar with these features. The main features are highlighted shortly.

45

The very first section at the top of your file gives a title to the published document. The comments that follow in your header are published as discussed in Recipe 2-2. Having a good header is important since this can be displayed at the command line, up until the first blank line of your function. However, you can also add more sections, text, equations, and images throughout your code. MATLAB automatically generates a table of contents of all the sections, and inserts the generated plots and command-line output in each section.

You need to be careful about putting section breaks inside loops, since this produces a snapshot of any figures at every iteration. This could be a desired behavior if you want to capture the evolution of a figure, but it could also accidentally produce hundreds of unwanted images. The following is an example script created to demonstrate publishing.

CREATE A TECHNICAL MEMO FROM YOUR CODE

```
%% Technical Memo Example
% Summary of example objective.
% Evaluate a function, in this case $\sin(x)$, in a loop. Show how the
% equation looks on its own line:
%
% $$ y = sin(x) $$

%% Section 1 Title
% Description of first code block.
% Define a customizable scale factor that is treated as a constant.
SCALE_FACTOR = 1.0;

%% Section 2 Title
% Description of second code block.
% Perform a for loop that updates a figure.
%
h = figure('Name','Example_Memo_Figure');
hold on;
y = zeros(1,100);
x = linspace(0,2*pi);
for k = 1:100
        %%% Evaluate the function. Comments not in a block after the title will
        %%% not be included in the main text.
        y(k) = sin(SCALE_FACTOR*x(k));
        plot(x(k),y(k),'.')
end

%% Conclusions
% You can add additional text throughout your script. You can insert lists,
% HTML, links, images, etc.
```

Figure 2-4 shows this script in the publishing tab of the MATLAB editor, with the pop-up menu opened to access the publishing options.

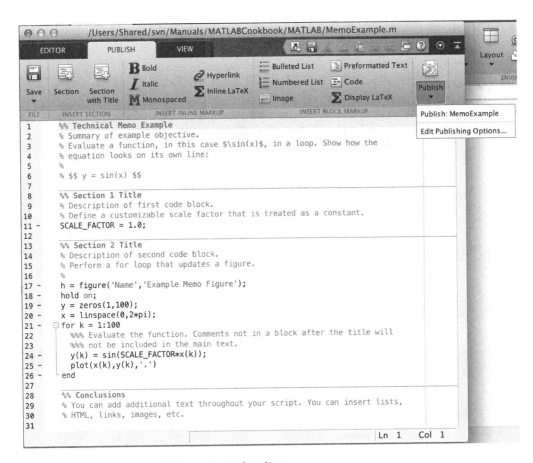

Figure 2-4. *Preparing to publish a script in the editor*

There are a number of settings that apply to publishing. You can save a set of settings with a name and easily reuse it for all of your files. The default settings for code are to both evaluate it and include the source code in the published document, but these may be turned off independently. To create a technical memo from a script without including the source code itself, you set the "Include code" option to *false*. You can set maximum dimensions on figures and select the format: JPEG, PNG, bitmap, or TIFF. You can even specify a MATLAB expression for a function to include input arguments, rather than just running it as a built-in demo.

Figure 2-5 shows the settings window with PDF selected as the output type. Note the Save As... button, which allows you to save settings. We set the maximum width of the figure to 200 pixels to enable the memo to fit on one page, for the purposes of this book.

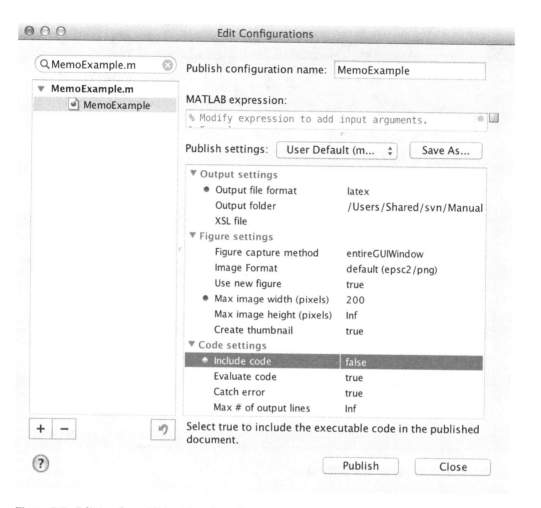

Figure 2-5. *Editting the publish settings for a file*

Figure 2-6 shows a LaTeX memo generated and compiled for the preceding listing, published without the code, with the figure generated in a loop. Note the table of contents, equation, and insertion of the graphic. We had to remove some extra \vspace commands that MATLAB added to the LaTeX to fit the memo on one page.

Technical Memo Example

Summary of example objective. Evaluate a function, in this case $sin(x)$, in a loop. Show how the equation looks on its own line:

$$y = sin(x)$$

Contents

- Section 1 Title
- Section 2 Title
- Conclusions

Section 1 Title

Description of first code block. Define a customizable scale factor that is treated as a constant.

Section 2 Title

Description of second code block. Perform a for loop that updates a figure.

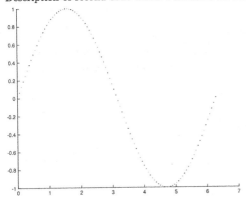

Conclusions

You can add additional text throughout your script. You can insert lists, HTML, links, images, etc.

Figure 2-6. *Technical memo published to LaTeX and compiled to PDF*

2-8. Integrating Toolbox Documentation into the MATLAB Help System

Problem

You would like to write a users' guide and provide it with your toolbox.

Solution

If you write HTML help files, you can, in fact, include them with your toolbox when you distribute it, and the help will show up in MATLAB's help browser.

How It Works

You are not limited to command-line help when providing documentation for your code or toolbox. MATLAB now provides an API for writing HTML documentation and displaying it to users in the help browser. You can write an entire HTML manual and include published versions of your demos.

In order to integrate your HTML help files into the MATLAB help system, you need to generate a few XML files. One provides a top-level table of contents for your toolboxes. Another provides a list of the demos or examples. The third identifies your product. The help topics to read are "Display Custom Documentation" and "Display Custom Examples." The help for third-party products is displayed in a separate section of the MATLAB help browser, entitled "Supplemental Software." The files you need to generate are listed in Table 2-1.

Table 2-1. *Custom Documentation Files*

info.xml	Identify your documentation
helptoc.xml	Table of contents
demos.xml	Table of examples

The MATLAB documentation describes the XML tags that you need. It provides template documents. Comments can be included within the files using standard HTML comments with `<!--` and `-->`.

The main purpose of the `info.xml` file is to provide a name for your toolbox, identify it as a toolbox or blockset, and provide a path to the remaining HTML documentation. The following is an example for our recipes code.

EXAMPLE INFO.XML

```
<productinfo xmlns:xsi="http://www.w3.org/2001/XMLSchema-instance"
    xsi:noNamespaceSchemaLocation="optional">
    <?xml-stylesheet type="text/xsl"href="optional"?>

    <matlabrelease>R2014b</matlabrelease>
    <name>MATLAB Recipes</name>
    <type>toolbox</type>
    <icon></icon>
    <help_location>Documentation</help_location>
    <help_contents_icon>$toolbox/matlab/icons/bookicon.gif</help_contents_icon>
</productinfo>
```

The table of contents file, `helptoc.xml`, must provide a listing of all the HTML files in your help. This is accomplished with a `<tocitem>` tag that can be nested. You generally provide a starting or main page for your toolbox, a "getting started" page, users' guide pages, release notes, and further pages that list the functions provided. `<tocitem>`'s can have references to HTML anchors; they do not all need to refer to separate HTML files.

A small set of icons is included, which can be displayed in the help contents. Consider the following `helptoc.xml`.

EXAMPLE HELPTOC.XML

```xml
<?xml version='1.0' encoding="utf-8"?>
<toc version="2.0">
<!-- First tocitem specifies top level page in Help browser Contents -->
    <tocitem target="index.html">Recipes Toolbox
        <!-- A Getting Started page is generally first -->
        <tocitem target="getting_started.html" image="HelpIcon.GETTING_STARTED">
            Getting Started
            <tocitem target="requirements.html">System Requirements</tocitem>
            <tocitem target="features.html">Features
                <!-- TOC levels may include anchor IDs -->
                <tocitem target="features.html#10187">Feature 1</tocitem>
                <tocitem target="features.html#10193">Feature 2</tocitem>
            </tocitem>
        </tocitem>
        <!-- There is a special icon for the User Guide -->
        <tocitem target="guide_intro.html"
            image="HelpIcon.USER_GUIDE">Recipes User Guide
            <tocitem target="setup.html">Setting Up</tocitem>
            <tocitem target="data_processing.html">Processing Data</tocitem>
            <tocitem target="verification.html">Verifying Outputs
                <tocitem target="test_failures.html">Handling Test Failures</tocitem>
            </tocitem>
        </tocitem>
        <!-- The function reference is next with the FUNCTION icon -->
        <!-- First item is page describing function categories, if any -->
        <tocitem target="function_categories.html"
                image="HelpIcon.FUNCTION">Function Reference
            <tocitem target="function_categories.html#1">Double Integrator
                <!-- Inside category, list the functions -->
                <tocitem target="function_1.html">function_1</tocitem>
                <tocitem target="function_2.html">function_2</tocitem>
                <!-- ... -->
            </tocitem>
            <tocitem target="function_categories.html#2">Aircraft
                <tocitem target="function_3.html">function_3</tocitem>
                <tocitem target="function_4.html">function_4</tocitem>
            </tocitem>
            <tocitem target="function_categories.html#3">Spacecraft
                <!-- ... -->
            </tocitem>
        </tocitem>
        <!-- Web links with the webicon.gif -->
        <tocitem target="http://www.psatellite.com"
                image="$toolbox/matlab/icons/webicon.gif">
        Web Site (psatellite.com)
        </tocitem>
    </tocitem>
</toc>
```

This produces the contents listing in the help browser shown in Figure 2-7. The major icons to delineate the help sections are used. Anchor IDs are used for both `features.html` and `function_categories.html`. There is even a reference to an external web site. Note that this means you will have written the following HTML files:

- index.html

- getting_started.html

- requirements.html

- features.html

- guide_intro.html

- setup.html

- data_processing.html

- verification.html

- test_failures.html

- function_categories.html

- function_1.html

- function_2.html

- ...

Figure 2-7. *Custom toolbox table of contents*

Clearly, generating a function list for a large toolbox by hand could be cumbersome. At PSS, we have functions to generate this XML automatically from a directory, using `dir`. You can use the functional form of `publish` to publish your functions and scripts to HTML automatically, as well.

The demos file is similar to the `toc` file in that it provides a nested list of demos or examples. There are two main tags: `<demosection>` and `<demoitem>`. Items can be m-files or videos. Published demos display a thumbnail for one of the figures from the demo, if any exist; the thumbnail image has the same name as the HTML file, but a different extension. The demos are completely independent from the HTML table of contents, and you can implement an examples listing without creating any other HTML help pages.

Here is a short example from our Cubesat Toolbox that includes a published demo called `MagneticControlDemo`.

```
EXAMPLE DEMOS.XML
```

```xml
<?xml version="1.0" encoding="utf-8"?>
<demos>
    <name>CubeSat</name>
    <type>toolbox</type>
    <icon>$toolbox/matlab/icons/demoicon.gif</icon>
    <description>Contains all the demo files for the CubeSat</description>
    <website>
        <a href="http://www.psatellite.com">For more info see psatellite.com</a>
    </website>
    <demosection>
        <label>AttitudeControl</label>
        <demoitem>
            <label>MagneticControlDemo: Magnetic control demand analysis</label>
            <callback>MagneticControlDemo</callback>
            <file>../CubeSat/Demos/AttitudeControl/html/MagneticControlDemo.html</file>
        </demoitem>
    </demosection>
</demos>
```

Once you have created a set of HTML files, you can create a database that will allow MATLAB to search them efficiently. To do this, you use `builddocsearchdb` with a path to the folder containing your help files; that is, the same path you enter in your `info.xml` file. This function creates a subfolder called `helpsearch` containing the database. With this subfolder added to your help installation, users will get results from your documentation when they search in the Help browser.

2-9. Structuring a Toolbox

Problem

You have a jumble of functions and scripts that you would like to organize into a toolbox that you can distribute to others.

Solution

A previous recipe showed you how to create or generate `Contents.m` files for individual folders in your toolbox. You can also create a top-level `Contents.m` file. We describe our usual toolbox structure, including placement of these files.

How It Works

We have a fixed structure for our commercial toolboxes that is used by our build tools and testing routines.

- Group-related functions together in folders
- Place scripts in separate folders
- Place script folders together in a Demos folder

- Use the same name for the function folder and corresponding demos folder

- Organize folder groups into Modules or Toolboxes

Once you create the help files, as described in the previous recipes, they will appear in the directory structure as shown next—not in literal alphabetical order. Note that the published demos are stored in the html directories within the demo folders. We do not display them all, but every folder should have its own Contents.m file.

```
Module
| Contents.m
| Folder1
| |      Contents.m
| |      Function1.m
| Folder2
| |      Function2.m
| Demos
| |      Folder1
| |      | Function1Demo.m
| |      | html
| |      Folder2
| |      | Function2Demo.m
| |      | html
| |      CombinedDemos
| |      | SuperDemo.m
| |      | html
| Documentation
| |      demos.xml
| |      info.xml
| |      ToolboxHelp
| |      |   helptoc.xml
| |      |   GettingStarted.html
| |      |   ...
```

You will note that there is a top-level Contents.m file within the Module, at the same level as the folders. MATLAB does not have any automated utility to make this for you. You can create one with a version line, the name of your toolbox, and any other information you would like displayed when the user types "help Module"; we generate a list of folders within the module using dir. Here is an example, noting that all lines in a Content.m file are comments:

```
% PSS Toolbox Folder NewModule
% Version 2015.1      05-Mar-2015
%
% Directories:
% Folder1
% Folder1
% Demos
% Demos/Folder1
% Demos/Folder1
```

Your toolbox module will now appear when the user types ver at the command. For example:

```
>> ver
----------------------------------------------------------------------------
MATLAB Version: 8.4.0.150421 (R2014b)
MATLAB License Number: 6xxxxx
Operating System: Mac OS X Version: 10.9.5 Build: 13F1066
Java Version: Java 1.7.0_55-b13 with Oracle Corporation Java HotSpot(TM) 64-Bit Server
   VM mixed mode
----------------------------------------------------------------------------
MATLAB                                    Version 8.4        (R2014b)
PSS Toolbox Folder NewModule              Version 2015.1
```

Summary

This chapter reviewed style guidelines for writing MATLAB code and highlighted some differences between styles for MATLAB and other languages. When establishing guidelines for your own toolboxes, consider the features you may want to use, such as automatic generation of contents files, publishing your results to HTML or Microsoft Word, and even incorporating HTML help in the web browser. Also, take the time to create proper headers and initialization when you generate code to avoid unpleasant surprises down the road! Table 2-2 lists the code developed in the chapter.

Table 2-2. *Chapter Code Listing*

File	Description
Dot	Dot product header example.
MemoExample	Example of a technical memo for publishing.
OverloadedFunction	An internally overloaded function.
ScriptDemo	Demo template for a script layout.

CHAPTER 3

■ ■ ■

Visualization

MATLAB provides extensive capabilities for visualizing your data. You can produce 2D plots, 3D plots, and animations; you can view images; and you can create histograms, contour and surfaces plots, and other graphical representations of your data. You are probably familiar with making simple 2D plots with lines and markers, and pie and bar charts, but you may not be aware of the additional possibilities made available by the low-level routines. There are also interactive capabilities for editing plots and figures, and adding annotations before printing or exporting them.

MATLAB excels in scientific visualization and in engineering the visualization of 3D objects. Three-dimensional visualization is used to visualize data that is a function of two parameters, for example, the height on the surface of the Earth, or to visualize three-dimensional objects. The former is used in all areas of science and engineering. The latter is particularly useful in the design and simulation of any kind of machine, such as robots, aircraft, automobiles, and spacecraft.

Three dimensional visualization of objects can be further divided into engineering visualization and photo-realistic visualization. The latter helps you understand what an object looks like and how it is constructed. When the inside of an object is considered, you move into the realm of solid modeling, which is used for creating models suitable for manufacturing of the object. The goal of photo-realistic visualization is to make the 3D view look like a photo. Photo-realistic rendering focuses the interaction of light with the object and the eye. MATLAB does provide some capabilities for lighting and camera interation, but it does not provide true photo-realistic rendering.

The main plotting routines are organized into several categories in the command line help:

graphics Low-level routines for figures, axes, lines, text, and other graphics objects.

graph2d Two-dimension graphs like linear plots, log scale plots, and polar plots.

graph3d Three-dimensional graphs like line, meshes, and surfaces; control of color, lighting, and the camera.

specgraph Specialized graphs, the largest category. Special 2D graphs, like bar and pie charts, histograms, contour plots, special 3D plots, volume and vector visualization, image display, movies, and animation.

The online help has an entire top-level section devoted to graphics, including plots, formatting and annotation, images, printing and saving, graphics objects and performance, and major changes to plotting internals that occurred in R2014b.

A good command of these functions allows you to create very sophisticated graphics, as well as to adapt them to different publication media, whether you need to adjust the dimensions, color, or font attributes of your plot. In this chapter, we present recipes that cover what you need to know to use MATLAB graphics effectively. There isn't space to discuss every available plotting routine, which is well-covered in the available help, but we do cover the basic functionality and provide recipes for common usage.

Electronic supplementary material The online version of this chapter (doi:10.1007/978-1-4842-0559-4_3) contains supplementary material, which is available to authorized users.

S. Thomas and M. Paluszek, *MATLAB Recipes*, DOI 10.1007/978-1-4842-0559-4_3

3-1. Plotting Data Interactively from the MATLAB Desktop

Problem

You would like to plot data in your workspace, but you aren't sure of the best method for visualizing it.

Solution

You can use the PLOTS tab in the MATLAB desktop to plot data directly by selecting variables in the workspace display. You select from a variety of plot options, and MATLAB automatically only shows you those that are applicable to the selected data set.

How It Works

Let's create some sample data to demonstrate this interactive capability, which is a fairly new feature in MATLAB. You'll start with some trigonometric functions to create sample data that oscillates.

```
theta = linspace(0, 4*pi);
y = sin(theta).*cos(2*theta) + 0.05*theta;
```

There are now two vector variables available in the workspace. Select the PLOTS tab in the desktop, and then select the y variable in the Workspace display (see Figure 3-1). The variable appears on the far left of the PLOTS tab area and various plot icons in the ribbon becomes active: plot, bar, area, pie, and so forth. Note the radio buttons on the far left, which are for either reusing the current figure for the plot or creating a new figure.

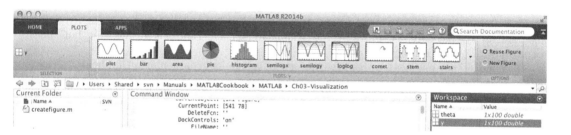

Figure 3-1. *PLOTS tab with plot icon ribbon*

Close any open figures with a `close all` and click the plot icon to create a new figure with a simple 2D plot of the data. Note that clicking the icon results in the plot command printing to the command line:

```
>> plot(y)
```

The data is printed with linear indices along the x axis, as shown in Figure 3-2.

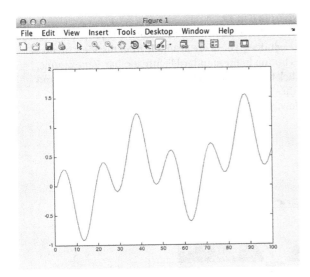

Figure 3-2. *Linear plot of trigonometric data*

You simply click another plot icon to replot the data using a different function, and again the function call is printed to the command line. The plot icons that are displayed are not all the plots available, but simply the default favorites from among all the many options; to see more icons, click the pop-up arrow at the right of the icon ribbon. The available plot types are organized by category. There is a Catalog button that you can press to bring up a dedicated plot catalog window with the documentation for each function.

To plot data y against input theta, you need to select both variables in the workspace view. They will be displayed in the plot ribbon, with a button to reverse their order. Now click an area plot to get a plot with the angle on the x axis, as shown in Figure 3-3.

```
>> area(theta, y)
```

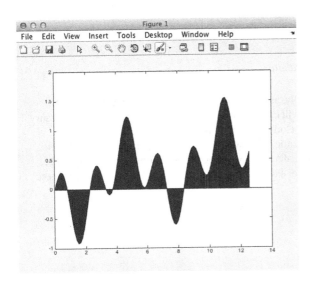

Figure 3-3. *Parametric area plot of trigonometric data*

59

Note that this time, as expected, the x-axis range is from 0 to 4π.

You can annotate the plot interactively with arrows and text, add subplots, change line properties, and more using the Plot Edit toolbar and the Figure Palette window. These are available from the View menu of the figure window and by clicking the Show Plot Tools button in the standard Figure toolbar. For example, using the plot tools, you can select the axes, double-click to open the property editor, type an X Label, and turn on grid lines. You can add another subplot, plot the values of theta against linear indices, and then change the plot type to a stem plot, all from this window. See Figure 3-4.

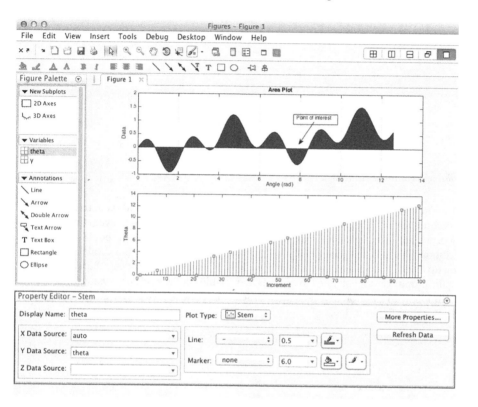

Figure 3-4. *Plot of trigonometric data in the Figure Palette*

The same changes can be made programmatically, as shown in following recipes. In fact, you can generate code from the Figure Palette and MATLAB will create a function with all the commands necessary to replicate your figure from your data. The Generate Code command is under the File menu of the window. It allows you to interactively create a visualization that works with some example data and then programmatically adapt it to your toolbox. MATLAB calls the new autogenerated function `createfigure`. You can see the use of the following functions: `figure`, `axes`, `box`, `hold`, `ylabel`, `xlabel`, `title`, `area`, `stem`, and `annotation`.

```matlab
function createfigure(X1, yvector1)
%CREATEFIGURE(X1, YVECTOR1)
%  X1:   area x
%  YVECTOR1:    area yvector

%  Auto-generated by MATLAB on 03-Jun-2015 14:32:43

% Create figure
figure1 = figure;

% Create axes
axes1 = axes('Parent', figure1, 'XGrid', 'on', 'OuterPosition', [0 0.5 1 0.5]);
box(axes1,'on');
hold(axes1,'on');

% Create ylabel
ylabel('Data');

% Create xlabel
xlabel('Angle_(rad)');

% Create title
title('Area_Plot');

% Create area
area(X1,yvector1,'DisplayName','Area','Parent',axes1);

% Create axes
axes2 = axes('Parent',figure1,'OuterPosition',[0 0 1 0.5]);
box(axes2,'on');
hold(axes2,'on');

% Create ylabel
ylabel('Theta');

% Create xlabel
xlabel('Increment');

% Create stem
stem(X1,'DisplayName','theta','Parent',axes2,'Marker','none',...
  'Color',[0 0.447 0.741]);

% Create textarrow
annotation(figure1,'textarrow',[0.609822646657571 0.568894952251023],...
  [0.827828828828829 0.717117117117118]);

% Create textbox
annotation(figure1,'textbox',...
  [0.553888130968622 0.814895792699917 0.120787482806052 0.0489690721649485],...
  'String',{'Point_of_interest'});
```

Note that this code did not, in fact, use the subplot function, but rather the option to specify the exact axes location in the figure with the 'OuterPosition' property. Also note that the units of the axes positions and the annotations are between 0 and 1; that is, normalized. This is, in fact, an option for axes, as seen in the following call using gca to get the handle to the current axes:

```
>> set(gca, 'units')
    'inches'
    'centimeters'
    'characters'
    'normalized'
    'points'
    'pixels'
```

Using other units may be helpful for certain applications, but normalized units are always the default. The following are additional interactive buttons in the Figure toolbar that should be mentioned:

- Zoom in
- Zoom out
- Hand tool to move an object in the plane of the figure
- Rotate tool to rotate the view
- Data cursor
- Brush/Select Data
- Colorbar
- Legend

The hand and rotate tools are very helpful with 3D data. The data cursor displays the values of a plot point right in the figure. The brush highlights a segment of data using a contrast color of your choosing using the colors pop-up. The colorbar and the legend buttons serve as on/off switches.

3-2. Incrementally Annotate a Plot

Problem

You need to annotate a curve in a plot at a subset of points on the curve.

Solution

Use the text function to notate the plot.

How It Works

Call text within a for loop in AnnotatePlot. Use sprintf to create the text for the annotations, which gives you control over the formatting of any numbers. In this case, use %d for integer display. linspace creates an evenly spaced index array into the data to give you the selected points to annotate; in this case, five points.

```matlab
%% Annotate a plot
% Add text annotations evenly spaced along a curve.

%% Parameters
nPoints = 5; % Number of plot points to have annotations

%% Create the line
v       = [1;2;3];
t       = linspace(0,1000);
r       = [v(1)*t;v(2)*t;v(3)*t];

%% Create the figure and plot
s = 'Annotated_Plot';
h = figure('name',s);
plot3(r(1,:),r(2,:),r(3,:));
xlabel('X');
ylabel('Y');
zlabel('Z');
title(s)
grid

%% Add the annotations
n       = length(t);
j       = ceil(linspace(1,n,nPoints));

for k = j
  text(r(1,k), r(2,k), r(3,k), sprintf ('-_Time_%d',floor(t(k))));
end
```

Note that you pass the index array j directly to the loop index k. Figure 3-5 shows the annotated plot. You create a three-dimensional straight line to annotate.

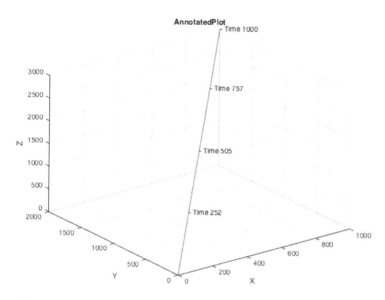

Figure 3-5. *Annotated three-dimensional plot*

3-3. Create a Custom Plot Page with Subplot

Problem

You need multiple plots of your data for a particular application, and as you rerun your script, they are cluttering your screen and hogging memory. We often create many dozens of plots as we work with our commercial toolboxes.

Solution

Create a single plot with several subplots on it so you only need one figure to see the results of one run of your application.

How It Works

The subplot function allows you to create a symmetric array of plots in a figure in two dimensions. You generate an m × n array of small axes that are spaced in the figure automatically. A good example is a 3D trajectory with views from different angles. You can create a plot with a 2 × 2 array of axes, with the 3D plot in the lower left-hand corner and views from each direction around it. The function is QuadPlot. It has a built-in demo, creating the figure shown in Figure 3-6.

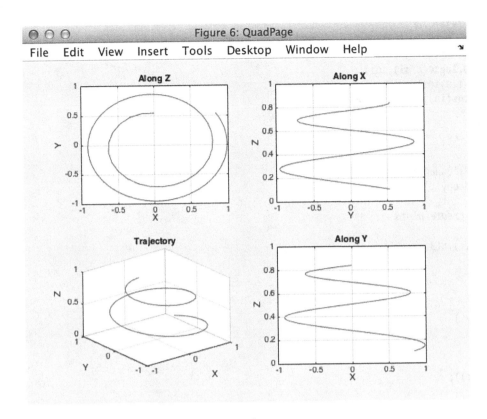

Figure 3-6. *QuadPlot using subplot for axes placement*

Note that you must use the size of your axes array—in this, case (2,2)—in each call to subplot.

```
%% QUADPLOT Create a quad plot page using subplot.
% This creates a 3D view and three 2D views of a trajectory in one figure.
%% Form
%   QuadPlot( x )
%% Input
%   x   (3,:)      Trajectory data
%
%% Output
% None. But you may want to return the graphics handles for further programmatic
% customization.
%
```

```matlab
function QuadPlot(x)
  if nargin == 0
    disp('Demo_of_QuadPlot');
    th = logspace(0,log10(4*pi),101);
    in = logspace(-1,0,101);
    x = [sin(th).*cos(in);cos(th).*cos(in);sin(in)];
    QuadPlot(x);
    return;
end

h = figure('Name','QuadPage');
set(h,'InvertHardcopy','off')

% Use subplot to create plots
subplot(2,2,3)
plot3(x(1,:),x(2,:),x(3,:));
xlabel('X')
ylabel('Y')
zlabel('Z')
grid on
title('Trajectory')
rotate3d on

subplot(2,2,1)
plot(x(1,:),x(2,:));
xlabel('X')
ylabel('Y')
grid on
title('Along_Z')

subplot(2,2,2)
plot(x(2,:),x(3,:));
xlabel('Y')
ylabel('Z')
grid on
title('Along__X')

subplot(2,2,4)
plot(x(1,:),x(3,:));
xlabel('X')
ylabel('Z')
grid on
title('Along__Y')
```

In the latest versions of MATLAB, you can easily access figure and axes properties using field names. For instance, let's get the figure generated by the demo using gcf, and then look at the children, which should include the four subplots.

```
>> h = gcf

h =

Figure (5: PlotPage) with properties:

      Number: 5
        Name: 'PlotPage'
       Color: [0.94 0.94 0.94]
    Position: [440 378 560 420]
       Units: 'pixels'

   Show all properties

>> h.Children

ans =
  5x1 graphics array:

  ContextMenu
  Axes            (Along Y)
  Axes            (Along X)
  Axes            (Along Z)
  Axes            (Trajectory)
```

Note that the titles of the axes are helpfully displayed. If you wanted to add additional objects or change the properties of the axes, you could access the handles this way. Or, you might want to provide the handles as an output for your function. You can also make a subplot in a figure of the current axes, just by calling subplot again with the array size and ID:

```
(2,2,1)
```

3-4. Create a Plot Page with Custom-Sized Axes

Problem

You would like to group some plots together in a figure, but not as evenly spaced subplots.

Solution

You can create custom-sized axes using the 'OuterPosition' property of the axes, placing them anywhere in the figure that you wish.

How It Works

You'll create a custom figure with two plots, one spanning the width of the figure and a second smaller axes, as in Figure 3-7. This leaves room for a block of descriptive text, which might describe the figure itself or display the results. In order to make the plots more interesting, you will add markers and text annotations using num2str.

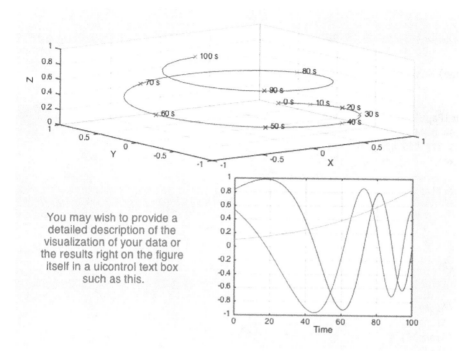

You may wish to provide a detailed description of the visualization of your data or the results right on the figure itself in a uicontrol text box such as this.

Figure 3-7. *PlotPage with custom-sized plots*

The function is PlotPage. Using 'OuterPosition' for the axes instead of 'Position' means the limits include the axes labels, so you can use the full range of the figure from 0 to 1 (normalized units).

```
%% PLOTPAGE Create a plot page with several custom plots in one figure.
% Specify axes with custom sizes on the figure.
%% Form
%  PlotPage( t, x )
%% Input
%  t  (1,:)    Time vector
%  x  (3,:)    Trajectory data
%
%% Output
% None. But you may want to return the graphics handles for further programmatic
% customization.

function PlotPage(t, x)

if nargin == 0
  disp('Demo of PlotPage');
  t = linspace(0,100,101);
  th = logspace(0,log10(4*pi),101);
  in = logspace(-1,0,101);
  x = [sin(th).*cos(in);cos(th).*cos(in);sin(in)];
end

h = figure('Name','PlotPage');
set(h,'InvertHardcopy','off')
```

```
% Specify the axes position as [left, bottom, width, height]
axes('outerposition',[0.5 0 0.5 0.5]);
plot(t,x);
xlabel('Time')
grid on

% Specify an additional axes and make a 3D plot
axes('outerposition',[0 0.5 1 0.5]);
plot3(x(1,:),x(2,:),x(3,:));
xlabel('X')
ylabel('Y')
zlabel('Z')
grid on

% add markers evenly spaced with time
hold on
for k=1:10:length(t)
    plot3(x(1,k),x(2,k),x(3,k),'x');
    % add a text label
    label = ['␣␣' num2str(t(k)) '␣s'];
    text(x(1,k),x(2,k),x(3,k),label);
end
hold off

uh = uicontrol('Style','text','String','Description␣of␣the␣plots',...
          'units','normalized','position',[0.05 0.1 0.35 0.3]);
set(uh,'string',['You␣may␣wish␣to␣provide␣a␣detailed␣description␣'...
              'of␣the␣visualization␣of␣your␣data␣or␣the␣results␣right␣on␣the␣figure
              ␣'...
              'itself␣in␣a␣uicontrol␣text␣box␣such␣as␣this.']);
set(uh,'fontsize',14);
set(uh,'foregroundcolor',[1 0 0]);
```

3-5. Plotting with Dates

Problem

You want to plot data as a function of time using dates on the x axis.

Solution

Access the tick labels directly using handles for the axis, or use datetick with serial date numbers.

How It Works

First, you can manually specify the tick labels. You plot the data as a function of the index and then replace the *x* labels with strings of your choice; in this case, specific months. For example, you plot the power consumption of a home in kilowatt-hours (kWh), see Figure 3-8. Note how the xlim, xtick, and xticklabel properties are set using set after generating the plot. The limits are set to [0 13] instead of [1 12] to accommodate the width of the bars.

```
%% Plot using months as the x label
% First we will set the labels manually. Then we will use MATLAB's serial date
% numbers to set the labels automatically.

%% Specify specific months as labels
kWh = [ 2500 2600 2900 1500 1300 1500 1600 1000 1400 1100 1200 2300];
month = {'Jan' 'Feb' 'Mar' 'Apr' 'May' 'Jun' 'Jul' 'Aug' 'Sep' 'Oct' 'Nov' 'Dec'};

figure('Name','Plotting_With_Manual_Date_Labels');
bar(1:12,kWh)
xlabel('Month');
ylabel('kWh')
title('Power_Consumption');
grid on

set(gca,'xlim',[0 13],'xtick',1:12,'xticklabel',month);
```

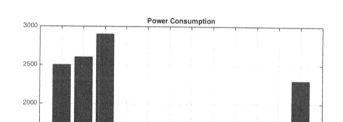

Figure 3-8. *Plotting with manual month labels*

If you are plotting data against complete dates, you can also use MATLAB's serial date numbers, which can be automatically displayed as tick marks using datetick. You can convert between calendar dates and serial numbers using datestr, datenum, and datevec. A date vector is the six-component date as [year month day hour minute second]. So, for instance, let's assign the data in the preceding example to actual dates in the year 2014. The default date tick marks show months just, like in the manual example, but for demonstration purposes, let's specify a format including the year: 'mmmyy'. See Figure 3-9.

```
%% Specify full dates and use serial dates to automatically produce labels
% Specifying only the month will use the current year by default. We will set
% the year to 2014 by using datevec.

N = datenum(month,'mmm');
```

```
V = datevec(N);
V(:,1) = 2014;
N = datenum(V);

figure('Name','Plotting_With_Serial_Dates');
bar(N,kWh)
xlabel('Date');
title('Power_Consumption_with_datetick');
datetick('x','mm/yy')
grid on
```

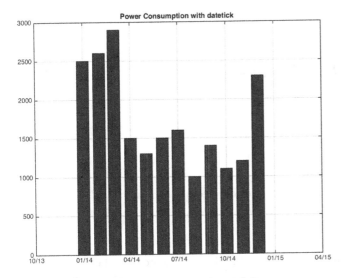

Figure 3-9. *Plotting using datetick with serial dates*

Note that the ticks themselves are no longer one per month; if you want to specify them manually, you now need to use date numbers. The properties are printed here, using get to show the XTicks used.

```
>> get(gca)
...
                    XLim: [735508 735965]
                XLimMode: 'manual'
              XMinorGrid: 'off'
              XMinorTick: 'off'
                  XScale: 'linear'
                   XTick: [735508 735600 735690 735781 735873 735965]
              XTickLabel: [6x5 char]
```

MATLAB's serial date numbers do not correspond to other serial date formats, like the Julian date. MATLAB simply counts days from Jan-1-0000, so the year 2000 starts at a serial number of 2000 * 365=730,000. The following quick example demonstrates this, as well as uses now to get the current date:

```
>> v = datevec(now)
v =
          2015           7          31          11          37      0.6198
>> n = datenum(v)
n =
     7.3618e+05
>> s = datestr(n,'local')
s =
31-Jul-2015 11:37:00
```

3-6. Generating a Color Distribution

Problem

You want to assign colors to markers or lines in your plot.

Solution

Specify the HSV components algorithmically from around the color wheel and convert to RGB.

How It Works

ColorDistribution chooses colors from around the color wheel, as shown in Figure 3-10. The colors are selected using the hue component of HSV, with a full range from 0 to 1. Parameters allow the user to separately specify the saturation and value, which are the same for all the colors generated. You could alternatively use these components to select a variety of colors of one hue.

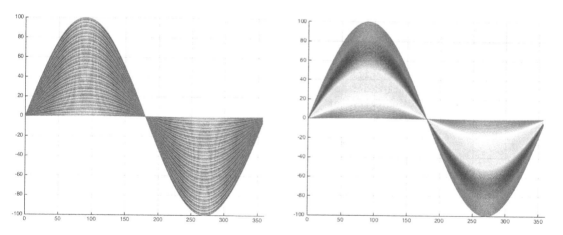

Figure 3-10. *Original lines and lines with a color distribution with values and saturation of 1*

Reducing the saturation (sat) lightens the colors while remaining on the same "spoke" of the color wheel. A saturation of 0 produces all grays. Value (val) keeps the ratio between RGB components remains the same, but lowering the magnitude makes colors darker; for example, [1 0.85 0] and [0.684 0.581 0].

```
%% Demonstrate a color distribution for an array of lines.
% Colors are calculated around the color wheel using hsv2rgb.

val    = 1;
sat    = 1;
n      = 100;
dTheta = 360/n;
thetaV = linspace(0,360-dTheta,n);

h      = linspace(0,1-1/n,n);
s      = sat*ones(1,n);
v      = val*ones(1,n);
colors = hsv2rgb([h;s;v]');
y      = sin(thetaV*pi/180);
h      = figure;
hold on;
set(h,'name','Color Wheel')
l      = gobjects(n);
for k = 1:n
  l(k) = plot(thetaV,k*y);
end
set(gca,'xlim',[0 360]);
grid on
pause

for k = 1:n
  set(l(k),'color',colors(k,:)*val);
end
```

3-7. Visualizing Data over 2D or 3D Grids

Problem

You need to perform a calculation over a grid of data and view the results.

Solution

The function meshgrid produces grids over x and y that can be used for calculations and subsequently input to surf. This is also useful for contour and quiver plots.

How It Works

First, you define the vectors in x and y that define your grid. You can perform your calculations in a `for` loop or in a vectorized function. The vectors do not have to be physical dimensions; indeed, in general they are quite different quantities involved in a parametric study. The classic example is an exponential function of two variables, which is viewed as a surface in Figure 3-11.

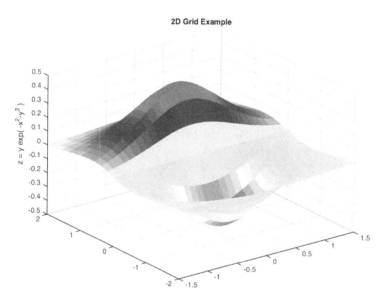

Figure 3-11. *3D surface generated over a 2D grid*

```
%% 2D example of meshgrid
figure('Name','2D_Visualization');
xv = -1.5:0.1:1.5;
yv = -2:0.2:2;
[X,Y] = meshgrid(xv, yv);
Z = Y .* exp(-X.^2 - Y.^2);

surf(X,Y,Z,'edgecolor','none')
title('2D_Grid_Example')
zlabel('z_=_y_exp(_-x^2-y^2_)')
colormap hsv

size(X)
size(Y)
```

The generated matrices are square and consist of the input vector replicated in the correct dimension. You could achieve the same result by hand using `repmat`, but `meshgrid` eliminates the need to remember the details.

```
>> size(X)
ans =
    41    41
>> size(Y)
ans =
    41    41
>> X(1:5,1:5)
ans =
          -2          -1.9          -1.8          -1.7          -1.6
          -2          -1.9          -1.8          -1.7          -1.6
          -2          -1.9          -1.8          -1.7          -1.6
          -2          -1.9          -1.8          -1.7          -1.6
          -2          -1.9          -1.8          -1.7          -1.6
>> Y(1:5,1:5)
ans =
          -2            -2            -2            -2            -2
        -1.9          -1.9          -1.9          -1.9          -1.9
        -1.8          -1.8          -1.8          -1.8          -1.8
        -1.7          -1.7          -1.7          -1.7          -1.7
        -1.6          -1.6          -1.6          -1.6          -1.6
```

For fun, you can plot contours of the data as well. You can use the gradient function to calculate the slope and plot this using quiver. See Figure 3-12.

```
figure('Name','Contour_and_Quiver')
[px,py] = gradient(Z,0.1,0.2);
contour(X,Y,Z), hold on
quiver(X,Y,px,py)
title('Contour_and_Quiver_Demo')
xlabel('x')
ylabel('y')
colormap hsv
axis equal
```

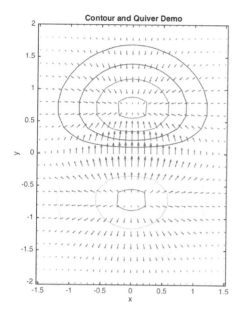

Figure 3-12. *3D surface visualized as contours*

You can also generate a 3D grid and compute data over the volume, for a fourth dimension. In order to view this extra data over the volume, you can use slice. This uses interpolation to draw slices at any location along the axes that you specify. If you want to see the exact planes in your data, you can use pcolor, surf, or contour in individual figures. quiver3 can be used to plot arrows in 3D space as well. The result is shown in Figure 3-13.

```
%% 3D example of meshgrid
% meshgrid can be used to produce 3D matrices, and slice can display selected
% planes using interpolation.
figure('Name','3D_Visualization');
zv = -3:0.3:3;
[x,y,z] = meshgrid(xv, yv, zv);
v = x .* exp(-x.^2 - y.^2 - z.^2);
slice(x,y,z,v,[-1.2 -0.5 0.8],[],[-0.25 1])
title('3D_Grid_Example')
zlabel('v_=_y_exp(_-x^2-y^2-z^2_)')
colormap hsv
```

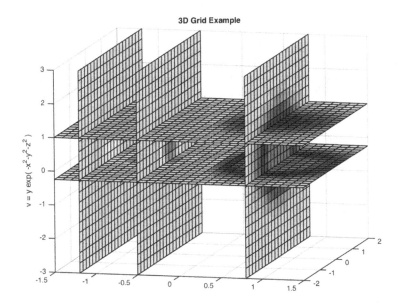

Figure 3-13. *3D Volume with slices*

3-8. Generate 3D Objects Using Patch

Problem

You would like to draw a 3D box.

Solution

You can create a 3D box as in Figure 3-14 using the patch function.

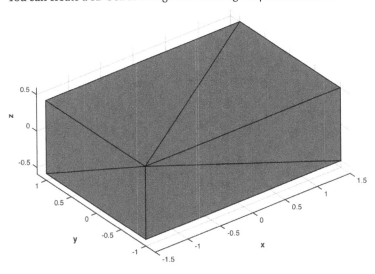

Figure 3-14. *Box generated using patch*

77

How It Works

The patch function in MATLAB uses vertices and faces to define an area in two or three dimensions. The vertex list is an n × 3 array specifying the vertex locations. The faces array is an n × m array, where m is the number of vertices per polygon. The faces array contains the row indices for the vertices. We usually set m to 3 since all graphics engines eventually reduce polygons to triangles. We draw a box in BoxPatch, shown next. Generally, when drawing a physical object, set axis to equal so that the aspect ratio is correct. patch has many properties. In this case, just set the color of the faces to gray using RGB. The edge color, which can also be specified, is black by default. The view(3) call sets the camera to a position with equal x, y, and z values. rotate3d on lets us move the camera around. This is very handy for inspecting the model.

```
%% Generate a cube using patch
% Create a figure a draw a cube in it. The vertices and faces are specified
% directly. Uses 'axis equal' to display the cube with an accurate aspect ratio.

%% Box design
x = 3;
y = 2;
z = 1;

% Faces
f   = [2 3 6;3 7 6;3 4 8;3 8 7;4 5 8;4 1 5;2 6 5;2 5 1;1 3 2;1 4 3;5 6 7;5 7 8];

% Vertices
v = [-x x x -x -x x x -x;...
      -y -y y y -y -y y y;...
      -z -z -z -z z z z z]'/2;

%% Draw the object
h = figure('name','Box');
patch('vertices',v,'faces',f,'facecolor',[0.5 0.5 0.5]);
axis equal
grid on
axis([-3 3 -3 3 -3 3])
xlabel('x')
ylabel('y')
zlabel('z')
view(3)
rotate3d on
```

3-9. Working with Light Objects

Problem

You would like to light the 3D box drawn in the previous recipe.

Solution

You can create ambient or directed light objects using the `light` function. Light objects affect both patch and surface objects, which are created by `surf`, `mesh`, `pcolor`, `fill`, `fill3`, and `patch`.

How It Works

The main properties for working with light objects are `Color`, `Style`, `Position`, and `Visible`. The style may be infinite, with the light shining in parallel rays from a specified direction, or local, with a point source shining in all directions. The `Position` property has a different meaning for each of these styles. `PatchWithLighting` adds a local light to the box script. You modify the box surface properties using `material` to get different effects.

```
%% Add lighting to the cube patch
% We use findobj to locate the patch drawn in Patch, then change its properties
% to be suitable for lighting. We add a local light.

%% Create the box patch object
BoxPatch;

%% Find and update the patch object
p = findobj(gcf,'type','patch');
c = [0.7 0.7 0.1];
set(p,'facecolor',c,'edgecolor',c,...
        'edgelighting','gouraud','facelighting','gouraud');
material('metal');

%% Lighting
l = light('style','local','position',[10 10 10]);
```

Figure 3-15 shows dull and metal material with the same lighting. The lighting produced by MATLAB is limited by being OpenGL lighting. Modern 3D graphics use textures and shaders for photo-realistic scene lighting. Also, you cannot generate shadows in MATLAB.

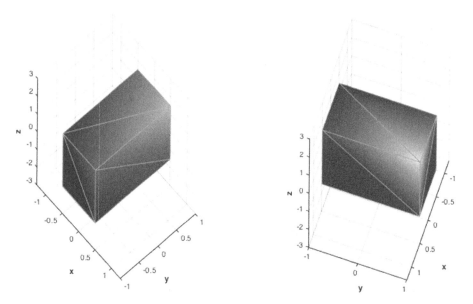

Figure 3-15. *Box illuminated with a local light object. The left box has "dull" material. The one on the right has "metal".*

The dull, shiny, and metal settings for material set the patch properties to produce these effects. You can easily print the effects to the command line using get.

```
>> material dull
>> get(p)
                      DiffuseStrength: 0.8
...
         SpecularColorReflectance: 1
                   SpecularExponent: 10
                   SpecularStrength: 0
>> material metal
>> get(p)
                      DiffuseStrength: 0.3
                  ...
         SpecularColorReflectance: 0.5
                   SpecularExponent: 25
                   SpecularStrength: 1

>> material shiny
>> get(p)
                      DiffuseStrength: 0.6
              ...
         SpecularColorReflectance: 1
                   SpecularExponent: 20
                   SpecularStrength: 0.9
```

Note that the AmbientStrength is 0.3 for all the settings material settings listed. If you want to see the effect of only your light objects without ambient light, you have to manually set this to 0. In Figure 3-16, the ambient strength is set to 0 and the shiny material is applied.

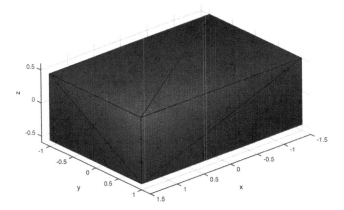

Figure 3-16. *Shiny box with ambient lighting removed (AmbientStrength is set to 0) and a different camera viewpoint*

MATLAB has a lighting function to control the lighting model with four settings: none, gouraud, phong, and flat. Gouraud interpolates the lighting across the faces gives the most realistic effect. Note that setting the lighting to Gouraud for our box sets the FaceLighting property to gouraud but the EdgeLighting to none, which gives a different effect than in our script, where the edge lighting was also set to Gouraud via its property. Flat lighting gives each entire face a uniform lighting, as seen in Figure 3-17, where we set the view to (-50,30) and the lighting to flat.

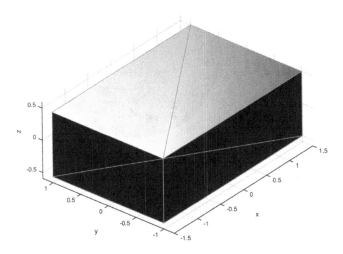

Figure 3-17. *Shiny box with flat lighting*

The MATLAB recommendations are to use flat lighting for faceted objects and gouraud lighting for curved objects. The easiest way to compare these is to create a sphere, which is simple using the sphere function and generating a surface. This is done as follows in SphereLighting. The infinite light object shines from the *x* axis.

```
%% Create and light a sphere

%% Make the sphere surface in a new figure
[X,Y,Z] = sphere(16);
figure('Name','Sphere Demo')
s = surf(X,Y,Z);
xlabel('x')
ylabel('y')
zlabel('z')
axis equal
view(70,15)

%% Add a lighting object and display the properties
light('position',[1 0 0])
disp(s)
title('Flat_Lighting')
pause

%% Change to Gouraud lighting and display again
lighting gouraud
title('Gouraud_Lighting')
disp(s)
```

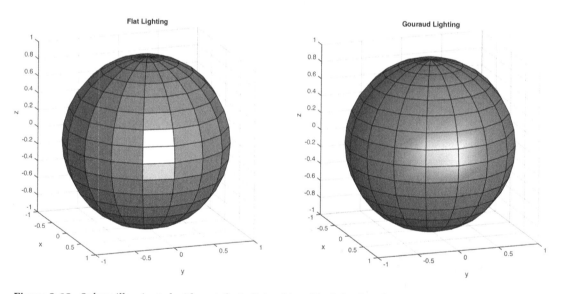

Figure 3-18. *Sphere illuminated with an infinite light object. The left sphere has flat lighting. The one on the right has gouraud*

In addition to a sphere function, MATLAB also provides cylinder and ellipsoid.

3-10. Programmatically Setting the Camera Properties

Problem

You would like to have a camera that can be pointed in your scene.

Solution

Use the MATLAB cam functions. These provide the same functionality as the buttons in the Camera toolbar, but with repeatability and the ability to pass in variables for the parameters.

How It Works

Make two boxes in the scene: one is scaled and displayed from the other by 5 in *x*. Use the MATLAB functions camdolly, camorbit, campan, camzoom, and camroll to control the camera. Put all of these functions in the PatchWithCamera.m script and provide examples of two sets of parameters. Note that without lighting, the edges disappear.

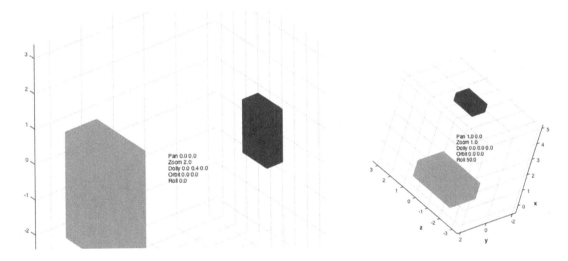

Figure 3-19. *Boxes with different camera parameters*

```
%% Generate two cubes using patch and point a camera at the scene
% The camera parameters will be set programmatically using the cam functions.

%% Camera parameters
% Orbit
thetaOrbit = 0;
phiOrbit = 0;

% Dolly
xDolly = 0;
yDolly = 0;
zDolly = 0;
```

```
% Zoom
zoom = 1;

% Roll
roll = 50;

% Pan
thetaPan = 1;
phiPan = 0;

%% Box design
x = 1;
y = 2;
z = 3;

% Faces
f = [2 3 6;3 7 6;3 4 8;3 8 7;4 5 8;4 1 5;2 6 5;2 5 1;1 3 2;1 4 3;5 6 7;5 7 8];

% Vertices
v = [-x x x -x -x x x -x;...
     -y -y y y -y -y y y;...
     -z -z -z -z z z z z]'/2;

%% Draw the object
h = figure('name','Box');

c = [0.7 0.7 0.1];
patch('vertices',v,'faces',f,'facecolor',c,'edgecolor',c,...
      'edgelighting','gouraud','facelighting','gouraud');

c = [0.2 0 0.9];
v       = 0.5*v;
v(:,1) = v(:,1) + 5;
patch('vertices',v,'faces',f,'facecolor',c,'edgecolor',c,...
      'edgelighting','gouraud','facelighting','gouraud');

material('metal');
lighting gouraud
axis equal
grid on
XLabelS('x')
YLabelS('y')
ZLabelS('z')
view(3)
rotate3d on

%% Camera commands
campan(thetaPan,phiPan)
camzoom(zoom)
camdolly(xDolly,yDolly,zDolly);
camorbit(thetaOrbit,phiOrbit);
camroll(roll);
```

84

```
s = sprintf('Pan_%3.1f_%3.1f\nZoom_%3.1f\nDolly_%3.1f_%3.1f %3.1f\nOrbit_%3.1f_%3.1f\
    nRoll_%3.1f',...
thetaPan,phiPan,zoom,xDolly,yDolly,zDolly,thetaOrbit,phiOrbit,roll);

text(2,0,0,s);
```

Additional functions for interacting with the scene camera include `campos` and `camtarget`, which can be used to set the camera position and target. This can be used to image one object from the vantage point of another. `camva` sets the camera view angle, so you can model a real camera's field of view. `camup`

3-11. Display an Image

Problem

You would like to draw an image.

Solution

You can read in an image directly from an image file and draw it in a figure window. MATLAB supports a variety of formats, including GIF, JPG, TIFF, PNG, and BMP.

How It Works

A black-and-white image is read using `imread` and displayed using `imagesc`. `imagesc` scales the color data into the colormap. It is necessary to apply the grayscale color map; otherwise, you'll get the colors in the default colormap. For the parula colormap, the colors are blue and yellow.

```
%% Draw a JPEG image in a figure multiple ways
% We will load and display an image of a mug.
%% See also
% imread, pcolor, imagesc, imshow, colormap

%% Read in the JPEG image
i = imread('Mug.jpg');

%% Draw the picture with imagesc
% This preserves an axes. Each pixel center of the image lies at integer
% coordinates ranging between 1 and M or N. Compare the result of imagesc to
% that of pcolor. axis image sets the aspect ratio so that tick marks on both
% axes are equal, and makes the plot box fit tightly around the data.
h = figure('name','Mug')
subplot(1,2,1)
pcolor(i)
shading('interp')
colorbar
axis image
title('pcolor_with_colorbar')
a = subplot(1,2,2)
```

```
% scale the image into the colormap
imagesc( i );
colormap(a,'gray')
axis image
grid on
title('imagesc_with_gray_colormap')
```

Figure 3-20 shows the mug first using pcolor, which creates a pseudocolor plot of a matrix, but is really a surf, with the view looking down from above. To highlight this fact, we added a colorbar. Then on the right, the image is drawn using imagesc with a gray colormap. Observe that imagesc has changed the direction of the axes so that the image appears right-side up. Both plots have axes with tick marks.

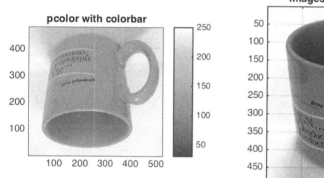
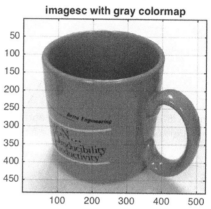

Figure 3-20. *Mug displayed using pcolor and imagesc*

MATLAB has another image display function called imshow, which is considered the fundamental image display function. It optimizes the figure, axes, and image object properties for displaying an image. If you have the Image Processing toolbox, imtool extends imshow with additional features. Notice how the image is displayed without the axes box. This function automatically scales and selects the gray colormap.

```
%% Draw with imshow
% The axes will be turned off. The image will be scaled to fit the figure if it
% is too large.
f = figure('Name','Mug_Image');
subplot(1,2,1)
imshow(i)
title('imshow')
subplot(1,2,2)
imshow(i,[30 200])
title('imshow_with_limits_[30_200]')
```

imshow

imshow with limits [30 200]

Figure 3-21. *Mug displayed using imshow, with color limits applied on the right*

Not all images use the full depth available; for instance, this mug image has a minimum value of 30 and a maximum of 250. imshow allows you to set the color limits of the image directly, and the pixels are scaled accordingly. You can darken the image by increasing the lower color limit, and brighten it by lowering the upper color limit.

3-12. Adding a Watermark

Problem

You have a lot of great graphics in your toolbox and you would like them marked to show that they were created by your company. Alternatively, or additionally, you may want to mark these images with a date or the version number of the software that generated it.

Solution

You can use low-level graphics functions to add a textual or image watermark to figures that you generate in your toolbox. The tricky part is adding the items to the figure in the correct order so that they are not overridden.

How It Works

The best way to add watermarks is to make a special axis for each text or image item you want to add. You turn the axis box off so that all you see is the text or image. In the first example, we added an icon and text to the lower left-hand corner of the plot. We added a color for the edge around the text so that it is nicely delineated. This is shown in Figure 3-22. In the example, we set the hard copy inversion to off, so that when we print the figure we will get a gray background; this makes it easier to see in the book.

```
>> h = figure;
>> set(h,'InvertHardCopy','off')
>> axes
>> Watermark(h)
```

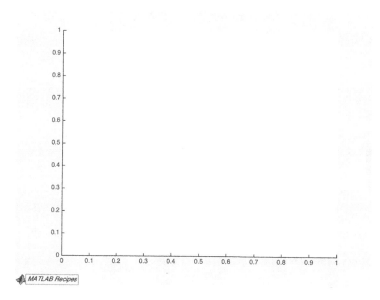

Figure 3-22. Company watermark

```matlab
function Watermark( fig, pos )

%% WATERMARK Add a watermark to a figure.
% This function creates two axes, one for the image and one for the text.
% Calling it BEFORE plotting can cause unexpected results. It will reset
% the current axes after adding the watermark. The default position is
% the lower left corner, (2,2).
%% Form
%   Watermark( fig, pos )
%% Inputs
%   fig         (1,1) Figure hangle
%   pos         (1,2) Coordinates, (left, bottom)
%% Outputs
% None.

if (nargin<1 || isempty(fig))
    fig = figure('Name','Watermark_Demo');
    set(fig,'color',[0.85 0.9 0.85]);
end

if (nargin<2 || isempty(pos))
    pos = [2 2];
end
```

```
string = 'MATLAB_Recipes';

% Save the current axes so we can restore it
aX = [];
if ~isempty(get(fig,'CurrentAxes'))
  aX = gca;
end

% Draw the icon
%--------------
[d,map] = imread('matlabicon','gif');
posIcon = [pos(1:2) 16 16];
a = axes( 'Parent', fig, 'box', 'off', 'units', 'pixels', 'position', posIcon );
image( d );
colormap(a,map)
axis off

% Draw the text
%--------------
posText = [pos(1)+18 pos(2)+1 100 15];
axes( 'Parent', fig, 'box', 'off', 'units', 'pixels', 'position', posText );
t = text(0,0.5,string,'fontangle','italic');
set(t,'edgecolor',[0.87 0.5 0])
axis off

% Restore current axes in figure
if ~isempty(aX)
  set(fig,'CurrentAxes',aX);
end

set(fig,'tag','Watermarked')
```

As an additional example, we added text along the left- and right-hand sides of a figure using text rotation. We gave the text a light color. This marks the figure as a draft. We create a blank figure and axis before adding the draft mark, as shown in Figure 3-23.

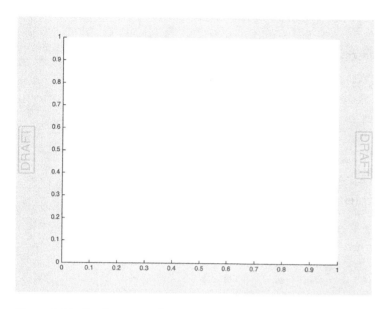

Figure 3-23. *Draft watermark*

```
>> h = figure('Name','Draftmark_Demo');
>> set(h,'color',[0.85 0.9 0.85]);
>> set(h,'InvertHardCopy','off')
>> axes;
>> Draftmark(h);

function Draftmark( fig, pos )
%% DRAFTMARK Add a draft marking to a figure.
% This function creates two axes, one each block of text.
% Calling it BEFORE plotting can cause unexpected results. It will reset
% the current axes after adding the watermark. The default position is
% the lower left corner, (2,2).
%% Form
%   Draftmark( fig, pos )
%% Inputs
%   fig (1,1) Figure hangle
%   pos (1,2) Coordinates, (left, bottom)
%% Outputs
% None.

if (nargin<1 || isempty(fig))
    fig = figure('Name','Draft_Demo');
    set(fig,'color',[0.85 0.9 0.85]);
end
```

```matlab
if (nargin<2 || isempty(pos))
    pos = [2 2];
end

string = 'DRAFT';

% Save the current axes so we can restore it
aX = [];
if ~isempty(get(fig,'CurrentAxes'))
    aX = gca;
end

% Draw the text
%--------------
pf = get(fig,'position');
posText = [pos(1)+5 pos(2)+0.5*pf(4)-40 20 80];
axes( 'Parent', fig, 'box', 'on', 'units', 'pixels', 'outerposition', posText );
t1 = text(0,0,string,'fontsize',20,'color',[0.8 0.8 0.8]);
set(t1,'rotation',90,'edgecolor',[0.8 0.8 0.8],'linewidth',2)
axis off

posText = [pos(1)+pf(3)-25 pos(2)+0.5*pf(4)-40 20 80];
axes( 'Parent', fig, 'box', 'on', 'units', 'pixels', 'outerposition', posText );
t2 = text(0,1,string,'fontsize',20,'color',[0.8 0.8 0.8]);
set(t2,'rotation',270,'edgecolor',[0.8 0.8 0.8],'linewidth',2)
axis off

% Restore current axes in figure
if ~isempty(aX)
    set(fig,'CurrentAxes',aX);
end
```

If you want to get very fancy, you could draw objects across the front of the figure and give them transparency, but they have to be fill or patch objects; text cannot be given transparency.

Summary

This chapter reviewed key features of MATLAB visualization, from basic plotting to 3D visualization, including objects and lighting. We demonstrated accessing figure and axes handles, and setting properties programmatically, as well as using the interactive tools for figures. Creating helpful visualization routines is a key part of any toolbox. MATLAB provides excellent data management routines, including those that can manage large grids of data, and many options for colorization. Table 3-1 lists the code developed in the chapter.

Table 3-1. *Chapter Code Listing*

File	Description
AnnotatePlot	Add text annotations evenly spaced along a curve.
Boxpatch	Generate a cube using patch.
ColorDistribution	Demonstrate a color distribution for an array of lines.
DraftMark	Add a draft marking to a figure.
GridVisualization	Visualize data over 2D and 3D grids.
PatchWithCamera	Generate two cubes using patch and point a camera at the scene.
PatchWithLighting	Add lighting to the cube patch.
PlotPage	Create a plot page with several custom plots in one figure.
PlottingWithDates	Plot using months as the x label.
QuadPlot	Create a quad plot page using subplot.
ReadImage	Draw a JPEG image in a figure multiple ways.
SphereLighting	Create and light a sphere.
Watermark	Add a watermark to a figure.

CHAPTER 4

■ ■ ■

Interactive Graphics

The previous chapter addressed generating static graphics. This chapter provides recipes for generating dynamic graphics. This includes animations of line and patch objects; utilizing `uicontrol` objects in figures; designing GUIs using the GUIDE development environment; and deploying your GUI as a MATLAB app. We present some tips for maximizing the performance of your dynamic graphics functions.

4-1. Creating a Simple Animation

Problem

You want a visualization that changes over time without generating hundreds of different figures.

Solution

You can create an animation by updating patch objects in a figure successively in a loop, Figure 4-1 shows one frame of such a animation.

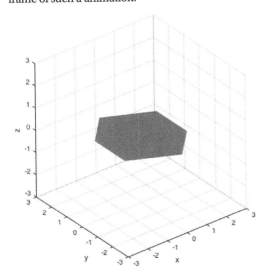

Figure 4-1. *Animation of a rotating box*

Electronic supplementary material The online version of this chapter (doi:10.1007/978-1-4842-0559-4_4) contains supplementary material, which is available to authorized users.

How It Works

First, you create a graphic involving the 3D box from the previous chapter. Then you update it in a loop. This is most efficient if you can assign new data to the existing graphics object. This could be changing the color, style, or physical location of the object. Alternatively, you can delete and re-create the object in the current axes. In both cases, you need to store the graphics handle for the updates.

In this case, you update the vertices by multiplying by a rotation matrix b. You then pass the vertices to the patch via the handle using set (p, 'vertices', vK). Note the use of the transposes as the vertices are stored in an n × 3 array. A light object makes the resulting animation more interesting. You set 'linestyle' to 'none' for the patch object to eliminate the lines between triangles.

```
%% Animate a cube using patch
% Create a figure and draw a cube in it. The vertices and faces are specified
% directly. We only update vertices to get a smooth animation.

%% Box design
x   = 3;
y   = 2;
z   = 1;

% Faces
f   = [2 3 6;3 7 6;3 4 8;3 8 7;4 5 8;4 1 5;2 6 5;2 5 1;1 3 2;1 4 3;5 6 7;5 7 8];

% Vertices
v = [-x x x -x -x x x -x;...
      -y -y y y -y -y y y;...
      -z -z -z -z z z z z]'/2;

%% Draw the object
h = figure('name','Box');
p = patch('vertices',v,'faces',f,'facecolor',[0.5 0.5 0.5],...
          'linestyle','none','facelighting','gouraud');
ax = gca;
set(ax,'DataAspectRatio',[1 1 1],'DataAspectRatioMode','manual')
axis([-3 3 -3 3 -3 3])
grid on
xlabel('x')
ylabel('y')
zlabel('z')
view(3)
rotate3d on
light('position',[0 0 1])

%% Animate
% We use tic and toc to time the animation. Pause is used with a fraction of a
% second input to slow the animation down.
tic
n = 10000;
a = linspace(0,8*pi,n);

c = cos(a);
s = sin(a);
```

```
for k = 1:n
  b = [c(k) 0 s(k);0 1 0;-s(k) 0 c(k)];
  vK = (b*v')';
  set(p,'vertices',vK);
  pause(0.001);
end
toc
```

The full animation of four rotations takes about 16 seconds on a MacBook Pro laptop. About 10 seconds of this is expected to be from the pause command; that is, 10000 steps * 0.001 seconds. Using pause allows you to slow down an animation that would otherwise be too fast to be useful. Remember that pause commands can be temporarily disabled by using pause off; this is useful when testing graphics functions that use pause.

■ **Tip**   Use pause to slow down animations as needed. Remember to use pause off to disable the pausing and run full speed during testing.

Check the execution time on your computer! Run the script twice, with pause turned off the second time.

```
>> pause on
>> PatchAnimation;
Elapsed time is 15.641664 seconds.
>> pause off
>> PatchAnimation;
Elapsed time is 0.780012 seconds.
```

Note that pause flushes the system graphics queue, drawing the updated patch to the screen. When pause is off, the graphics don't update, and you see just the initial frame in the window. Also note that actual increase in time from the pause and the graphics updates was almost 15 seconds. To force a graphics update without using pause, use drawnow.

This script uses cells to allow the individual sections to be run independently. This means you can rerun the animation without re-creating the figure, by re-executing that cell. This can be done from the Run Section toolbar button or by keyboard command, such as Command-Enter on a Mac.

Suppose you want to add a text item to the animation that displays the angle of rotation. You can do this using title easily enough:

```
title(sprintf('Angle: %f deg',a(k)*180/pi));
```

However, you will be surprised at the performance impact. The animation now takes over 90 seconds! Displaying text is much less efficient than updating the graphics vertices. First, you can try directly using the handle to the axis title object and setting the string. However, this makes little difference, still taking about 90 seconds. Another solution would be to add an inner loop to update the title less often. Trial and error shows that an update every 50 steps has little impact on the runtime. The figure with the title is shown in Figure 4-2.

```
if rem(k,50)==0
  set(ax.Title,'string',sprintf('Angle: %.5g deg',a(k)*180/pi));
end
```

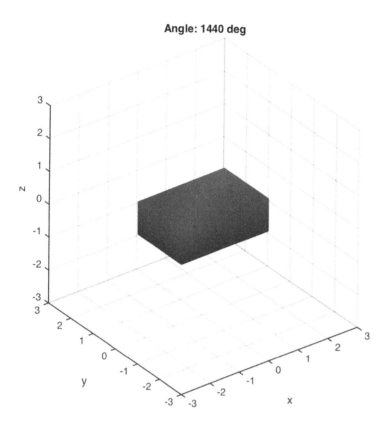

Figure 4-2. *Animation of the box with a changing title*

Table 4-1 is a summary of the execution times on the reference MacBook. The times are as printed from toc; they are from a single run, not an average. Expect a variation in execution time of up to 10% across multiple runs.

Table 4-1. *Execution Times for PatchAnimation*

No title	
pause off	0.780154 sec
pause on (0.001 sec)	17.254507 sec

With title	
Title	90.761500 sec
Set every step	90.213318 sec
Set every 50 steps	20.218774 sec

4-2. Playing Back an Animation

Problem

You want to store and play back an animation.

Solution

Save each frame of the animation into an AVI file using the VideoWriter class.

How It Works

In the following listing, you use VideoWriter to save the animation and read it into an AVI file. This line of code opens an AVI file:

```
vObj = VideoWriter('RotatingBox.avi');
```

The script is PatchAnimationStorage.m. The sections creating the box and figure aren't shown because they are the same as the previous recipe. In this case, you only use 100 points for the four rotations; the execution time, including saving the movie, is about 4 seconds with pause off. Running the script in the Profiler shows that almost 90% of the execution time is spent in the writeVideo command.

```
%% Animate a cube using patch and store as an AVI file
% The figure and box are created as in PatchAnimation. This time we use a
% VideoWriter to store the frames in a movie.

    .
    .
    .

%% Animate
n = 100;
a = linspace(0,8*pi,n);
c = cos(a);
s = sin(a);

% Create a video file
vObj = VideoWriter('RotatingBox.avi');
open(vObj);
tic
for k = 1:n
  pause(0.01);
  b = [c(k) 0 s(k);0 1 0;-s(k) 0 c(k)];
  vK = (b*v')';
  set(p,'vertices',vK);
  writeVideo(vObj,getframe(h));
end
toc

close(h)
close(vObj)
```

You can then play back your animation in any movie player, as shown in Figure 4-3.

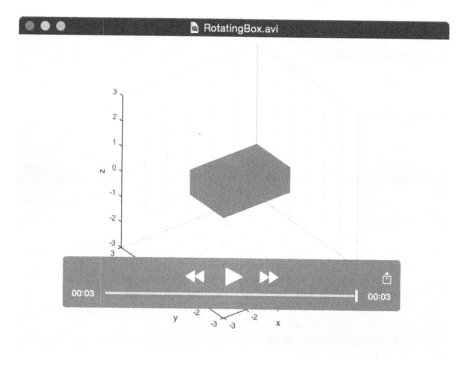

Figure 4-3. *Movie file playing back in a video player*

4-3. Animate Line Objects

Problem

You would like to update a plot with line objects in a loop.

Solution

This is similar to Recipe 4-1, but you will update different properties of the graphics object. You'll use the quad plot from Chapter 3 and add animation of a marker along the trajectory. This will also demonstrate adding a menu to a figure using uimenu.

How It Works

Start with the QuadPlot.m function. This creates four subplots to view a trajectory: one in 3D and three 2D views from different directions (see Figure 4-4). You must do a few things to add a marker that you can animate:

1. Add a time input.

2. Add a marker to each subplot and save the handles.

3. Add a text uicontrol to display the current time as the animation progresses.

4. Store the trajectory data and handles in the figure UserData.

5. Turn off the regular figure menu, and add an Animate menu with a Start function.

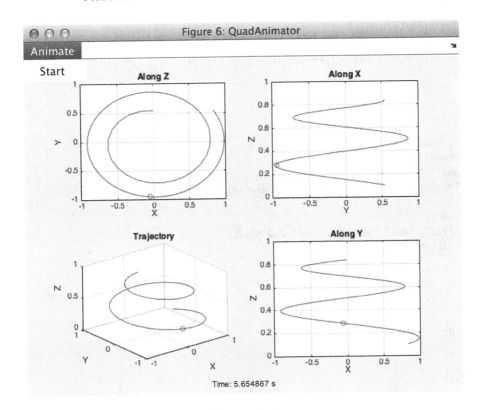

Figure 4-4. *Frame of an animation of the quad plot*

You use a nargin check to determine if you are creating the figure using t and x data, or entering a callback using the input 'update'. An alternative is to place the callback in a separate function; the figure executing the callback can be identified using a Tag property or using gcbf, as done here.

```
%% QUADANIMATOR Create a quad plot page with animation.
% This creates a 3D view and three 2D views of a trajectory in one figure. A
% menu is provided to animate the trajectory over time.
%% Form
%   QuadAnimator( t, x )
%% Input
%   t (1,:) Time data
%   x (3,:) Trajectory data
%
%% Output
% None.
```

```
function QuadAnimator(t,x)

if nargin == 0
  disp('Demo of QuadAnimator');
  t = linspace(0,4*pi,101);
  th = logspace(0,log10(4*pi),101);
  in = logspace(-1,0,101);
  x = [sin(th).*cos(in);cos(th).*cos(in);sin(in)];
  QuadAnimator(t,x);
  return;
end

if nargin==2
  h = figure('Name','QuadAnimator');
  set(h,'InvertHardcopy','off','menubar','none')
  ma = uimenu(h,'Label','Animate');
  ms = uimenu(ma,'Label','Start','Callback','QuadAnimator(''update'')');
  m = Plot(x);
  p = get(h,'position');
  ut = uicontrol('Style','text','String','Time: 0.0 s',...
                 'Position',[0 0 p(3) 20]);

  d.t = t;
  d.x = x;
  d.m = m;
  d.ut = ut;
  set(h,'UserData',d);
else
  h = gcbf;
  d = get(h,'UserData');
  Animate(d);
end

function m = Plot(x)
% Use subplot to create four plots of a trajectory

subplot(2,2,3)
plot3(x(1,:),x(2,:),x(3,:));
hold on
m(3) = plot3(x(1,1),x(2,1),x(3,1),'o');
hold off
xlabel('X')
ylabel('Y')
zlabel('Z')
grid on
title('Trajectory')
```

```
subplot(2,2,1)
plot(x(1,:),x(2,:));
hold on
m(1) = plot(x(1,1),x(2,1),'o');
hold off
xlabel('X')
ylabel('Y')
grid on
title('Along_Z')

subplot(2,2,2)
plot(x(2,:),x(3,:));
hold on
m(2) = plot(x(2,1),x(3,1),'o');
hold off
xlabel('Y')
ylabel('Z')
grid on
title('Along_X')

subplot(2,2,4)
plot(x(1,:),x(3,:));
hold on
m(4) = plot(x(1,1),x(3,1),'o');
hold off
xlabel('X')
ylabel('Z')
grid on
title('Along_Y')

function Animate( d )
% Animate the markers on the subplots over time

for k = 1:length(d.t)
  x = d.x(:,k);
  set(d.m(3),'XData',x(1),'YData',x(2),'ZData',x(3));
  set(d.m(1),'XData',x(1),'YData',x(2));
  set(d.m(2),'XData',x(2),'YData',x(3));
  set(d.m(4),'XData',x(1),'YData',x(3));
  set(d.ut,'string',sprintf('Time: %f s',d.t(k)));
  drawnow;
end
```

As can be seen, two subfunctions segregate the plotting and animating functionality. The animation sets the XData, YData, and ZData of the markers for the current time, and updates the text control. We used a drawnow to flush the events queue. The animation runs at a nice speed without requiring a pause command, but this may be different on your computer, so be prepared to experiment!

4-4. Implementation of a uicontrol Button

Problem

You want to use a button in a dialog box to stop a script as it is running.

Solution

Use uicontrol and figure to create a pop-up window with control, as shown in Figure 4-5.

Figure 4-5. *UIControlDemo window*

How It Works

Use two uicontrol calls in the script, UIControlDemo.m. The first puts a text box in the window. The second puts a button in the window. You don't have to specify a style for a button, as this is the default style, but you may choose to specify it for clarity. The button control has a callback. A callback can be any MATLAB code or a function handle. In this case, just set the global stop to *true* to stop the loop. Note that we used true and false for the global boolean for clarity, although 1 and 0 will work.

```
%% Demonstrate the use of a uicontrol button with a callback
% Create a window with a button that interacts with a global variable in the script.

%% Build the GUI
% This is a global to communicate the button push from the GUI
global stop;
stop = false;

% Build the GUI
set(0,'units','pixels')
p = get(0,'screensize');
bottom = p(4) - 190;
fig = figure('name','UIControlDemo','position',[340 bottom 298 90],...
             'NumberTitle','off','menubar','none',...
             'resize','off');

% The display text
speed = uicontrol( 'Parent', fig, 'position', [ 20 40 280 15],...
                   'style', 'text','string','Waiting to start.');

% This has a callback setting stop to 1
step = uicontrol( 'parent', fig, 'position',[ 40 40 40 20],...
                  'string','Stop', 'callback','stop = true;');
```

```
%% Run the GUI
for k = 1:1000
  pause(0.01)
  set( speed, 'String', k );
  if( stop )
    break; %#ok<UNRCH>
  end
  %drawnow % alternative to pause
end
```

The position input is defined as

```
[left bottom width height]
```

The purpose of obtaining the computer's screen size is to place the window near the top of the screen by assigning the bottom position parameter to the screen size minus the figure size (90 pixels tall), plus a 100 pixel margin; that is, p(4) - 190.

MATLAB's code analyzer places an alert on the line with the break saying that the line is unreachable when stop is false. This is, in fact, the case, but you have the uicontrol to change that parameter. MATLAB can't ascertain that, so you can add the %#ok<UNRCH> comment to suppress the warning. This comment can be automatically added by MATLAB (i.e., Autofixed), if you right-click the line with the warning and select "Suppress this statement..." in the pop-up menu.

■ **Tip**   Suppress warnings on lines with code that is reachable only by changes in your boolean logic.

Let's check the execution time. Run the script with tic and toc twice, with pause turned off the second time.

```
>> tic; UIControlDemo; toc
Elapsed time is 11.601678 seconds.
>> pause off
>> tic; UIControlDemo; toc
Elapsed time is 0.147663 seconds.
```

If you want the animation to last more or less than the 11 seconds, you can adjust the pause time. You can see that the graphics loop alone takes only a small fraction of a second, despite updating 1000 times! This is because with pause off, the graphics are not forced to update every step of the loop. MATLAB flushes the graphics only when the script ends, unless you have one of the commands that flushes the system queue, such as pause, drawnow, or getframe. If you don't want or need pause, use drawnow to force a graphics update every step of the loop. Table 4-2 shows the execution times with pause on or off and using drawnow instead. These are the times from a single run on the reference MacBook, not an average; expect a variation in runtimes of up to 10%.

Table 4-2. Execution Times for PatchAnimation

pause off	0.147663 sec
pause on (0.01 sec)	11.601678 sec
drawnow	2.642504 sec
pause AND drawnow	13.785564 sec

4-5. Display Status of a Running Simulation or Loop

Problem

You want to display the time remaining for a time-consuming task done in a loop.

Solution

Create a window with a text uicontrol to display the time remaining (see Figure 4-6).

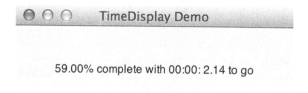

Figure 4-6. *Time Display window*

How It Works

TimeDisplayGUI implements the time window. It uses three actions with varargin. A persistent variable, hGUI, stores the steps and increments automatically for every update call. The following are some things to notice in this function:

- The MATLAB function now is used to get the current date for timing purposes.

- The number of steps completed is stored in hGUI.stepsDone.

- The GUI only updates the text string every half second of real time.

- It calculates an estimated amount of real time until script completion, assuming all steps take the same amount of time.

- The built-in demo uses pause.

```
function TimeDisplayGUI( action, varargin )

%% TimeDisplayGUI Displays an estimate of time to go in a loop.
% Call TimeDisplayGUI('update') each step; the step counter is incremented
% automatically using a persistent variable. Updates at 0.5 sec intervals.
%
%   TimeDisplayGUI( 'initialize', nameOfGUI, totalSteps )
%   TimeDisplayGUI( 'update' )
%   TimeDisplayGUI( 'close' )
%
% You can only have one TimeDisplayGUI operating at once. The built-in demo uses
% pause to run for about 5 seconds.
%% Form:
%   TimeDisplay( action, varargin )
```

```
%% Inputs
%   action        (1,:)   'initialize', 'update', or 'close'
%   nameOfGUI     (1,:)   Name to display
%   totalSteps    (1,1)   Total number of steps
%
%% Outputs
%   None

persistent hGUI
if nargin == 0
  % Demo
  disp('Initializing_demo_window_with_100_steps.')
  TimeDisplayGUI( 'initialize', 'TimeDisplay_Demo', 100 );
  for k = 1:100
    pause(0.05)
    TimeDisplayGUI( 'update' );
  end
  return;
end

switch action
  case 'initialize'
    hGUI              = BuildGUI( varargin{1} );
    hGUI.totalSteps = varargin{2};
    hGUI.stepsDone  = 0;
    hGUI.date0      = now;
    hGUI.lastDate   = now;
  case 'update'
    if( isempty( hGUI ) )
      return
    end
    hGUI.stepsDone = hGUI.stepsDone + 1;
    hGUI = Update( hGUI );
  case 'close'
    if ~isempty(hGUI) && ishandle(hGUI.fig)
      delete( hGUI.fig );
    else
      delete(gcf)
    end
    hGUI = [];
end

function hGUI = Update( hGUI )
% Update the display

thisDate = now;
dTReal   = thisDate-hGUI.lastDate; % days
if (dTReal > 0.5/86400)
  % Increment every 1/2 second
  stepPer  = hGUI.stepsDone/(thisDate - hGUI.date0);
  stepsToGo = hGUI.totalSteps - hGUI.stepsDone;
  tToGo     = stepsToGo/stepPer;
```

105

```
  datev     = datevec(tToGo);
  str       = FormatString( hGUI.stepsDone/hGUI.totalSteps, datev );

  set( hGUI.percent, 'String', str );
  drawnow;
  hGUI.lastDate = thisDate;
end

function h = BuildGUI( name )
% Initialize the GUIs

set(0,'units','pixels')
p          = get(0,'screensize');
bottom     = p(4) - 190;
h.fig      = figure('name',name,'Position',[340 bottom 298 90],'NumberTitle','off',...
                    'menubar','none','resize','off','closerequestfcn',...
                    'TimeDisplayGUI(''close'')');

v          = {'Parent',h.fig,'Units','pixels','fontunits','pixels'};

str = FormatString( 0, [0 0 0 0 0 0] );
h.percent = uicontrol( v{:}, 'Position',[ 20 35 260 20], 'Style','text',...
                        'fontsize',12,'string',str,'Tag','StaticText2');
drawnow;

function str = FormatString( fSteps, date )
% Format the time to go string

str = sprintf('%4.2f%% complete with %2.2i:%2.2i:%5.2f to go',...
                    100*fSteps,date(4),date(5),date(6));
```

The following script, TimeDisplayDemo, shows how the function is used. Figure 4-6 shows the resulting window.

```
%% Demonstrate a GUI that shows the time to go in a process
%% See also
% TimeDisplayGUI

%% Script constants
n  = 10000;
dT = 0.1;
a  = rand(10,10);

%% Initialize the time display
TimeDisplayGUI( 'initialize', 'SVD', n )

%% Loop
for j = 1:n
```

```
    % Do something time consuming
    for k = 1:100
      svd(a);
    end

    % Display the status message
    TimeDisplayGUI( 'update' );
end

%% Finish
TimeDisplayGUI( 'close' );
```

4-6. Create a Custom GUI with GUIDE

Problem

You have a repeating workflow and you would like to build a GUI to avoid changing parameters in your script repeatedly. For example, let's take the rotating cube animation from Recipe 4-1 and put it in a GUI, so you can easily see the effect of different pause lengths.

Solution

You will use the GUI Design Environment (GUIDE) to create a GUI, starting from a blank figure. You need an edit box for the pause length, plus buttons for interaction.

How It Works

Type **guide** to start the GUIDE Quick Start window. From the Create New GUI tab, choose Blank GUI. This opens a blank figure entitled untitled1.fig in the editor, as seen in Figure 4-7.

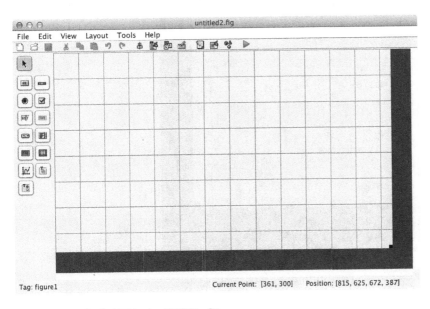

Figure 4-7. *Blank GUI in the GUIDE editor*

Create the following items in the GUI using the buttons on the left:

- Edit box for entering the pause time

- Text label for the box

- Button to start the animation

Start with the text label, which looks like a box with TXT inside. Click the button, then drag with the mouse until you have a good-sized box. It fills in with the words "Static Text". Double-click the text box to open the control Inspector. From here, you can change the style and content of the text. Change the String to "Pause Duration (s)" and tab out of the field or hit Enter.

Next, add the edit box. This button looks like a box with EDIT inside. Draw the box for the edit box to the right of your text label. Double-click it to open the Inspector. Change the String to "0.01", the default pause duration. Note that there is a Tag field below the String field. This is something like "edit1" by default. It is the identifier of the handle to this edit box in the GUI code. Change it to "pauseDur".

Finally, add the button. This looks like a button with the letters OK on it. Place the button under your text and edit boxes. It reads "Push Button" by default. In the Inspector, change it to "Start". Change the Tag to "startButton".

You can change parameters of the figure itself as well by double-clicking the background, outside of your controls. Change the Color to the background color of your choice. Uncheck the box for InvertHardcopy, which allows your background color to show when you print the figure. The controls you added will be much easier to see with the altered background color.

There are options for implementing the animation. You can add an axes directly in the GUI, or maintain a separate window for the animation so that it looks the same as before. For now, you will use a separate figure window for the animation.

Resize the figure smaller if you like. Align your controls using Tools ➤Align Objects.... and save your new figure. Your figure should now look something like Figure 4-8.

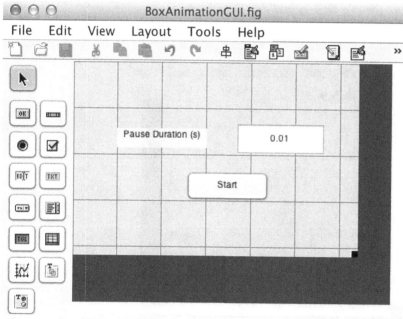

Figure 4-8. *Newly saved GUI*

At this time, MATLAB creates an m-file to control the figure. The FIG-file maintains the geometry, style, and tag data that you saw in the Inspectors. The m-file handles the execution of the control callbacks. Figure 4-9 shows the list of functions in your new m-file, using the Tag names you specified when you edited the controls.

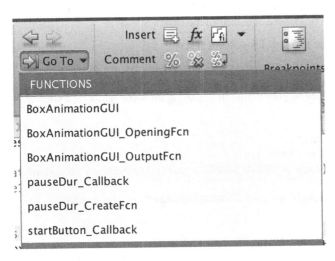

Figure 4-9. *Functions in the newly saved GUI m-file*

The main function, BoxAnimationGUI, contains a section of initialization code labeled DO NOT EDIT. You can add additional initialization code after this section, or in the OpeningFcn, where you have access to the handles data. The edit box, your control for entering the pause duration, has two related functions: a callback and a create function. The Start button has only a callback.

You need to do the following in the code:

1. Create the figure window and draw the cube in BoxAnimationGUI_OpeningFcn, storing the handle to the patch object so that you can access the vertices.

2. Convert the string in the edit box to a number and store it.

3. Run the animation in startButton_Callback.

There are two choices for converting the edit box contents string to a number. You can do it in the edit box callback, activated when the user tabs out of the box or hits Enter when it is active, or wait and convert the data only when the user pushes Start. This is an architectural decision that may, in a larger GUI, be impacted by relationships between the different parameters the user might be entering. In this simple case, it doesn't make much difference, and you will convert it in the edit box callback. This does, however, bring up the issue of initialization of the data; you have to convert the default string for the pause duration into a double during initialization, or the user won't be able to run the animation until activating the callback for the first time. Therefore, you need to add the following step to your list of coding tasks:

4. Initialize the value of the pause duration in pauseDur_CreateFcn.

Finally, you are creating an external figure with the GUI. With this default list of functions, there is no way to close the extra GUI when the main window closes. However, it is possible to add a close function that can take care of this cleanup step. From the FIG window, in the figure Inspector, the default CloseRequestFcn is closereq. If you click the small button to the left of this, MATLAB creates a close function and adds it to your m-file. This is your final piece of coding in the GUI:

5. Close the extra figure window in the figure1_CloseRequestFcn.

The fully realized GUI function is shown next. Note that the custom data fields that are added to the handles data structure are grouped together in a data substructure called data to avoid name clashes with the uicontrol handles. It is very easy to introduce bugs by inadvertently using the same name for a control object and the related parameter.

```
function varargout = BoxAnimationGUI(varargin)
% BOXANIMATIONGUI MATLAB code for BoxAnimationGUI.fig
%       BOXANIMATIONGUI, by itself, creates a new BOXANIMATIONGUI or raises the existing singleton*.
%
%       H = BOXANIMATIONGUI returns the handle to a new BOXANIMATIONGUI or the handle to
%       the existing singleton*.
%
%       BOXANIMATIONGUI('CALLBACK',hObject,eventData,handles,...) calls the local
%       function named CALLBACK in BOXANIMATIONGUI.M with the given input arguments.
%
%       BOXANIMATIONGUI('Property','Value',...) creates a new BOXANIMATIONGUI or raises the
%       existing singleton*. Starting from the left, property value pairs are
%       applied to the GUI before BoxAnimationGUI_OpeningFcn gets called. An
%       unrecognized property name or invalid value makes property application
%       stop. All inputs are passed to BoxAnimationGUI_OpeningFcn via varargin.
%
%        *See GUI Options on GUIDE's Tools menu. Choose "GUI allows only one
%       instance to run (singleton)".
%
% See also: GUIDE, GUIDATA, GUIHANDLES

% Edit the above text to modify the response to help BoxAnimationGUI

% Last Modified by GUIDE v2.5 25-Aug-2015 15:10:40

% Begin initialization code - DO NOT EDIT
gui_Singleton = 1;
gui_State = struct('gui_Name',        mfilename, ...
                   'gui_Singleton',   gui_Singleton, ...
                   'gui_OpeningFcn',  @BoxAnimationGUI_OpeningFcn, ...
                   'gui_OutputFcn',   @BoxAnimationGUI_OutputFcn, ...
                   'gui_LayoutFcn',   [], ...
                   'gui_Callback',    []);
if nargin && ischar(varargin{1})
    gui_State.gui_Callback = str2func(varargin{1});
end
```

```matlab
if nargout
    [varargout{1:nargout}] = gui_mainfcn(gui_State, varargin{:});
else
    gui_mainfcn(gui_State, varargin{:});
end
% End initialization code - DO NOT EDIT


% --- Executes just before BoxAnimationGUI is made visible.
function BoxAnimationGUI_OpeningFcn(hObject, eventdata, handles, varargin)
% This function has no output args, see OutputFcn.
% hObject    handle to figure
% eventdata  reserved - to be defined in a future version of MATLAB
% handles    structure with handles and user data (see GUIDATA)
% varargin   command line arguments to BoxAnimationGUI (see VARARGIN)


% ADDED CUSTOM CODE FOR RECIPE
% Design the box
x   = 3;
y   = 2;
z   = 1;
f   = [2 3 6;3 7 6;3 4 8;3 8 7;4 5 8;4 1 5;2 6 5;2 5 1;1 3 2;1 4 3;5 6 7;5 7 8];
v = [-x x x -x -x x x -x;...
     -y -y y y -y -y y y;...
     -z -z -z -z z z z z]'/2;


% Create the figure
h = figure('name','Box');
p = patch('vertices',v,'faces',f,'facecolor',[0.5 0.5 0.5],...
          'linestyle','none','facelighting','gouraud');
ax = gca;
set(ax,'DataAspectRatio',[1 1 1],'DataAspectRatioMode','manual')
grid on
axis([-3 3 -3 3 -3 3])
xlabel('x')
ylabel('y')
zlabel('z')
view(3)
light('position',[0 0 1]);


% Choose default command line output for BoxAnimationGUI
handles.output = hObject;


% Additional variables required
handles.data.box = p;
handles.data.vertices = v;
handles.data.axis = ax;
handles.data.figure = h;
% END CUSTOM CODE
```

```matlab
% Update handles structure
guidata(hObject, handles);
% UIWAIT makes BoxAnimationGUI wait for user response (see UIRESUME)
% uiwait(handles.figure1);


% --- Outputs from this function are returned to the command line.
function varargout = BoxAnimationGUI_OutputFcn(hObject, eventdata, handles)
% varargout  cell array for returning output args (see VARARGOUT);
% hObject    handle to figure
% eventdata  reserved - to be defined in a future version of MATLAB
% handles    structure with handles and user data (see GUIDATA)

% Get default command line output from handles structure
varargout{1} = handles.output;


function pauseDur_Callback(hObject, eventdata, handles)
% hObject    handle to pauseDur (see GCBO)
% eventdata  reserved - to be defined in a future version of MATLAB
% handles    structure with handles and user data (see GUIDATA)

% Hints: get(hObject,'String') returns contents of pauseDur as text
%        str2double(get(hObject,'String')) returns contents of pauseDur as a double

% ADDED CUSTOM CODE FOR RECIPE
pauseDur = str2double(get(hObject,'String'));
% Optional: add checking of pause value; can't be negative
handles.data.pauseVal = pauseDur;
guidata(hObject, handles);


% --- Executes during object creation, after setting all properties.
function pauseDur_CreateFcn(hObject, eventdata, handles)
% hObject    handle to pauseDur (see GCBO)
% eventdata  reserved - to be defined in a future version of MATLAB
% handles    empty - handles not created until after all CreateFcns called

% Hint: edit controls usually have a white background on Windows.
%       See ISPC and COMPUTER.
if ispc && isequal(get(hObject,'BackgroundColor'), get(0,'defaultUicontrolBackgroundColor'))
    set(hObject,'BackgroundColor','white');
end

% ADDED CUSTOM CODE FOR RECIPE
pauseDur = str2double(get(hObject,'String'));
% Optional: add checking of pause value; can't be negative
handles.data.pauseVal = pauseDur;
guidata(hObject, handles);
```

```matlab
% --- Executes on button press in startButton.
function startButton_Callback(hObject, eventdata, handles)
% hObject    handle to startButton (see GCBO)
% eventdata  reserved - to be defined in a future version of MATLAB
% handles    structure with handles and user data (see GUIDATA)

% ADDED CUSTOM CODE FOR RECIPE
dT = handles.data.pauseVal;    % pause duration from our edit box
p = handles.data.box;          % handle to the patch object
v0 = handles.data.vertices;    % initial vertices, before rotation
ax = handles.data.axis;        % axis, for updating title
n = 1000;
a = linspace(0,8*pi,n);

c = cos(a);
s = sin(a);

for k = 1:n
  b    = [c(k) 0 s(k);0 1 0;-s(k) 0 c(k)];
  vK   = (b*v0')';
  set(p,'vertices',vK);
  if rem(k,25)==0
    title(ax,sprintf('Angle: %.5g deg',a(k)*180/pi));
  end
  pause(dT);
end

% --- Executes when user attempts to close figure1.
function figure1_CloseRequestFcn(hObject, eventdata, handles)
% hObject    handle to figure1 (see GCBO)
% eventdata  reserved - to be defined in a future version of MATLAB
% handles    structure with handles and user data (see GUIDATA)

% Hint: delete(hObject) closes the figure
delete(hObject);

% ADDED CUSTOM CODE FOR RECIPE
delete(handles.data.figure)
```

■ **Tip**   Store your added data in a unique substructure, so it can't be confused with any of your graphics handles.

To run the GUI, either execute the m-file or use the Run button from the GUIDE figure editor. The GUI with the plot window opens, as shown in Figure 4-10.

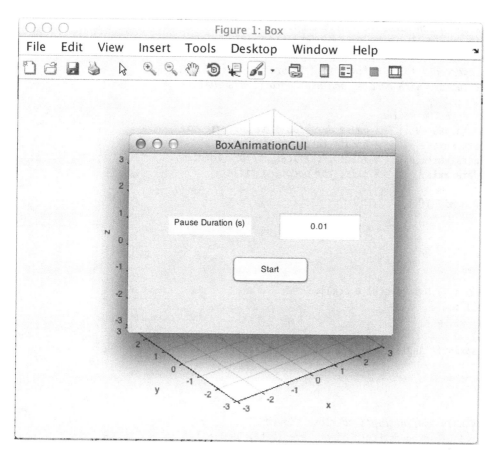

Figure 4-10. *Completed GUI with plot window*

You can verify that changing the pause duration and running the animation works. Closing the GUI closes the plot with it. However, if you close the plot and try to run the GUI, you get an error; this is not a case that has been handled with this implementation. You could add a close function to the plot figure to either ask the user for confirmation using questdlg or close the GUI with it. Alternatively, the GUI could check that the figure window exists, and re-create it if it was inadvertently closed. In order to do this, the initialization code needs to be moved to its own function.

As an exercise, try implementing the pause time via a slider instead of an edit box, with a range of 0 to 0.1 seconds. You may also want to try adding additional controls for the number of steps in the animation.

4-7. Build a MATLAB App from Your GUI

Problem

You would like to share your new GUI with others as a packaged app.

Solution

MATLAB provides a utility to package a GUI (or script) as an *app*, which can then easily be installed and uninstalled by users. You will use the GUI created in the previous recipe as an example.

How It Works

You create an app by specifying the main file that runs it, or in this case, the main function for the BoxAnimationGUI from the previous recipe. The packaging utility performs a dependency check and includes any other related functions and files in your path. The resulting binary file can then be distributed and installed by others.

The app utilities are accessed from the Apps tab of the MATLAB Command Window. This tab has buttons to Get More Apps, Install App, and most importantly for this recipe, Package App. The tab also has a ribbon showing any apps you currently have installed. Clicking Package App opens a window where you enter the file and metadata information for your app.

The first step, starting from the upper left of the Package App window, is to select the main file for your app. Keep in mind that this doesn't have to be a GUI; for instance, you could have a script that gathers user input from the command line using input or inputdlg. Click "Add main file" and select BoxAnimationGUI.m. MATLAB automatically fills in the name of the app from the name of your main file and does a dependency check. In this case, the only dependency is the corresponding FIG-file, BoxAnimationGUI.fig. In the bottom left you can add any additional shared resources that can't be found by MATLAB's search utility, such as files called via eval or load with string names.

In the center of the Package App window, you add additional information to describe the app. You can select an icon, including a custom icon if you have one; assign a version number; write a summary and a longer description; and provide a screenshot. The icon you choose is displayed in the Apps toolbar of MATLAB when users install your app.

Once you have entered all the information for the app and verified the dependencies, you package the files into the app on the right of the Package App window. You can change the output folder before creating the package; the app installer that is generated is saved with the .mlappinstall extension.

Your package data is saved in a project file with a .prj extension. This allows you to repackage your app as needed during development; you can increment the version number for bug fixes or major version changes.

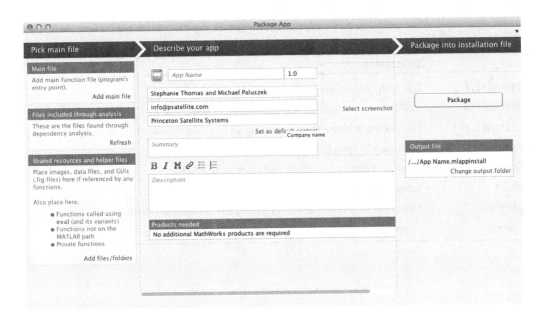

Figure 4-11. *Package app window*

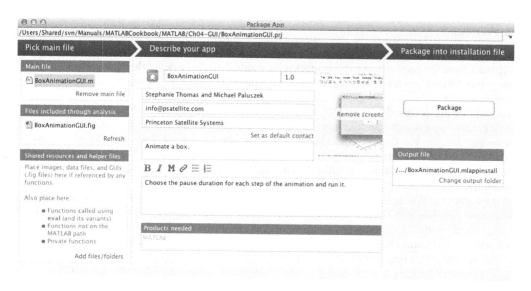

Figure 4-12. *Packaged app results with project file*

Summary

This chapter introduced figure controls and updating graphics in a loop. MATLAB provides a rich GUI building environment, including buttons, sliders, list boxes, menus, and plot axes. You can create uicontrols directly or use the GUIDE tool to place controls with the mouse. It is important to consider performance when designing graphics that update, as some operations have widely disparate performance, such as strings vs. object geometry. Table 4-3 lists the code developed in the chapter.

Table 4-3. *Chapter Code Listing*

File	Description
BoxAnimationGUI.fig	File with GUI definition.
BoxAnimationGUI.m	MATLAB code implementing BoxAnimationGUI.fig.
BoxAnimationGUI.prj	File storing information for creating an app from BoxAnimationGUI.m.
PatchAnimation	Animate a 3D patch in a for loop.
PatchAnimationStorage	Animate a cube using patch and store as an AVI file.
QuadAnimator	Create a quad plot page with animation.
TimeDisplayDemo	Demonstrate a GUI that shows the time remaining in a process.
UIControlDemo	Demonstrate the use of a uicontrol button with a callback.

CHAPTER 5

■ ■ ■

Testing and Debugging

The MATLAB unit test framework now allows you to incorporate testing into your MATLAB software, just as you would your C++ or Java packages. Since entire textbooks have been written on testing methodologies, this chapter is limited to covering the mechanics of using the test framework itself. We also present a couple of recipes that are useful for debugging.

We should, however, say a few words about the goal of software testing. Testing should determine if your software functions as designed. The first step is to have a concrete design against which you are coding. The functionality needs to be carefully described as a set of requirements. The requirements need to specify which inputs the software expects and what outputs it will generate. Testing needs to verify that for all valid inputs, it generates the expected outputs. A second consideration is that the software should handle expected errors and warn the user. For example, a simple function adds two MATLAB variables:

```
c = a + b;
```

You need to verify that it works for any numeric a and b. You generally do not need to warn the user if a or b is not numeric; that would just fill your code up with unneeded tests. A case where you might want a check is a function containing

```
b = acos(a);
```

If it is supposed to return a real number (perhaps as part of another function), you might want to limit a to have a magnitude less than 1. If you have the code,

```
if( abs(a) > 1 )
  a = sign(a);
end
b = acos(a);
```

In this case, your test code needs to pass in values of a that are greater than one. This is also a case where you might want to add a custom warning to the user if the magnitude limiting code is exercised, as shown next. If you have custom warnings and errors in your code, you also need to test them.

```
if( abs(a) > 1 )
  warning('MyToolbox:MyFunction:OutOfBounds','Input_a_is_out_of bounds');
  a = sign(a);
end
b = acos(a);
```

Electronic supplementary material The online version of this chapter (doi:10.1007/978-1-4842-0559-4_5) contains supplementary material, which is available to authorized users.

For engineering software, your test code should include known outputs generated by known inputs. In the preceding code, you might include inputs of 1.1, 1, 0.5, 0, −0.5 − 1, and −1.1. This would span the range of expected inputs. You might also be very thorough and input `linspace (−1.1, 1.1)` and test against another source of values for the inverse cosine. As shown in the later chapters, we usually include a demo function that tests the function with an interesting set of inputs. Your test code can use the code from the demo function as part of the testing.

All test procedures should employ the MATLAB code coverage tools. The Coverage Report, used in conjunction with the MATLAB Profiler, keeps track of which lines of code are exercised during execution. For a given function or script, it is essential that all code be exercised in its test. Studies have shown that testing done without coverage tools typically exercises only 55 % of the code. In reality, it is impossible to actually test every path in anything but the simplest software, and this must be factored into the software development and quality assurance processes. MATLAB does not currently support running the coverage tools on a suite of tests, or during your regression testing, so you should exercise the coverage tools on a per-test basis as you design them.

Once you start using your software, any bug you find should be used to add an additional test case to your tests.

5-1. Creating a Unit Test

Problem

Your functions require unit tests.

Solution

Use MATLAB's built-in test capabilities (now available using Java classes) to write and execute unit test functions. Test functions and scripts are identified by using the word *test* as a prefix or suffix to the file name, and are run via the `runtests` function.

How It Works

The `matlab.unittest` package is an xUnit-style, unit-testing framework for MATLAB. You can write scripts with test cases separated using cell titles, or functions with test cases in subfunctions, and execute them using the framework. We will show an example of each. There is extensive documentation of the framework and examples in the MATLAB documentation; these lists will get you started:

These are the relevant MATLAB packages implementing the framework:

- matlab.unittest
- matlab.unittest.constraints
- matlab.unittest.fixtures
- matlab.unittest.qualifications

The qualifications package provides all the methods for checking function results, including numerical values, errors, and warnings. The fixtures package allows you to provide setup and teardown code for individual tests or groups of tests.

Here are the relevant classes you will use when coding tests:

- matlab.unittest.TestCase
- matlab.unittest.TestResult
- matlab.unittest.TestSuite
- matlab.unittest.qualifications.Verifiable

TestCase is the superclass for writing test classes.
Here are the relevant functions:

- assert
- runtest
- functiontests
- localfunctions

The simplest way to implement tests for a function is to write a script. Each test case is identified with a cell title, using %%. Use the assert function to check function output. The script can then be run via runtest, which runs each test, even if a prior test fails, and collates the output into a useful report.

Let's write tests for an example function, CompleteTriangle, that computes the remaining data for a triangle given two sides and the interior angle:

```
function [A,B,c] = CompleteTriangle (a,b,C)

c = sqrt(a^2 + b^2 - 2*a*b*cosd(C));
sinA = sind(C)/c*a;
sinB = sind(C)/c*b;
cosA = (c^2+b^2 - a^2)/2/b/c;
cosB = (c^2+a^2-b^2)/2/a/c;
A = atan2(sinA,cosA)*180/pi;
B = atan2(sinB,cosB)*180/pi; % insert typo: change a B to A

end
```

This is similar to the right triangle function used as an example in the MATLAB documentation, but you need the four quadrant inverse tangent, as you are allowing obtuse triangles. Since there are very similar lines of code for the two angles, A and B, there is a note that having a typo in one of these lines would be likely, especially if you use copy/paste while writing the function; we'll demonstrate the effect of such a typo via our tests.

Now let's look at a script that defines a few test cases for this function, TriangleTest. Each check uses assert with a logical statement.

```
%% Test1: sum of angles
% Test that the angles add up to 180 degrees.
C = 30;
[A,B] = CompleteTriangle(1,2,C);
theSum = A+B+C;
assert(theSum == 180,'PSS:Book:triangle','sum_of_angles:_%f',theSum)
```

```
%% Test 2: isosceles right triangles
% Test that if sides a and b are equal, angles A and B are equal.
C = 90;
[A,B] = CompleteTriangle(2,2,C);
assert(A ==B,'PSS:Book:triangle','Isoceles_Triangle')

%% Test 3: 3-4-5 right triangle
% Test that if side a is 3 and side b is 4, side c (hypotenuse) is 5.
C=90;
[~,~,c] = CompleteTriangle(3,4,C);
assert(c == 5,'PSS:Book:triangle','3-4-5_Triangle')

%% Test 4: equilateral triangle
% Test that if sides a and b are equal, all angles are 60.
[A, B, c] = CompleteTriangle(1,1,60);
assert(A == 60,'PSS:Book:triangle','Equilateral_Triangle_%d',1)
assert(B == 60, 'PSS:Book:triangle','Equilateral_Triangle_%d',2)
assert(c == 1,'PSS:Book:triangle','Equilateral_Triangle_%d',3)
```

Note how the additional inputs available to assert are used to add a message ID string and an error message. The error message can take formatted strings with any of the specifiers supported by sprintf, such as %d and %f.

You can simply execute this script, in which case it exits on the first assert that fails. Even better, you can run it with runtests, which automatically distinguishes between the test cases and runs them independently should one fail.

```
>> runtests('TriangleTest');

Running TriangleTest
...
================================================================================
Error occurred in TriangleTest/Test4_EquilateralTriangle and it did not run to
    completion.

    --------------
    Error Details:
    --------------
    Equilateral Triangle 1
================================================================================
.
Done TriangleTest
_____


Failure Summary:
      Name                                    Failed   Incomplete   Reason(s)
      ==================================================================
      TriangleTest/Test4_EquilateralTriangle    X          X        Errored.
```

The equilateral triangle test failed. You can tell it was the first assert in that case due to the index that was printed, Equilateral Triangle 1. If you run the code for that test at the command line, you see that the output does, in fact, look correct:

```
>> [A,B,c] = CompleteTriangle (1,1,60)
A =
            60
B =
            60
c =
     1
```

If you actually subtract the expected value, 60, from A and B, you see why the test has failed.

```
>> A - 60
ans =
    7.1054e - 15
>> B - 60
ans =
    7.1054e - 15
```

You are within the tolerances of the trigonometric functions in MATLAB, but the assert statement did not take that into account. You can add a tolerance, like so:

```
assert(abs (A - 60) < 1e - 10,'PSS:Book:triangle', 'Equilateral_Triangle_%d',1)
assert(abs (B - 60) < 1e - 10,'PSS:Book:triangle','Equilateral_Triangle_%d',2)
```

And now the tests all pass:

```
>> runtests('TriangleTest')
Running TriangleTest
....
Done TriangleTest
_____


ans  =
  1x4 TestResult array with properties:

    Name
    Passed
    Failed
    Incomplete
    Duration
Totals:
    4 Passed, 0 Failed, 0 Incomplete.
    0.012243 seconds testing time.
```

Note that the terminating semicolon is left off; so in addition to the brief report, you see that runtests returns an array of TestResult objects and prints additional totals information, including the test duration.

Now let's consider the case of a typo in the function that you have not yet debugged. You change a B to an A on the last line of the function, so that it reads:

```
B = atan2(sinB, cosA)*180/pi; % insert typo: change a B to A
```

Run the tests again, using the tolerance check. Use the table class with the TestResult output to get a nicely formatted version of the test results.

```
>> tr = runtests('TriangleTest');
>> table(tr)
ans =
```

Name	Passed	Failed	Incomplete	Duration
'TriangleTest/Test1_SumOfAngles'	False	true	true	0.0040209
'TriangleTest/Test2_IsoscelesRightTriangles'	true	false	false	0.002971
'TriangleTest/Test3_3_4_5RightTriangle'	true	false	false	0.0027831
'TriangleTest/Test4_EquilateralTriangle'	true	false	false	0.0031556

Despite this being a major error in the code, only one test has failed: the sum of angles test. The isosceles and equilateral triangle tests still passed because A and B are equal in both cases. You could introduce errors into each line of your code to see if your tests catch them!

Now let's consider the other possibility for the unit tests: a test function, as opposed to the script. In this case, each test case has to be in its own subfunction, and the main function has to return an array of test function objects. This provides you the opportunity to write setup and teardown functions for the tests. It also makes use of the TestCase class and the qualifications package. Here is what the tests look like in this format:

```
function tests = TriangleFunctionTest
% Create an array of local functions
tests = functiontests(localfunctions);
end

%% Test Functions
function testAngleSum(testCase)%#ok<*DEFNU>
C       = 30;
[A,B]   = CompleteTriangle(1, 2, C);
theSum = A+B+C;
testCase.verifyEqual (theSum,180)
end

function testIsosceles(testCase)
C       = 90;
[A,B] = CompleteTriangle(2,2,C);
testCase.verifyEqual(A,B)
end

function test345(testCase)
C       = 90;
[~,~,c] = CompleteTriangle(3,4,C);
testCase.verifyEqual(c,5)
end
```

```matlab
function testEquilateral(testCase)
[A,B,c] = CompleteTriangle(1,1,60);
assert(abs(A-60)<testCase.TestData.tol)
testCase.verifyEqual(B,60,'absTol',1e-10)
testCase.verifyEqual(c,1)
end

%% Optional file fixtures
function setupOnce(testCase)  % do not change function name
% set a tolerance that can be used by all tests
testCase.TestData.tol=1e-10;
end

function teardownOnce(testCase)  % do not change function name
% change back to original path, for example
end

%% Optional fresh fixtures
function setup(testCase)  % do not change function name
% open a figure, for example
end

function teardown(testCase)  % do not change function name
% close figure, for example
end
```

If you just run this function, you get an array of the four test methods.

```matlab
>> TriangleFunctionTest
ans =
  1x4 Test array with properties:

    Name
    Parameterization
    SharedTestFixtures
```

Two methods for setting a tolerance for the tests in testEquilateral have been shown; in one case, you hardcode a tolerance in using the absTol parameters, and in the other, you use a setup function to pass a tolerance in via TestData. There are two types of setup and teardown functions to choose from: *file* fixtures, which run just once for the entire set of tests in the file, and *fresh* fixtures, which run for each test case. The file fixtures are identified with the *Once* suffix. In the case of this tolerance, the setupOnce function is appropriate.

To run the tests, use runtests as for the script. Happily, the tests all pass!

```matlab
>> runtests('TriangleFunctionTest')
Running TriangleFunctionTest
....
Done TriangleFunctionTest

_____

...
Totals:
   4 Passed, 0 Failed, 0 Incomplete.
   0.043001 seconds testing time.
```

You can run either set of tests in the Profiler (i.e., Run and Time) to verify coverage of the function being tested. It is a bit easier to navigate to the results for CompleteTriangle using the script version of the tests; the results from the test function lists many functions from the test framework. The result in the Profiler, showing 100 % coverage of the function, is shown in Figure 5-1.

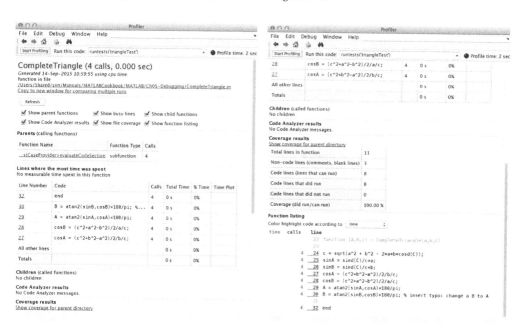

Figure 5-1. *Triangle tests in the Profiler*

After you have run the Profiler, you can run a Coverage Report. To run the report, you have to use the Current Folder pane of the Editor, and select Reports/Coverage Report from the context menu. An example is shown in Figure 5-2. The example function runs too quickly to take any measurable time, but generally, this report gives you insight into the time taken by your function, as well as the coverage you achieved.

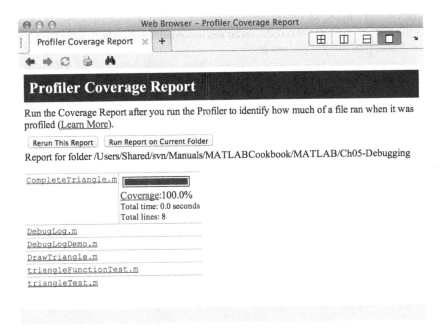

Figure 5-2. *Coverage Report for CompleteTriangle*

5-2. Running a Test Suite

Problem

Your toolbox has dozens or hundreds of functions, each with unit tests. You need an efficient way to run them all, or even better, run subsets.

Solution

MATLAB's test framework includes the construction of test suites.

How It Works

After you have generated tests for the functions in your toolbox, you can group them into suites in several ways. The help for the TestSuite class lists the options:

```
TestSuite methods:
    fromName    - Create a suite from the name of the test element
    fromFile    - Create a suite from a TestCase class filename
    fromFolder  - Create a suite from all tests in a folder
    fromPackage - Create a suite from all tests in a package
    fromClass   - Create a suite from a TestCase class
    fromMethod  - Create a suite from a single test method
```

You can also concatenate test suites made using these methods and pass the array to the test runner. In this way, you can easily generate subsets of your tests to run.

In the previous recipe, you created two test files for `CompleteTriangle`: a test script and a test function. You can create a test suite for the folder containing this code, and it will automatically find both sets of test cases. Assume that the current folder contains the two test files.

```
>> import matlab.unittest.TestSuite
>> testSuite = TestSuite.fromFolder(pwd);
>> result = run(testSuite)

Running TriangleFunctionTest
....
Done TriangleFunctionTest
_____


Running TriangleTest
.......
Done TriangleTest
_____
result =
  1×8 TestResult array with properties:

    Name
    Passed
    Failed
    Incomplete
    Duration
Totals:
  8 Passed, 0 Failed, 0 Incomplete.
  0.04218 seconds testing time.
```

As you can see, test suites are really quite simple. Some advanced features include the ability to apply selectors to a suite to obtain a subset of tests. To see the full documentation of `TestSuite` at the command line, type either

```
>> help matlab.unittest.TestSuite
```

or

```
>> import matlab.unittest.TestSuite
>> help TestSuite
```

The function for performing selections is `select If`. Here is an example that selects the two tests of an equilateral triangle from the suite:

```
>> subSuite = testSuite.selectIf('Name','*Equilateral*');
>> subSuite
subSuite =
  1×2 Test array with properties:

    Name
    Parameterization
    SharedTestFixtures
```

```
>> subSuite.Name
ans =
TriangleFunctionTest/testEquilateral
ans =
TriangleTest/Test4_EquilateralTriangle
```

You can run the tests in the resulting suite, or concatenate with other suites, as before.

5-3. Setting Verbosity Levels in Tests

Problem

The printouts from your tests are getting out of control, but you don't want to just delete or comment out all the information you have needed as you are developing the tests. If a test fails in the future, you may need those messages.

Solution

The test framework includes a logging feature that has four levels of verbosity. To utilize it, you create a test runner using the logging plugin and add log calls in your test cases.

How It Works

The four verbosity levels supported are Terse, Concise, Detailed, and Verbose, which are enumerated in Table 5-1.

Table 5-1.

1	Terse	Minimal amount of information
2	Concise	Typical amount of information
3	Detailed	Supplemental amount of information
4	Verbose	Surplus of information

The default test runner uses the lowest verbosity setting, Terse. The log function you use in your test cases is a method of TestCase, so to access the help, you need to use the fully qualified name:

```
>> help matlab.unittest.TestCase/log
```

The following is the log method syntax from the help:

> log(TESTCASE, LEVEL, DIAG) logs the diagnostic at the specified LEVEL. LEVEL can be either a numeric value (1, 2, 3, or 4) or a value from the matlab.unittest. Verbosity enumeration. When level is unspecified, the log method uses level Concise (2).

Logging requires a TestCase object. The diagnostic data for DIAG can be a string or an instance of matlab.unittest.diagnostics.Diagnostic. Let's write an example test for eig that demonstrates verbosity.

```
%% VerboseEigTest Demonstrate verbosity levels in tests
% Run a test of the eig function using log messages. Demonstrates
% all four levels of verbosity. To run the tests, at the command line use
% a TestRunner configured with the LoggingPlugIn:
%
%    import matlab.unittest.TestRunner;
%    import matlab.unittest.plugins.LoggingPlugin;
%    runner = TestRunner.withNoPlugins;
%    runner.addPlugin(LoggingPlugin.withVerbosity(4));
%    results = runner.run(VerboseEigTest);
%% Form
%    tests = VerboseEigTest
%% Inputs
% None.
%% Outputs
%    tests (:) Array of test functions

function tests = VerboseEigTest
% Create an array of local functions
tests = functiontests (localfunctions);
end


%% Test Functions
function eigTest (testCase)
log(testCase,'Generating_test_data'); % default is level 2
m = rand(2000);
A = m'*m;
log(testCase,'About_to_call_eig.');
[V,D,W] = eig(A);
log(testCase, 4, 'Eig_finished.');
assert(norm(W'*A-D*W')<1e-6)
log(testCase,3, 'Test_of_eig_completed.');
end


% If you want to use the Verbose enumeration in your code instead of numbers,
% import the class matlab.unittest.Verbosity
function eigWithEnumTest(testCase)
import matlab.unittest.Verbosity
m = rand(1000);
A = m'*m;
log(testCase, Verbosity.Detailed, 'About_to_call_eig_(with_enum).');
[V,D,W] = eig(A);
assert(norm(W'*A-D*W')<1e-6)
log(testCase, Verbosity.Terse, 'Test_of_eig_(with_enum)_completed.');
end
```

If you just run this test with runtests, you get the Terse level of output. Note that the system time is displayed along with your log message.

```
>> runtests('VerboseEigTest');
Running VerboseEigTest
   [Terse] Diagnostic logged (2015-09-14 T12:15:29): About to call eig.
.  [Terse] Diagnostic logged (2015-09-14 T12:15:40): Test of eig (with enum) completed

.
Done VerboseEigTest
```
_____

To get a higher level of verbosity requires a test runner with the logging plugin. This requires a few imports at the command line (or in your script). You need to generate a "plain" runner, with no plugins, and then add the logging plugin with the desired level of verbosity. The verbosity level of the message is displayed in the output.

```
>> import matlab.unittest.TestRunner;
>> import matlab.unittest.plugins.LoggingPlugin;
>> runner = TestRunner.withNoPlugins;
>> runner.addPlugin (LoggingPlugin.withVerbosity(4));
>> results = runner.run(VerboseEigTest);
  [Concise] Diagnostic logged (2015-09-14 T12:19:57): Generating test data
    [Terse] Diagnostic logged (2015-09-14 T12:19:57): About to call eig.
  [Verbose] Diagnostic logged (2015-09-14 T12:20:01): Eig finished.
 [Detailed] Diagnostic logged (2015-09-14 T12:20:07): Test of eig completed.
 [Detailed] Diagnostic logged (2015-09-14 T12:20:07): About to call eig (with enum).
    [Terse] Diagnostic logged (2015-09-14 T12:20:08): Test of eig (with enum) completed.
```

5-4. Create a Logging Function to Display Data

Problem

It is easy and convenient to print variable values by removing the semicolons from statements, but code left in this state can produce unwanted printouts that are very difficult to track down. Even using disp and fprintf can make unwanted printouts hard to find, because you probably use these functions elsewhere.

Solution

Create a custom logging function to display a variable with a helpful identifying message. You can extend this to a logging mechanism with verbosity settings similar to that described in the previous recipe, as used in the MATLAB testing framework, and in most C++ and Java testing frameworks.

How It Works

An example logging function is implemented in DebugLog. DebugLog prints out a message, which can be anything, and before that displays, the path to where DebugLog is called. The backtrace is obtained using dbstack.

```matlab
%% DEBUGLOG Logging function for debugging
% Use this function instead of adding disp() statements or leaving out semicolons.
%% Form
%   DebugLog( msg, fullPath )
%% Description
% Prints out the data in in msg using disp() and shows the path to the message.
% The full path option will print a complete backtrace.
%% Inputs
%   msg         (.)      Any message
%   fullPath    (1,1)    If entered, print the full backtrace
%% Outputs
%   None

function DebugLog( msg, fullPath )

% Demo
if( nargin < 1 )
  DebugLog(rand(2,2));
  return;
end

% Get the function that calls this one
f = dbstack;

% The second path is only if called directly from the command line
if(length(f) > 1)
  f1 = 2;
else
  f1 = 1;
end

if( nargin > 1 && fullPath )
  f2 = length(f);
else
  f2 = f1;
end

for k = f1:f2
  disp(['- >_' f(k).name]);
end
disp(msg);
```

DebugLog is demonstrated in DebugLogDemo. The function has a subfunction to demonstrate the backtrace.

```matlab
%% Demonstrate DebugLog
% Log a variable to the command window using DebugLog.

function DebugLogDemo
```

```
y = linspace(0,10);
i = FindInY(y);

function I = FindInY(y)

i = find(y < 0.5);
DebugLog( i, true );
```

This the output of the demo:

```
>> DebugLogDemo
-> FindInY
-> DebugLogDemo
     1    2    3    4    5
```

One extension of this function is to add the name of the variable being logged, if msg is a variable, using the function inputname. This additional lines of code look like this:

```
str = inputname(1);
if ~isempty(str)
  disp(['Variable:␣' str]);
end
```

The demo output now looks like this:

```
>> DebugLogDemo
-> FindInY
-> DebugLogDemo
Variable: i
     1    2    3    4    5
```

Consistently using your own logging functions for displaying messages to the user and printing debug data will make your code easier to maintain.

5-5. Generating and Tracing MATLAB Errors and Warnings

Problem

You would like to display errors and warnings to the user in an organized fashion.

Solution

Always use the additional inputs to warning and error to specify a message ID. This allows your message to be traced back to the function in the code that generated it, as well as controlling the display of certain warnings.

How It Works

The warning function has several helpful parameters for customizing and controlling warnings displays. When you are generating a warning, use the full syntax with a message identifier:

```
warning('MSGID','MESSAGE', A, B, ...)
```

The MSGID is a mnemonic in the form <component>[:<component>]:<mnemonic>, such as PSS:FunctionName:IllegalInput. The ID is not normally displayed when you give a warning, unless you have turned verbose display on, via warning on verbose and warning off verbose. This is easy to demonstrate at the command line:

```
>> warning('PSS:Example:DemoWarning', 'This_is_an_example_warning')
Warning: This is an example warning
>> warning verbose on
>> warning('PSS:Example:DemoWarning','This_is_an_example_warning')
Warning: This is an example warning
(Type "warning off PSS:Example:DemoWarning" to suppress this warning.)
```

As displayed, you can turn a given warning off using its message ID by using the command form shown or the functional form, warning('off','msgid').

The lastwarn function can also return the message ID if passed an additional output, as in:

```
>> [lastmsg, lastid] = lastwarn
lastmsg =
This is an example warning
lastid =
PSS:Example:DemoWarning
```

The error and lasterr functions work the same way. An added benefit of using message identifiers is that you can select them when debugging, as an option when stopping for errors or warnings. The debugger is integrated into the editor window, and the debugger options are grouped under the Breakpoints toolbar button. The button and the More Options pop-up window are shown in Figure 5-3. In this case, we entered an example PSS message identifier.

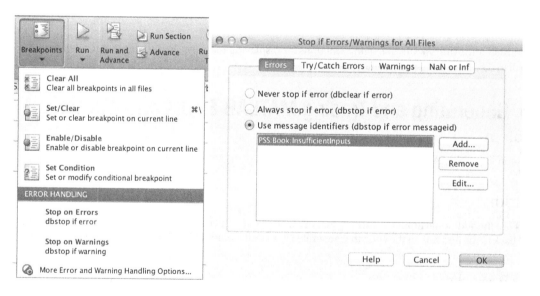

Figure 5-3. *Option to stop on an error in debugger*

Remember, you should always mention any warnings and errors that may be generated by a function in its header!

5-6. Testing Custom Errors and Warnings

Problem

You have code that generates warnings or errors for problematic inputs and you need to test it.

Solution

You have two possibilities for testing the generation of errors in your code: try/catch blocks with assert and the verifyError method available to a TestCase. With warnings, you can either use lastwarn or verifyWarning.

How It Works

A comprehensive set of tests for your code should include all paths, or as close to all paths, as possible; and it must exercise all the warnings and errors that can be generated by your code. You can do this manually by using try/catch blocks to catch errors and comparing the error (MException object) to the expected error. For warnings, you can check lastwarn to see that a warning was issued, like so:

```
>> lastwarn('');
>> warning('PSS:Book:id','Warning!')
Warning: Warning!
>> [anywarn, anyid] = lastwarn;
>> assert(strcmp (anyid, 'PSS:Book:wrongid'))
Assertion failed.
```

Here is an example of a try/catch block with assert to detect a specific error:

```
%% Test that we get the expected error, and pass
errFun = @() error('PSS:Book:id','Error!');
try
  feval(errFun);
catch ME
  assert(strcmp(ME.identifier,'PSS:Book:id'));
end
```

This test verifies that the error thrown is the one expected; however, it does not detect if no error is thrown at all. For this, you need to add a boolean variable to the try block.

```
%% This time we don't get any error at all
wrongFun = @() disp('some error-free code.');
tf = false;
try
  feval(wrongFun);
  tf = true;
catch ME
  assert(strcmp(ME.identifier,'PSS:Book:id'));
end
if (tf)
  assert(false,'CatchErrorTest: No error thrown');
end
```

When you run this code segment, you get the following output:

```
Some error-free code.
CatchErrorTest: No error thrown
```

If you run the test as part of a test script with runtests, the test fails.

A far better way to test for warnings and errors is to use the unit test framework's qualifiers to check that the desired warning or error is generated. Here is an example of verifying a warning, with a test that will pass and a test that will fail; note that you need to pass a function handle to the verifyWarning function.

```
function tests = WarningsTest
% Create an array of local functions
tests = functiontests (localfunctions);
end

%% Test Functions
function passTest (testCase)
warnFun = @()warning('PSS:Book:id','Warning!');
testCase.verifyWarning(warnFun,'PSS:Book:id');
end

function failTest (testCase)
warnFun = @() warning ('Wrong:id','Warning!');
testCase.verifyWarning (warnFun,'PSS:id','Wrong_id');
end
```

When you run this test function with runtests, you can see that failTest did, in fact, fail.

```
>> runtests('WarningsTest')
Running WarningsTest
.Warning: Warning!

================================================================
Verification failed in WarningsTest/failTest.

    ----------------
    Test Diagnostic:
    ----------------
    Wrong id

    --------------------
    Framework Diagnostic:
    --------------------
    verifyWarning failed.
    --> The function handle did not issue the expected warning.

        Actual Warnings:
                Wrong:id
        Expected Warning:
                PSS:id
```

```
    Evaluated Function:
            @()warning('Wrong:id','Warning!')
    -----------------
    Stack Information:
    -----------------
    In /Users/Shared/svn/Manuals/MATLABCookbook/MATLAB/Ch05-Debugging/WarningsTest.m
        (failTest) at 12
========================================================
.
Done WarningsTest
_____

Failure Summary:
    Name                    Failed    Incomplete    Reason(s)
    ================================================================
    WarningsTest/failTest    X                      Failed by verification.

Totals:
    1 Passed, 1 Failed, 0 Incomplete.
    0.047691 seconds testing time.
```

verifyError works the same way. In practice, you need to make a function handle that includes the inputs that cause the error or warning to be generated.

For advanced programmers, there is a further mechanism for constructing tests using verifyThat with the Constraint class. You can supply your own Diagnostic objects as well. For more information, see the reference pages for these classes along with the Verifiable class.

5-7. Testing Generation of Figures

Problem

Your function generates a figure instead of an output variable. How do you test it?

Solution

Although you may need a human to verify that the figure looks correct, you can at least verify that the correct set of figures is generated by your function using findobj.

How It Works

Routinely assigning names to your figures makes it easy to test that they have been generated, even if you don't have access to the handles. You can also assign tags to figures, such as having a single tag for your entire toolbox, which allows you to locate sets of figures.

```
>> figure ('Name', 'Figure_1', 'Tag', 'PSS');
>> figure ('Name', 'Figure_2', 'Tag', 'PSS')
>> h = findobj('Tag', 'PSS')
h =
   2×1 Figure array:
```

```
   Figure    (PSS)
   Figure    (PSS)
>> h = findobj('Name','Figure_1')
h =
   Figure (PSS) with properties:

        Number: 1
          Name: 'Figure_1'
         Color: [0.94 0.94 0.94]
      Position: [440 378 560 420]
         Units: 'pixels'
```

In your test, you can then check that you have the correct number of figures generated using length(h) or that each specific named figure exists using strcmp. If you are storing any data in your figures using UserData, you can test that as well.

If you are not using tags or need to check for figures that do not have names or tags, you can find all figures currently open using the type input to findobj:

```
>> findobj('type','figure')
ans =
   2×1 Figure array:

   Figure    (PSS)
   Figure    (PSS)
```

Note that figures are only returned by findobj if they are visible to the command line via their HandleVisibility property. This property can have the values 'on', 'off', and 'callback'. GUIs generated by the design tool GUIDE are generally hidden to prevent users from accidentally altering the GUI using plot or similar commands; these figures use the value 'callback'. Regular figures have the value 'on' and can be located. A figure with HandleVisibility set to 'off' can only be accessed using its handle.

Summary

This chapter demonstrated how to use MATLAB's unit test framework and provided recipes to help you debug your functions. Table 5-2 lists the code files.

Table 5-2. *Chapter Code Listing*

File	Description
CatchErrorTest	Script showing how to catch errors in a try block.
CompleteTriangle	Example function calculating angles in a triangle.
DebugLog	Custom data logging function.
DebugLogDemo	Demo of DebugLog showing a backtrace.
TriangleFunctionTest	A function with test cases for CompleteTriangle.
TriangleTest	A script with test cases for CompleteTriangle.
VerboseEigTest	A test function showing all levels of verbosity.
WarningsTest	A test function using verifyWarning

PART II

■ ■ ■

Applications

In this part of the book we will explore the use of MATLAB for dynamical systems and control system design in a number of technologies. In each area we will derive the equations of motion for the system. A system is defined by its state equations, states and parameters. The equations of motion are the equations of the states of a system. The state variables are the set of variables that evolve with time that completely define the current state of the system and allow for future prediction of the state without any knowledge of the past. We also need parameters that are independent of the states to fully define the system along with the inputs to the system. The state vector will always be represented by an n-by-1 MATLAB array.

In the equations that we present, we will use the dot notation for derivatives, i.e.

$$\dot{r} = \frac{dr}{dt}$$

State equations are of the form

$$\dot{x} = ax + bu$$
$$y = cx + du$$

x is the state and is an $n \times 1$ vector represented by an n row by 1 column MATLAB array. u is the input matrix and is $m \times 1$. y is the measurement. a relates the state to the state derivative and is an $n \times n$ array. b is the input array and is $n \times m$ where the number of inputs, u, is m. c relates the state the to measurement and d relates the input to the measurement.

We are not going to delve into control theory in detail. That would require a complete textbook by itself, or many textbooks if you wanted to explore control system design in depth. We will provide an intuitive approach to allow you to get control systems up and running quickly without too much code!

CHAPTER 6

■ ■ ■

The Double Integrator

A *double integrator* is a dynamical model for a wide variety of physical systems. This includes a mass moving in one dimension and an object rotating around a shaft. It represents a broad class of systems with two states. In this chapter, you will learn how to model a double integrator and how to control it. In the process, you will create some very important functions for implementing control systems, plotting, and performing numerical integration. This will provide a springboard to other, more complex systems in later chapters.

6-1. Writing Equations for the Double Integrator Model

Problem

A double integrator is a second-order model, with a second derivative, where the derivative is independent of the state. This model appears in many engineering disciplines.

Solution

You will write the equations for the model dynamics and implement these in a function.

How It Works

One-dimensional linear motion can be modeled with the following differential equations:

$$\dot{r} = v \tag{6.1}$$

$$m\dot{v} = F \tag{6.2}$$

r and v are states; m, the mass, is a parameter; and F, the force, is an input. The state vector is

$$x = \begin{bmatrix} r \\ v \end{bmatrix} \tag{6.3}$$

The variable x is represented by a MATLAB two rows × one column array. The first element of the array is r and the second is v.

Electronic supplementary material The online version of this chapter (doi:10.1007/978-1-4842-0559-4_6) contains supplementary material, which is available to authorized users.

S. Thomas and M. Paluszek, *MATLAB Recipes*, DOI 10.1007/978-1-4842-0559-4_6

■ **Tip** This equation works equally well for rotational motion. Just replace m with I for inertia, r with θ for angle, v with ω for angular velocity, and F with T for torque.

To write a function for the derivatives, divide by m to isolate the derivatives on the left-hand side of the equations. The terms on the right-hand side are what you will calculate in this so-called RHS function.

$$\dot{r} = v \tag{6.4}$$

$$\dot{v} = \frac{F}{m} \equiv a \tag{6.5}$$

Writing these equations in vector notation, you have

$$\dot{x} = \begin{bmatrix} v \\ a \end{bmatrix} \tag{6.6}$$

Now you can write the function, RHSDoubleIntegrator, for the derivative of the state vector x. Note the prefix of RHS in the name, which you use to identify all functions that can be integrated. The velocity term is the second element of state x, and is passed as the derivative of the position state r. The derivative of the velocity state is the acceleration a. The RHS function has a placeholder ~ for the first argument, where the integrator will pass the time t, which this function doesn't require.

```
function xDot = RHSDoubleIntegrator(~, x, a)

xDot = [x(2);a];
```

6-2. Creating a Fixed-Step Numerical Integrator

Problem

You need to use numerical integration in the simulations to evolve the state of the systems.

Solution

You will review the equations for a fourth-order Runge-Kutta integrator and develop a function to perform fixed-step integration.

How It Works

Let's look at a simple model for linear motion. You need to put the equations in state equation form, which is a set of first-order differential equations with the derivatives on the left-hand side. Take, for example, the one-dimensional motion model from Recipe 6-1, with the derivative terms for r and v on the left-hand side of the equations.

$$\frac{dr}{dt} = v \tag{6.7}$$

$$\frac{dv}{dt} = \frac{F}{m} \tag{6.8}$$

Multiply both sides by dt.

$$dr = v\,dt \tag{6.9}$$

$$dv = \frac{F}{m}\,dt \tag{6.10}$$

Replace dt with the fixed-time interval h. You can now write the simplest type of numerical integrator for computing the state at step $k + 1$ from the state at step k.

$$r_{k+1} = r_k + v_k h \tag{6.11}$$

$$v_{k+1} = v_k + \frac{F_k}{m} h \tag{6.12}$$

Step k is at time t_k and step $k + 1$ is at time t_{k+1}, where $t_{k+1} = t_k + h$.

This simple integrator is called *Euler integration*. It assumes that the force F_k is constant over the time interval h. Euler integration works fairly well for simple systems, like the preceding one. For example, for a spring system

$$\ddot{r} + \omega^2 r = a \tag{6.13}$$

the natural frequency of oscillation is ω. If the time step is greater than half the period of the oscillation $2\pi/\omega$, the numerical integration cannot capture the dynamics. In practice, the time step, h, must be much lower than half.

Euler integration is rarely used for engineering due to its limited accuracy. One of the most popular methods used for control system simulation is the fourth-order Runge-Kutta method. The equations are as follows:

$$
\begin{aligned}
k_1 &= f\left(x, u(t), t\right) \\
k_2 &= f\left(x + \frac{h}{2}k_1, u(t) + \frac{h}{2}, t + \frac{h}{2}\right) \\
k_3 &= f\left(x + \frac{h}{2}k_2, u(t) + \frac{h}{2}, t + \frac{h}{2}\right) \\
k_4 &= \left(x + hk_3, u(t + h - \varepsilon), t + h\right) \\
x &= x + \frac{h}{6}\left(k_1 + 2\left(k_2 + k_3\right) + k_4\right) + O\left(h^4\right)
\end{aligned}
\tag{6.14}
$$

$f(x, u, t)$ is the right-hand side of the differential equations. $O(h^4)$ means the truncation error due to the order of the integration goes as the fourth power of the time step. This means that if you halve this time step, the error drops to 0.0625 of the error with the bigger time step. In the preceding system, the right-hand sides are computed at four different points, twice at $h/2$ and once at t and $t + h$.

141

$$f(x,F,t) = \begin{bmatrix} v \\ \dfrac{F}{m} \end{bmatrix}$$
(6.15)

■ **Note** There are other fourth-order Runge-Kutta methods with different coefficients.

MATLAB has many numerical integrators. They are designed to integrate over any interval. Some, such as ode113, adjust the step size and the order of the integration (Euler is first-order, the preceding Runge-Kutta is fourth-order), between the desired interval. For digital control, you need to integrate between the step size of the digital controller. You could use ode113 for this, but usually the fourth-order Runge-Kutta is sufficient. This method is used for all of the examples in this book.

You next want to look at the RungeKutta function that implements equation 6.14. Note the use of feval to evaluate the right-hand-side function in the following code.

```
function x = RungeKutta( Fun, t, x, h, varargin )

hO2    = 0.5*h;
tPHO2  = t + hO2;

k1    = feval( Fun,    t,     x,              varargin{:} );
k2    = feval( Fun,    tPHO2, x + hO2*k1, varargin{:} );
k3    = feval( Fun,    tPHO2, x + hO2*k2, varargin{:} );
k4    = feval( Fun,    t+h,   x + h*k3,   varargin{:} );

x     = x + h*(k1 + 2*(k2+k3) + k4)/6;
```

Fun is a pointer to the right-hand-side function. varargin is passed to that function, which enables the dynamics model to have any number of parameters. This RungeKutta function is used in all of the examples in this book. You precompute all values that are used multiple times, such as $t + h/2$. This is particularly important in functions that are called repeatedly.

You pass this function a handle to the right-hand-side function, RHSDoubleIntegrator, which implements equation 6.1.

■ **Tip** Replace unused variables in function calls with the tilde.

In order to integrate the model one step, you call

```
xNew = RungeKutta( @RHSDoubleIntegrator, ~, x, h, a )
```

Our RungeKutta function, and all MATLAB integrators, have the dependent variable first, which is t in this case. Since it isn't used here, you replace it with the tilde. MATLAB's code analyzer will suggest this for efficiency for all unused function inputs and outputs in your code.

6-3. Implement a Discrete Proportional-Derivative Controller

Problem

You want digital control software that can control a double integrator system and other dynamical systems.

Solution

You will derive the equations for a damped second-order system in the time domain and then create a sampled data version and implement it a MATLAB function.

How It Works

If a constant force F is applied to the system, the mass m will accelerate and its position will change with the square of time. The analytical solution for the two states, r and v, is

$$r(t) = r(0) + v(0)(t - t(0)) + \frac{1}{2}\frac{F}{m}(t - t(0))^2 \qquad (6.16)$$

$$v(t) = v(0) + \frac{F}{m}(t - t(0)) \qquad (6.17)$$

If you wish to have the position of mass stay close to zero, you can use a control system known as a *regulator*. You will use a proportional-derivative regulator. This regulator measures position and applies a control force proportional to the position error and to the derivative of the position error. Let's look at a particularly simple form of this control:

$$F_c = -k_r r - k_v v \qquad (6.18)$$

F_c is the control force. You don't have to be able to measure the disturbance force, F, for this to work. Picking the gains, k_r and k_v, is easy if you write the dynamical system as a second-order system:

$$m\ddot{r} = F_c + F \qquad (6.19)$$

$$m\ddot{r} = F - k_r r - k_v v \qquad (6.20)$$

$$m\ddot{r} + k_v \dot{r} + k_r r = F \qquad (6.21)$$

The controlled system is a damped second-order oscillator. You can write the desired differential equation as

$$\ddot{r} + 2\zeta\sigma\dot{r} + \sigma^2 r = \frac{F}{m} \qquad (6.22)$$

143

where the gains are

$$k_r = m\sigma^2 \tag{6.23}$$

$$k_v = m\zeta\sigma \tag{6.24}$$

σ is the undamped natural frequency and ζ is the damping ratio. This system will always be stable as long as the gains are positive. If F if constant the position will settle to an offset. This is

$$r = \frac{F}{m\sigma^2} \tag{6.25}$$

This method of control design is called "pole-placement".

Virtually all control systems are implemented on digital computers, so you must transform this controller into a digital form. Assume that you only measure position. The first step is to assemble the control in a continuous time state space form. For this implementation, you add a rate filter to the PD controller.

$$\omega = \omega_r + 2\zeta\omega_n \tag{6.26}$$

$$k = \omega_r \omega_n^2 m / w \tag{6.27}$$

$$\tau = \left(\frac{m}{k} \omega_n (\omega_n + 2\zeta\omega_r) - 1 \right) / \omega \tag{6.28}$$

$$a = -\omega \tag{6.29}$$

$$b = \omega \tag{6.30}$$

$$c = -k\omega\tau \tag{6.31}$$

$$d = k * (\tau\omega + 1) \tag{6.32}$$

where ω_r is the cutoff frequency for the first-order filter on the rate term; ω_n is the undamped natural frequency for the controller; and ζ is the controller damping ratio. m is the "mass" or inertia. You can always set this to 1 and scale the control output. The undamped natural frequency gives the bandwidth of the controller. The higher the bandwidth, the faster it responds to errors. The higher the bandwidth, the smaller the offset error will be due to a constant input.

$$\dot{x} = ax + bu \tag{6.33}$$

$$y = -cx - du \tag{6.34}$$

x is the controller state and u is the position measurement. The state space form is convenient for computation but still assumes that you are sampling continuously. There are many ways to convert this to digital form. You will use a zero-order-hold, meaning you will compute the control each sample and hold the value over that sample period. You convert this using the matrix exponential function in MATLAB, expm. If T is the sample period, you assemble the matrix

$$\sigma = \begin{bmatrix} aT & bT \\ 0 & 0 \end{bmatrix} \tag{6.35}$$

The sampled time versions of a and b are

$$\begin{bmatrix} a_d \\ b_d \end{bmatrix} = e^{\sigma} \tag{6.36}$$

The digital controller is now

$$x_{k+1} = a_d x_k + b_d u_k \tag{6.37}$$

$$y_k = -c x_k - d u_k \tag{6.38}$$

Let's now look at PDControl. This function designs and implements the control system derived in equation 6.26. The name stands for Proportional-Derivative Control. It has several child functions. The header is shown below. It has a link to the help for one of the subfunctions, which is active when the header is displayed at the command line. You list each data structure field for the input and output.

```
%% PDCONTROL Design and implement a PD Controller in sampled time.
%% Forms
%   d = PDControl( 'struct' )
%   d = PDControl( 'initialize', d )
%   [y, d] = PDControl( 'update', u, d )
%
%% Description
% Designs a PD controller and implements it in discrete form.
%
%   y = -c*x - d*u
%   x = a*x + b*u
%
% where u is the input and y is the output. This controller has a first
% order rate filter on the derivative term.
%
% Set the mode to initialize to create the state space matrices for the
% controller. Set the mode to update to update the controller and get a
% new output.
%
% Utilizes the subfunction C2DZOH to discretize, see <a href="matlab: help PDControl>
      CToDZOH">CToDZOH help</a>
%
%% Inputs
% mode        (1,1) 'initialize' or 'update'
% u           (1,1) Measurement
% d           (.) Data structure
%                 .m      (1,1) Mass
%                 .zeta   (1,1) Damping ratio
%                 .wN     (1,1) Undamped natural frequency
%                 .wD     (1,1) Derivative term filter cutoff
```

145

```
%                       .tSamp    (1,1) Sampling period*
%                       .x        (1,1) Controller state
%
%% Outputs
%   y          (1,1) Control
%   d          (.)  Data structure additions
%                       .a        (1,1) State transition matrix
%                       .b        (1,1) Input matrix
%                       .c        (1,1) State output matrix
%                       .d        (1,1) Feedthrough matrix
%                       .x        (1,1) Updated controller state
```

Next, the body of the function. Note the switch statement and the two child functions, CToDZOH and DefaultStruct, at the bottom.

```
function [y, d] = PDControl( mode, u, d )
% Demo
if( nargin < 1 )
  disp('Demo_of_PDControl_using_the_default_struct')
  d = PDControl('struct');
  d = PDControl('initialize',d);
  disp(d)
  return
end

switch lower(mode)
  case 'initialize'
    d                = u;
    w                = d.wD + 2*d.zeta*d.wN;
    k                = d.wD*d.wN^2*d.m/w;
    tau              = ((d.m/k)*d.wN*(d.wN + 2*d.zeta*d.wD) - 1 )/w;
    d.a              = -w;
    d.b              = w;
    d.c              = -k*w*tau;
    d.d              = k*(tau*w + 1);

    [d.a, d.b]  = CToDZOH(d.a,d.b,d.tSamp);
    y                = d;

  case 'update'
    y    = -d.c*d.x - d.d*u;
    d.x = d.a*d.x + d.b*u;

  case 'struct'
    y = DefaultStruct;

  otherwise
    error('%s_is_not_a_valid_mode',mode);
end
```

```
function [f, g] = CToDZOH( a, b, T )
%% CToDZOH
% Continuous to discrete transformation using a zero order hold. Discretize
% using a matrix exponential, <matlab:doc('expm') expm>.
%
% [f, g] = C2DZOH( a, b, T )
%
% *Inputs*
%
% a   (1,1)   Continuous plant matrix
% b   (1,1)   Input matrix
% T   (1,1)   Time step
%
% *Outputs*
%
% f   (1,1)   Discrete plant
% g   (1,1)   Discrete input
%
% See also
% expm

q = expm([a*T b*T;zeros(1,2)]);

f = q(1,1);
g = q(1,2);

function d = DefaultStruct

d.m      = 1.0;
d.zeta   = 0.7;
d.wN     = 0.1;
d.wD     = 0.5;
d.tSamp  = 1.0;
d.x      = 0.0;
d.a      = [];
d.b      = [];
d.c      = [];
d.d      = [];
```

This is our standard format for an engineering function. The following are its important features:

- It combines design and implementation in one function.
- It returns the default data structure that it uses.
- It has modes.
- It has a built-in demo.
- It has nested functions.

The built-in demo uses the default values. The default values give the user an idea of reasonable parameters for the function. This built-in demo generates the state space matrices, which are scalars in this case.

```
Demo of PDControl using the default struct
       m: 1
    zeta: 0.7000
      wN: 0.1000
      wD: 0.5000
   tSamp: 1
       x: 0
       a: 0.5273
       b: 0.4727
       c: -0.0722
       d: 0.0800
```

A more elaborate demo, with a simulation, could have been added. The built-in demos are very useful because they show the user a simple example of how to use the function. It also is helpful in developing the function, because you can test the function by just typing the function name in the command line.

The first argument is the mode variable that indicates which case in the switch statement the function should execute. The "initialize" mode must always be run first. The initialization modifies the data structure, which is used as the function's memory. You could also have used persistent variables for the function memory. Using an output makes it easier to programmatically inspect the contents of memory. The "update" is used to update the controller as new inputs arrive. The switch statement has an "otherwise" case to warn the user of mode errors. This throws an error, stopping execution of the script. You may not always want to do this and may just use a warning to warn the user.

The nested function CToDZOH converts the continuous control system to a sampled-data control system using equation 6.35. The name stands for Continuous to Discrete Zero-Order Hold. A non-controls expert wouldn't immediately understand the acronym, but the expanded name is too long to be a useful function name.

■ **Tip** Make function names consistent in form and use terms that are standard for your field. Remember that not all readers of your code will be native English-language speakers!

If you were building a toolbox, the CToDZOH function would likely be a separate file. For this book, it is only used by PDControl, so you put it into that function file.

6-4. Simulate the Double Integrator with Digital Control

Problem

You want to simulate digital control of the double integrator model.

Solution

You will write a script that calls the control function and integrator sequentially in a loop and plots the results.

How It Works

Table 6-1 presents the nominal values for the control parameters that you will use for the double integrator simulation.

Table 6-1. *Control Parameters*

Zeta	Damping ratio	1.0
wN	Undamped natural frequency	0.1 rad/sec
wD	Derivative term filter cutoff	1.0 rad/sec
dT	Time step	0.1 sec

The simulation script is implemented in DoubleIntegratorSim.m. Note the use of cell breaks to divide the script into sections that can be run independently. The "See also" section lists the functions used, which are links when the header is displayed via the command-line help.

```
%% Double Integrator Demo
% Demonstrate control of a double integrator.
%% See also
% PDControl, RungeKutta, RHSDoubleIntegrator, TimeLabel

%% Initialize
tEnd        = 100; % Simulation end time (sec)
dT          = 0.1; % Time step (sec)
aD          = 1.0; % Disturbance acceleration (m/s^2)
controlIsOn = false; % True if the controller is to be used
x           = [0;0]; % [position;velocity]

% Controller parameters
d       = PDControl( 'struct' );
d.zeta  = 1.0;
d.wN    = 0.1;
d.wD    = 1.0;
d.tSamp = dT;
d       = PDControl( 'initialize', d );

%% Simulation
nSim  = tEnd/dT+1;
xPlot = zeros(3,nSim);

for k = 1:nSim
  if( controlIsOn )
    [u, d] = PDControl('update',x(1),d);
  else
    u = 0;
  end
```

```
  xPlot(:,k) = [x;u];
    x          = RungeKutta( 'RHSDoubleIntegrator', 0, x, dT, aD+u );
end

%% Plot the results
yL     = {'r_(m)' 'v_(m/s)' 'u_(m/s^2)'};
[t,tL] = TimeLabel(dT*(0:(nSim-1)));

PlotSet( t, xPlot, 'x_label', tL, 'y_label', yL );
```

The first code block sets up simulation parameters that the user can change. The controlIsOn variable is set to true if the controller is to be used. This makes it easy to test the script without the controller. When the controller is disabled, you get the "open loop" response. It is a good idea to make sure that the open-loop response makes sense before testing the controller.

■ **Tip** Put all parameters that the user can change at the beginning of the script.

The second block sets up the controller. Recall that PDControl has three arguments: 'struct' 'initialize', 'update'. The first returns the data structure required by the function. You fill the structure fields with the values selected for the problem in the lines that follow that statement. At the end of this block, you initialize the controller. This sets the controller state to zero and creates the sampled time state space matrices, which in this case are four scalars.

The third block is the simulation with the check to see if the controller is on. Note the sequential use of the control function followed by the integrator. This is discrete control because the control, u, is constant over the integration time step. The final block plots the results.

Figure 6-1 shows the open-loop response obtained by setting the controlIsOn flag to false and executing DoubleIntegratorSim. The velocity increases linearly and the position increases with the square of time, as it should. The output agrees with the analytical solution in equation 6.16. Figure 6-2 shows the closed-loop response, with controlIsOn set to true. The velocity goes to zero and the position reaches a constant, though not zero. The control acceleration u exactly matches the disturbance acceleration a. You could have eliminated the position offset by using a proportional integral differential (PID) controller.

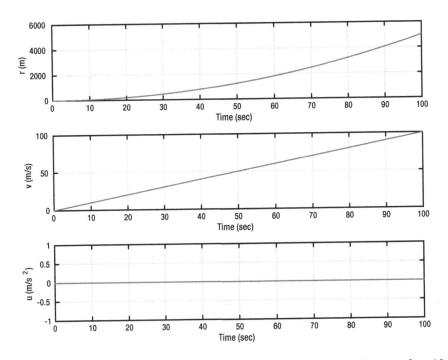

Figure 6-1. *The open-loop response with a constant disturbance acceleration of 1 m/s²*

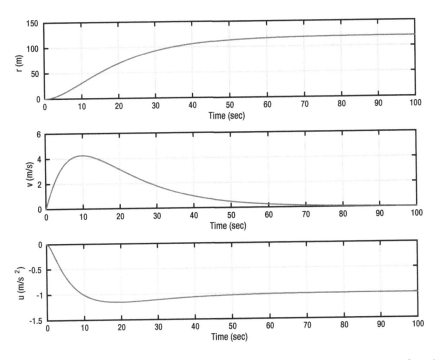

Figure 6-2. *The closed-loop response with a constant disturbance acceleration of 1 m/s²*

The two examples show that the simulation works without the control and that the control performs as expected. This script is an integrated test of all of the functions listed in the header. It does a good job of testing their functionality. However, one test isn't sufficient to understand the controller. Let's make the controller underdamped by setting ζ in the field d.zeta, to 0.2. Now the response oscillates (see Figure 6-3). You set tEnd to 300 to show that it damps.

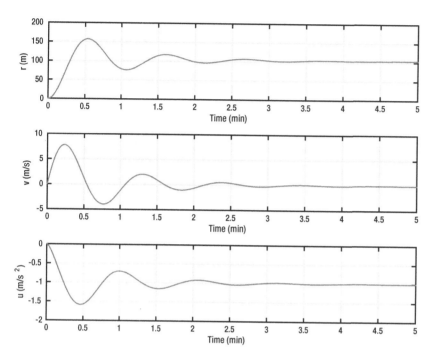

Figure 6-3. *The closed-loop response with a constant disturbance acceleration of 1 m/s² and ζ equal to 0.2*

Another thing to try is setting the bandwidth really high. Set ω_n, in field d.wN, to 8, and the rate filter bandwidth d.wD to 50. The result is shown in Figure 6-4. The controller is unstable because the bandwidth is much higher than that allowed by the sampling rate.

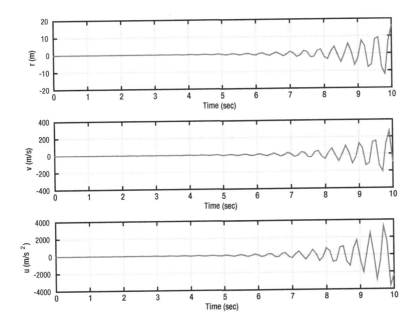

Figure 6-4. *The closed-loop response using a bandwidth too high for the sampling*

Your bandwidth has to be less than half the sampling bandwidth, which is

$$\omega_s = \frac{2\pi}{T} \tag{6.39}$$

All the results are expected behavior. The last case is what is known as an edge or corner case that shows that the expected instability does happen. These four cases are a minimalist set of tests for this admittedly simple control system example.

6-5. Create Time Axes with Reasonable Time Units

Problem

You want your time axes to have easy-to-read units, not just seconds.

Solution

You will create a function that checks the duration and converts from seconds to minutes, hours, days, or years.

How It Works

You check the maximum time in the array of times and scale it to larger time units. The time units implemented are seconds, minutes, hours, days, and years. You return the scaled time vector, the label string, and the units string, as it might be useful.

153

```
function [t, c, s] = TimeLabel( t )

secInYear   = 365.25*86400;
secInDay    = 86400;
secInHour   =  3600;
secInMinute =    60;

tMax        = max(t);

if( tMax > secInYear )
  c = 'Time (years)';
  s = 'years';
  t = t/secInYear;
elseif( tMax > 3*secInDay )
  c = 'Time (days)';
  t = t/secInDay;
  s = 'days';
elseif( tMax > 3*secInHour )
  c = 'Time (hours)';
  t = t/secInHour;
  s = 'hours';
elseif( tMax > 3*secInMinute )
  c = 'Time (min)';
  t = t/secInMinute;
  s = 'min';
else
  c = 'Time (sec)';
  s = 'sec';
end
```

6-6. Create Figures with Multiple Subplots

Problem

You frequently generate figures with multiple subplots during control analysis, and this results in large blocks of repetitive code at the bottom of every script.

Solution

You make a function that can easily generate subplots with a single line.

How It Works

You will write a function that uses parameter pairs to flexibly create subplot figures in a single function call. The y input can have multiple rows, and the x input can have one row or the same number of rows as y. You supply default labels so that the function can be called with just two inputs.

The only parameters supported in this version are various labels and the plot type—standard `plot`, `semilogx`, `semilogy`, and `loglog`—but you can easily add functionality for line thickness, plot markers, shading, and so forth. You use a `for` loop to check every other component of `varargin` in a switch statement. Remember that `varargin` provides a cell array of arguments.

Note the use of a built-in demo showing both main branches of the function, for one x series and for two.

The plotting code creates subplots in the figure for each plot based on the number of rows in x and y. This function assumes the subplots are in a single column, but you could extend the logic to create multiple columns or any arrangement of subplots that suits your application. The grid is turned on.

```
function PlotSet( x, y, varargin )

% Demo
%-----
if( nargin < 1 )
  x = linspace(1,1000);
  y = [sin(0.01*x);cos(0.01*x)];
  disp('PlotSet:_One_x_and_two_y_rows')
  PlotSet( x, y )
  disp('PlotSet:_Two_x_and_two_y_rows')
  PlotSet( [x;y(1,:)], y )

  return;
end

% Defaults
nCol      = 1;
n         = size(x,1);
m         = size(y,1);

yLabel    = cell(1,m);
xLabel    = cell(1,n);
plotTitle = cell(1,n);
for k = 1:m
  yLabel{k} = 'y';
end
for k = 1:n
  xLabel{k}    = 'x';
  plotTitle{k} = 'y_vs._x';
end
figTitle = 'PlotSet';
plotType = 'plot';

% Handle input parameters
for k = 1:2:length(varargin)
  switch lower(varargin{k} )
    case 'x_label'
      for j = 1:n
        xLabel{j}      = varargin{k+1};
      end
```

155

```
    case 'y_label'
      temp        = varargin{k+1};
      if( ischar(temp) )
        yLabel{1} = temp;
      else
        yLabel    = temp;
      end
    case 'plot_title'
      plotTitle{1}  = varargin{k+1};
    case 'figure_title'
      figTitle      = varargin{k+1};
    case 'plot_type'
      plotType      = varargin{k+1};
    otherwise
      fprintf(1,'%s is not an allowable parameter\n',varargin{k});
    end
  end

h = figure;
set(h,'Name',figTitle);

% First path is for just one row in x
if( n == 1 )
  for k = 1:m
    subplot(m,nCol,k);
    plotXY(x,y(k,:),plotType);
    xlabel(xLabel{1});
    ylabel(yLabel{k});
    if( k == 1 )
      title(plotTitle{1})
    end
    grid on
  end
else
  for k = 1:n
    subplot(n,nCol,k);
    plotXY(x(k,:),y(k,:),plotType);
    xlabel(xLabel{k});
    ylabel(yLabel{k});
    title(plotTitle{k})
    grid on
  end
end

%% Implement different plot types
function plotXY(x,y,type)

switch type
  case 'plot'
    plot(x,y);
  case {'log' 'loglog' 'log_log'}
    loglog(x,y);
```

```
case {'xlog' 'semilogx' 'x_log'}
    semilogx(x,y);
case {'ylog' 'semilogy' 'y_log'}
    semilogy(x,y);
otherwise
    error('%s_is_not_an_available_plot_type',type);
end
```

This function allows DoubleIntegratorSim.m to generate its plots with one line of code.

Summary

The double integrator is a very useful model for developing control systems, as it represents an ideal version of many systems, such as a spring attached to a mass. In this chapter, you developed the mathematical model for the double integrator and wrote the dynamics in a right-hand-side function. You were introduced to numerical integration and wrote the Runge-Kutta integrator, which will be used throughout the remaining applications in this book. The recipe for the control function combines design and implementation, contains a built-in demo, and defines a data structure that is used for memory between calls. The first demo script showed how to initialize a controller for a double integrator, simulate it, and plot the results. Table 6-2 lists the code developed in the chapter. This is the basis for almost any mathematical or control analysis that you will do in MATLAB!

Table 6-2. *Chapter Code Listing*

File	Description
RHSDoubleIntegrator	Dynamical model for the double integrator.
RungeKutta	Fourth-order Runge-Kutta integrator.
PDControl	Proportional-derivative controller.
DoubleIntegratorSim	Simulation of the double integrator with discrete control.
PlotSet	Create two-dimensional plots from a data set.
TimeLabel	Produce time labels and scaled time vectors.

CHAPTER 7

Robotics

The SCARA robot (Selective Compliance Articulated Robot Arm) is a simple industrial robot used for placing components in a two-dimensional space. You will learn the equations of motion for a SCARA robot arm that has two rotational joints and one prismatic joint. Each joint has a single degree of freedom. A SCARA robot is broadly applicable to work where a part needs to be inserted in a two-dimensional space or where drilling needs to be done.

The input to the robot system will be a new location for the arm end effector. You have to solve two control problems. One is to determine which angles you need to place the arm at a particular *xy* coordinate. This is the inverse kinematics problem. The second is to control the two joints so that you get a smooth response to commands to move the arm. You will also develop a custom visualization function that can be used to create animations of the robot motion.

For more information on the dynamics used in this chapter, see example 9.8.2 (p. 405) in Lung-Wen Tsai's book *Robot Analysis: The Mechanics of Serial and Parallel Manipulators* (John Wiley & Sons, 1999).

7-1. Creating a Dynamic Model of the SCARA Robot

Problem

The robot has two rotational joints and one linear "joint." You need to write the dynamics that link the forces and torques applied to the arm to its motion so that you can simulate the arm.

Solution

The equations of motion are written as second order differential equations. The right hand side involves solving a set of linear equations.

How It Works

The SCARA robot is shown in Figure 7-1. It has two arms that move in the *xy*-plane and a plunger that moves in the *z* direction. The angles θ_1 and θ_2 are measured around the z_0 and z_1 axes.

Electronic supplementary material The online version of this chapter (doi:10.1007/978-1-4842-0559-4_7) contains supplementary material, which is available to authorized users.

© Stephanie Thomas and Michael Paluszek 2015
S. Thomas and M. Paluszek, *MATLAB Recipes*, DOI 10.1007/978-1-4842-0559-4_7

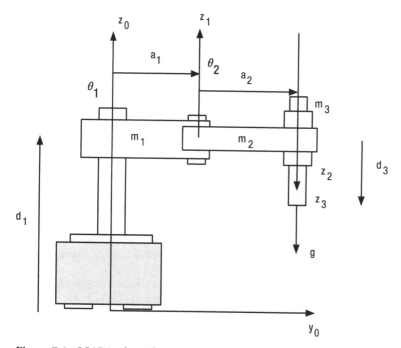

Figure 7-1. *SCARA robot. The two arms move in a plane. The plunger moves perpendicular to the plane*

The equations of motion for the SCARA robot are

$$
I\begin{bmatrix} \ddot{\theta}_1 \\ \ddot{\theta}_2 \\ \ddot{d}_3 \end{bmatrix} + \begin{bmatrix} -(m_2 + 2m_3)a_1 a_2 \sin\theta_2 \left(\dot{\theta}_1 \dot{\theta}_2 + \frac{1}{2}\dot{\theta}_2^2\right) \\ \left(\frac{1}{2}m_2 + m_3\right)a_1 a_2 \sin\theta_2 \dot{\theta}_1^2 \\ -m_3 g \end{bmatrix} = \begin{bmatrix} T_1 \\ T_2 \\ F_3 \end{bmatrix}
\tag{7.1}
$$

The first term is the product of the generalized inertia matrix and the acceleration vector. The second array contains the rotational coupling terms. The final array is the control vector. The generalized inertia matrix, I, is

$$
\begin{bmatrix} I_{11} & I_{21} & 0 \\ I_{21} & I_{22} & 0 \\ 0 & 0 & I_{33} \end{bmatrix}
\tag{7.2}
$$

where

$$
I_{11} = \left(\frac{1}{3}m_1 + m_2 + m_3\right)a_1^2 + (m_2 + 2m_3)a_1 a_2 \cos\theta_2 + \left(\frac{1}{3}m_2 + m_3\right)a_2^2
\tag{7.3}
$$

$$I_{21} = \left(\frac{1}{2}m_2 + m_3\right)a_1 a_2 \cos\theta_2 + \left(\frac{1}{3}m_2 + m_3\right)a_2^2 \tag{7.4}$$

$$I_{22} = \left(\frac{1}{3}m_2 + m_3\right)a_2^2 \tag{7.5}$$

$$I_{33} = m_3 \tag{7.6}$$

Note that in developing this inertia matrix, the author is treating the links as point masses and not solid bodies.

The matrix is symmetric, as it should be. There is coupling between the two rotational degrees of freedom but no coupling between the plunger and the rotational hinges.

First, define a data structure for the robot, defining the length and mass of the links, and with fields for the forces and torques that can be applied. The function can supply a default structure to be filled in, or the fields can be specified a priori.

```
%   d = SCARADataStructure
%   d = SCARADataStructure( a1, a2, d1, m1, m2, m3 )
%
%% Description
% Create a SCARA robot data structure. Type d = SCARADataStructure for
% default arguments. The forces and torques are set to zero.
%
%% Inputs
%    a1 (1,1) Link 1 length
%    a2 (1,1) Link 2 length
%    d1 (1,1) Distance of link 1 from ground
%    m1 (1,1) Link 1 mass
%    m2 (1,1) Link 2 mass
%    m3 (1,1) Link 3 mass
%    t1 (1,1) Joint 1 torque
%    t2 (1,1) Joint 2 torque
%    f3 (1,1) Joint 3 force
%
%% Outputs
%    d (.) Data structure

function d = SCARADataStructure( a1, a2, d1, m1, m2, m3 )

if( nargin < 1 )
   d = struct('a1',0.1,'a2',0.1,'d1',0.05,'m1',1,'m2',1,'m3',1,'t1',0,'t2',0,'f3',0);
else
   d = struct('a1',a1,'a2',a2,'d1',d1,'m1',m1,'m2',m2,'m3',m3,'t1',0,'t2',0,'f3',0);
end
```

Then write the right-hand-side (RHS) function from the equations. You need to solve for the state derivatives $\ddot{\theta}_1, \ddot{\theta}_2, \ddot{d}_3$, which you do with a left matrix divide. This is easily done in MATLAB with a backslash, which uses a QR, triangular, LDL, Cholesky, Hessenberg, or LU solver, as appropriate for the inputs. The function does not have a built-in demo, as this impacts performance in RHS functions, which are called repeatedly by integrators. Note the definition of the constant for gravity at the top of the file. The inertia matrix is returned as an additional output.

161

```
%% RHSSCARA Right hand side of the SCARA robot arm equations.
%
%% Form
%  [xDot, i] = RHSSCARA( t, x, d )
%
%% Description
% Generates an acceleration vector given the current state, time, and data
% structure describing the SCARA robot's configuration.
%  function [xDot, i] = RHSSCARA( t, x, d )
%
%% Description
% Generates an acceleration vector.
%
%% Inputs
%  t          (1,1)   Time (s)
%  x          (6,:)   State vector [theta1;theta2;d3;omega1;omega2;v3]
%  d          (.)     SCARA data structure
%
%% Outputs
%  xDot       (6,:)   State derivative
%  i          (3,3)   Generalized inertia matrix
%
%% See also
% SCARADataStructure

function [xDot, i] = RHSSCARA( ~, x, d )
g    = 9.806;   % The acceleration of gravity (m/s^2)

c2   = cos(x(2));
s2   = sin(x(2));

theta1Dot = x(4);
theta2Dot = x(5);

% Inertia matrix
i        = zeros(3,3);
a1Sq     = d.a1^2;
a2Sq     = d.a2^2;
a12      = d.a1*d.a2;
m23      = 0.5*d.m2 + d.m3;
i(1,1)   = (d.m1/3 + d.m2 + d.m3)*a1Sq + 0.5*m23*a12*c2 + (d.m2/3 + d.m3)*a2Sq;
i(2,2)   = (d.m2/3 + d.m3)*a2Sq;
i(3,3)   = d.m3;
i(1,2)   = m23*a12*c2 + (d.m2/3 + d.m3);
i(2,1)   = i(1,2);

% Right hand side
u = [d.t1;d.t2;d.f3];
f = [-(d.m2 + 2*d.m3)*a12*s2*(theta1Dot*theta2Dot + 0.5*theta2Dot^2);...
      0.5*m23*a12*s2*theta1Dot^2;...
      -d.m3*g];

xDot = [x(4:6);i\(f - u)];
```

7-2. Customize a Visualization Function for the Robot

Problem

You would like to be able to visualize the motion of the robot arm in three dimensions.

Solution

You will write a function to draw a 3D SCARA robot arm. This will allow you to easily visualize what is happening with the robot arm.

How It Works

This function demonstrates the use of the low-level plotting functions patch and light. You create box and cylinder shapes for the components of the robot arm. This function also demonstrates how to produce MATLAB movies of the robot motion using getframe. The resulting visualization is shown in Figure 7-2.

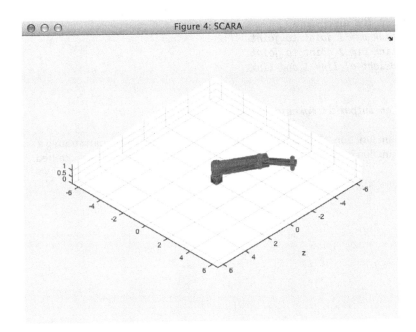

Figure 7-2. *SCARA robot visualization using patch*

This function's first argument is an action. You define an initialization action to generate all the patch objects, which are stored in a persistent variable. Then, during the update action, you only need to update the patch vertices. The function has one output, which is movie frames from the animation. Note that the input *x* is vectorized, meaning you can pass a set of states to the function and not just one at a time. The following is the header of the function.

```
%% DRAWSCARA Draw a SCARA robot arm.
%
%% Forms
%       DrawSCARA( 'initialize', d )
%  m = DrawSCARA( 'update', x )
%
%% Description
% Draws a SCARA robot using patch objects. A persistent variable is used to
% store the graphics handles in between update calls.
%
% The SCARA acronym stands for Selective Compliance Assembly Robot Arm
% or Selective Compliance Articulated Robot Arm.
%
% Type DrawSCARA for a demo.
%
%% Inputs
%  action  (1,:) Action string
%  x       (3,:) [theta1;theta2;d3]
%    or
%  d       (1,1) Data structure for dimensions
%                   .a1 (1,1) Link arm 1 joint to joint
%                   .a2 (1,1) Link arm 2 joint to joint
%                   .d1 (1,1) Height of link 1 and link2
%
%% Outputs
%  m       (1,:) If there is an output it makes a movie using getframe
```

Next, show the body of the main function. Note that the function has a built-in demo demonstrating a vector input with 100 states. The function initializes itself with default data if the data structure d is omitted.

```
function m = DrawSCARA( action, x )

persistent p

% Demo
%-----
if( nargin < 1 )
  DrawSCARA( 'initialize' );
  t          = linspace(0,100);
  omega1   = 0.1;
  omega2   = 0.2;
  omega3   = 0.3;
  x          = [sin(omega1*t);sin(omega2*t);0.01*sin(omega3*t)];
  m          = DrawSCARA( 'update', x );
  if( nargout < 1 )
    clear m;
  end
  return
end
switch( lower(action) )
  case 'initialize'
```

```
    if( nargin < 2 )
      d = SCARADataStructure;
    else
      d = x;
    end

    p = Initialize( d );

  case 'update'
    if( nargout == 1 )
      m = Update( p, x );
    else
      Update( p, x );
    end
end
```

Note that subfunctions were used for the Initialize and Update actions. This keeps the switch statement clean and easy to read. In the Initialize function, you define additional parameters for creating the box and cylinder objects you use to visualize the entire robot arm. Then you use patch to create the graphics objects, using parameter pairs instead of the (x,y,z) input. Specifying the unique vertices this way can reduce the size of the data needed to define the patch, and it is simple conceptually. See the "Introduction to Patch Objects" and the "Specifying Patch Object Shapes" sections of MATLAB help for more information. The handles are stored in the persistent variable p.

```
%---------------------------------------------------------------------------
%   Initialize the picture. The robot is defined using these parameters:
%        .b  (1,3) Box dimensions [x y z] See Box
%        .l1 (1,5) Link arm 1 dimensions [x y z t d] See UChannel
%        .l2 (1,3) Link arm 2 dimensions [x y z] See Box
%        .c1 (1,2) Cylinder 1 [r l]
%        .c2 (1,2) Cylinder 2 [r l]
%        .c3 (1,2) Cylinder 3 [r l]
%        .c4 (1,2) Cylinder 4 [r l]
%---------------------------------------------------------------------------
function p = Initialize( d )

p.fig = figure( 'name','SCARA' );

% Create parts
c = [0.5 0.5 0.5]; % Color
r = [1.0 0.0 0.0];

% Store for use in updating
p.a1 = d.a1;
p.a2 = d.a2;

% Physical parameters for drawing
d.b  = [1 1 1]*d.d1/2;
d.l1 = [0.12 0.02 0.02 0.005 0.03]*10*d.a1;
d.l2 = [0.12 0.02 0.01]*10*d.a2;
d.c1 = [0.1 0.4]*d.a1;
```

```
d.c2 = [0.06 0.3]*d.a1;
d.c3 = [0.06 0.5]*d.a2;
d.c4 = [0.05 0.6]*d.a2;

% Base
[vB, fB] = Box( d.b(1), d.b(2), d.b(3) );
[vC, fC] = Cylinder( d.c1(1), d.c1(2) );
F        = [fB;fC+size(vB,1)];
vB(:,3)  = vB(:,3) + d.b(3)/2;
vC(:,3)  = vC(:,3) + d.b(3);
v        = [vB;vC];
p.base   = patch('vertices', v, 'faces', f,...
                 'facecolor', c, 'edgecolor', c,...
                 'facelighting', 'phong' );

% Link 1

% Arm
[vA, fA]   = UChannel( d.l1(1), d.l1(2), d.l1(3), d.l1(4), d.l1(5) );
vA(:,3)    = vA(:,3) + d.d1;
vA(:,1)    = vA(:,1) - d.b(1)/2;

% Pin
[vC, fC]   = Cylinder( d.c2(1), d.c2(2) );
vC(:,3)    = vC(:,3) + d.d1 - d.c2(2)/2;
vC(:,1)    = vC(:,1) + d.a1 - d.c2(1);
p.v1       = [vC;vA];
f          = [fC;fA+size(vC,1)];
p.link1    = patch('vertices', p.v1, 'faces', f,...
                   'facecolor', r, 'edgecolor', r,...
                   'facelighting', 'phong' );
% Find the limit for the axes
zLim       = max(vC(:,3));

% Link 2
[vB, fB]   = Box(d.l2(1), d.l2(2), d.l2(3) );
[vC, fC]   = Cylinder( d.c3(1), d.c3(2) );
vC(:,1)    = vC(:,1) + d.l2(1)/2 - 2*d.c3(1);
vC(:,3)    = vC(:,3) - d.c3(2)/2;
p.v2       = [vC;vB];
p.v2(:,1)  = p.v2(:,1) + d.l2(1)/2 - 2*d.c3(1);
p.v2(:,3)  = p.v2(:,3) + d.d1;
f          = [fC;fB+size(vC,1)];
v2         = p.v2;
v2(:,1)    = v2(:,1) + d.a1;
p.link2    = patch('vertices', v2, 'faces', f,...
                   'facecolor', r, 'edgecolor', r,...
                   'facelighting', 'phong' );
```

```
% Link 3
[vC, fC]      = Cylinder( d.c4(1), d.c4(2) );
p.v3          = vC;
p.r3          = d.l2(1) - 4*d.c3(1);
p.v3(:,3)     = p.v3(:,3) + d.d1/4;
vC(:,1)       = vC(:,1) + p.r3 + d.a1;
f             = fC;
p.link3       = patch('vertices', vC, 'faces', f,...
                       'facecolor', c, 'edgecolor', c,...
                       'facelighting', 'phong' );

xLim          = 1.3*(d.a1+d.a2);
xlabel('x');
ylabel('y');
zlabel('z');
grid on
rotate3d on
axis([-xLim xLim - xLim xLim 0 zLim])
set(gca,'DataAspectRatio',[1 1 1],'DataAspectRatioMode','manual')
s = 10*max(Mag(v'));
light('position',s*[1 1 1])
view([1 1 1])
```

The Update function updates the vertices for each patch object. The nominal vertices are stored in the persistent variable p and are rotated using a transformation matrix calculated from the sine and cosine of the link angles. If there is an output argument, the function uses getframe to grab the figure as a movie frame.

```
%--------------------------------------------------------------------------
% Update the picture and get the frame if requested
%--------------------------------------------------------------------------
function m = Update( p, x )

for k = 1:size(x,2)

  % Link 1
  c        = cos(x(1,k));
  s        = sin(x(1,k));
  b1       = [c - s 0;s c 0;0 0 1];
  v        = (b1*p.v1')';
  set(p.link1,'vertices',v);

  % Link 2
  r2       = b1*[p.a1;0;0];
  c        = cos(x(2,k));
  s        = sin(x(2,k));
  b2       = [c - s 0;s c 0;0 0 1];
  v        = (b2*b1*p.v2')';
  v(:,1)   = v(:,1) + r2(1);
  v(:,2)   = v(:,2) + r2(2);
  set(p.link2,'vertices',v);
```

```
% Link 3
r3      = b2*b1*[p.r3;0;0] + r2;
v       = p.v3;
v(:,1)  = v(:,1) + r3(1);
v(:,2)  = v(:,2) + r3(2);
v(:,3)  = v(:,3) + x(3,k);
set(p.link3,'vertices',v);

if( nargout > 0 )
  m(k) = getframe(p.fig);
else
  drawnow;
end

end
```

The subfunctions Box, Cylinder, and UChannel create the vertices and faces for each type of 3D object. Faces are defined using indices of the vertices; in this case, triangles. The Box function is shown here to demonstrate how the vertices and faces matrices are created.

```
%-----------------------------------------------------------------------
%   Inputs
%   ------
%   Box
%   x              (1,1)  x length
%   y              (1,1)  y length
%   z              (1,1)  z length
%
%   Outputs
%   -------
%   v              (:,3) Vertices
%   f              (:,3) Faces
%-----------------------------------------------------------------------
function [v, f] = Box( x, y, z )

f  = [2 3 6;3 7 6;3 4 8;3 8 7;4 5 8;4 1 5;2 6 5;2 5 1;1 3 2;1 4 3;5 6 7;5 7 8];
x  = x/2;
y  = y/2;
z  = z/2;

v = [-x  x  x -x -x  x  x -x;...
     -y -y  y  y -y -y  y  y;...
     -z -z -z -z  z  z  z  z]';
```

7-3. Using Numerical Search for Robot Inverse Kinematics

Problem

The goal of the robot controller is to place the end effector at a desired position. You need to know the link states corresponding to this position.

Solution

You will use a numerical solver to compute the robot states. The MATLAB solver is `fminsearch`, which implements a Nelder – Mead minimizer.

How It Works

The goal of our control system is to position the end effector and a desired position $[x,y,z]$. z is determined by d_1–d_3 from Figure 7-1 in Recipe 7-1. x and y are found from the two angles, a_1 and a_2. The position vector for the arm end effector is

$$\begin{bmatrix} x \\ y \\ z \end{bmatrix} = \begin{bmatrix} a_1 \sin\theta_1 + a_2 \sin(\theta_1 + \theta_2) \\ a_1 \cos\theta_1 + a_2 \cos(\theta_1 + \theta_2) \\ d_1 - d_3 \end{bmatrix} \tag{7.7}$$

While these equations don't seem complicated, they can't be used to solve for x and y directly. First of all, if a_2 is less than a_1 there will be a region around the origin that cannot be reached. In addition, there may be more than one solution for each x, y pair.

You use this equation for the position to create a cost function that can be passed to `fminsearch`. This computes the state, which results in the desired position. The resulting function demonstrates a nested cost function, a built-in demo, and a default plot output. Note that you use a data structure as returned by `optimset` to pass parameters to `fminsearch`.

```
%% SCARAIK Generate SCARA states for desired end effector position and angle.
%
%% Form:
%   x = SCARAIK( r, d )
%
%% Description
% Uses fminsearch to find the link states given the effector location. The
% cost function is embedded. Type SCARAIK for a demo which creates a plot
% and a video.
%
%% Inputs
%   r               (3,:) End effector position [x;y;z]
%   d               (.)   Robot data structure
%                         .a1 (1,1) Link 1 length
%                         .a2 (1,1) Link 2 length
%                         .d1 (1,1) Distance of link 1 from ground
%
%% Outputs
%   x               (3,:) SCARA states [theta1;theta2;d3]

function x = SCARAIK( r, d )

% Demo
%-----
if( nargin < 1 )
    r = [linspace(0,0.2);zeros(2,100)];
    d = SCARADataStructure;
```

```
    SCARAIK( r, d );
    return;
end

n = size(r,2);
xY = zeros(2,n);

TolX        = 1e - 5;
TolFun      = 1e - 9;
MaxFunEvals = 1500;
Options = optimset('TolX',TolX,'TolFun',TolFun,'MaxFunEvals',MaxFunEvals);

x0 = [0;0];
for k = 1:n
  d.xT     = r(1:2,k);
  xY(:,k) = fminsearch(@Cost, x0, Options, d );
  x0       = xY(:,k);
end

x = [xY;d.d1 - r(3,:)];

% Default output is to create a plot
%----------------------------------
if( nargout == 0 )
  DrawSCARA( 'initialize', d );
  m = DrawSCARA( 'update', x );
  vidObj = VideoWriter('SCARAIK.avi');
  open(vidObj);
  writeVideo(vidObj,m);
end

%--------------------------------------------------------------------------
%   Cost function
%   The cost is the difference between the position as computed from the
%   states and the target position xT.
%--------------------------------------------------------------------------
function y = Cost( x, d )

xE = d.a1*cos(x(1)) + d.a2*cos(x(1)+x(2));
yE = d.a1*sin(x(1)) + d.a2*sin(x(1)+x(2));
y  = sqrt((xE-d.xT(1))^2+(yE-d.xT(2))^2);
```

The function creates a video using a VideoWriter object and the frame data returned by DrawSCARA. Before VideoWriter was introduced, this could be done with movie2avi.

7-4. Developing a Control System for the Robot

Problem

Robot arm control is a critical technology in robotics. You need to be able to smoothly and reliably change the location of the end effector. The speed of the control determines the number of operations that you can do in a given amount of time, thus determining the productivity of the robot.

Solution

This problem is solved using the inverse kinematics function discussed earlier, and then feed the desired angles into two PD controllers, as developed in Chapter 6.

How It Works

Apply the PD controller described in Chapter 6 using the c array as the desired angle and position vector. You compute control accelerations, not torques, and then multiply by the inertia matrix to get control torques,

$$T = Ia \qquad (7.8)$$

where T is the control torque, I is the inertia matrix, and a is the computed control acceleration. You need to do this because there are cross-coupling terms in the inertia matrix, and I_{11} changes as the position of the outer arm changes. You neglect the nonlinear terms in the equations of motion. These terms are functions of the angles and the angular rates. If you move slowly, this should not pose a problem. If you move quickly, you could feedforward the nonlinear torques and cancel them.

The first step is to specify a desired position for the end effector and use the inverse kinematics function to compute the target states corresponding to this location.

```
% Pick the location to place the end effector, [x;y;z]
r = [4;2;0];

% Find the two angles for the joints
setPoint = SCARAIK( r, d );
```

Next is the code that designs the controllers, one for each joint, using PDControl. Note that identical parameters are used for both controllers. Set the damping ratio, zeta, to 1.0 to avoid overshoot. Recall that wN, the undamped natural frequency, is the bandwidth of the controller; the higher this frequency, the faster the response. wD, the derivative term filter cutoff, is set to 5–10 times wN, so that filter doesn't cause lag below wN. The dT variable is the timestep of the simulation.

```
%% Control Design
% We will use two PD controllers, one for each rotational joint.

% Controller parameters
dC1          = PDControl( 'struct' );
dC1.zeta    = 1.0;
dC1.wN      = 0.6;
dC1.wD      = 60.0;
dC1.tSamp   = dT;
dC2          = dC1;
```

```
% Create the two controllers
dC1        = PDControl( 'initialize', dC1 );
dC2        = PDControl( 'initialize', dC2 );
```

This is the portion that computes and applies the control. You eliminate the inertia coupling by computing joint accelerations and multiplying by the inertia matrix, which is computed each time step, to get the desired control torques. Note that you use the feature of the RHS that computes the inertia matrix from the current state.

```
[acc(1,1), dC1] = PDControl('update',thetaError(1),dC1);
[acc(2,1), dC2] = PDControl('update',thetaError(2),dC2);
torque          = inertia(1:2,1:2)*acc;
```

You can run these lines at the command line to see what the acceleration and torque magnitude looks like for an example robot. Note that, assuming MKS units, you have links of 1 meter in length and masses of 1 kg.

```
>> dC1          = PDControl( 'struct' );
>> dC1.zeta     = 1.0;
>> dC1.wN       = 0.6;
>> dC1.wD       = 60.0;
>> dC1.tSamp    = 0.025;
>> dC2          = dC1;
>> dC1          = PDControl( 'initialize', dC1 );
>> dC2          = PDControl( 'initialize', dC2 );
>> d = SCARADataStructure(1,1,1,1,1,1);
>> x = zeros(6,1);
>> [~,inertia] = RHSSCARA( 0, x, d );
>> inertia
inertia =

    4.4167      2.8333         0
    2.8333      1.3333         0
         0           0         1

>> thetaError = [0.1;0.1];
>> [acc(1,1), dC1] = PDControl('update',thetaError(1),dC1);
>> [acc(2,1), dC2] = PDControl('update',thetaError(2),dC2);
>> acc
acc =

    -7.236
    -7.236

>> torque = inertia(1:2,1:2)*acc
torque =

    -52.461
    -30.15
```

7-5. Simulating the Controlled Robot

Problem

You want to test the robot arm under control. The input will be the desired *xy* coordinates of the end effector.

Solution

The solution is to build a MATLAB script in which you design the PD controller matrices as you did earlier, and then simulate the controller in a loop, applying the calculated torques until the states match the desired angles. You will not control the vertical position of the end effector in this recipe.

How It Works

This is a discrete simulation, with a fixed-time step and the control torque calculated separately from the dynamics. The simulation runs in a loop, calling first the controller code from Recipe 7-4 and the right-hand side from the fourth-order Runge-Kutta function. When the simulation ends, the angles and angle errors are plotted and a 3D animation is displayed. You could plot more variables, but all the essential information is in the angles and errors.

With a very small time step of 0.025 seconds, you could have increased the bandwidth of the controller to speed the response. Remember that the cutoff frequency of the filter must also be below the Nyquist frequency. Any signals above the Nyquist Frequency will be observed at an alias of their true frequency, not their true frequency.

Notice that you do not handle large angle errors; that is, errors greater than 2π. In addition, if the desired angle is $2\pi - \varepsilon$ and the current position is $2\pi + \varepsilon$, it will not necessarily go the shortest way. This can be handled by adding code that computes the smallest error between two points on the unit circle. The reader can add code for this to make the controller more robust.

The script SCARARobotSim.m follows, skipping the control design lines from Recipe 7-4. First, you initialize the simulation data, including the time parameters and the robot geometry. You initialize the plotting arrays using zeros before entering the simulation loop. There is a control flag that allows the simulation to be run open loop or closed loop. The integration occurs in the last line of the loop.

```
%% Initialize
% Specify the time, robot geometry and the control target.

% Simulation time settings
tEnd        = 20.0;     % sec
dT          = 0.025;
nSim        = tEnd/dT+1;
controlIsOn = true;

% Robot parameters
d = SCARADataStructure(3,2,1,4,6,1);

% Set the initial arm states
x0      = zeros(6,1);
%x0(5) = 0.05;

% Pick the location to place the end effector, [x;y;z]
r = [4;2;0];
```

```
% Find the two angles for the joints
setPoint = SCARAIK( r, d );

%% Simulation
% The simulation can be run with or without control, i.e. closed or open
% loop.
x        = x0;
xPlot   = zeros(4,nSim);
tqPlot  = zeros(2,nSim);
inrPlot = zeros(2,nSim);

for k = 1:nSim
  % Control error
  thetaError  = setPoint(1:2) - x(1:2);
  [~,inertia] = RHSSCARA( 0, x, d );
  acc         = zeros(2,1);

  % Apply the control
  if( controlIsOn )
    [acc(1,1), dC1] = PDControl('update',thetaError(1),dC1);
    [acc(2,1), dC2] = PDControl('update',thetaError(2),dC2);
    torque          = inertia(1:2,1:2)*acc;
  else
    torque = zeros(2,1);
  end
  d.t1 = torque(1);
  d.t2 = torque(2);

  % Plotting array
  xPlot(:,k)   = [x(1:2);thetaError];
  tqPlot(:,k)  = torque;
  inrPlot(:,k) = [inertia(1,1);inertia(2,2)];

  % Enter the motor torques into the dynamics model
  x = RungeKutta( @RHSSCARA, 0, x, dT, d );
end

%% Plot the results
% Plot a time history and perform an animation.
% Plot labels
yL = {'\theta_1_(rad)' '\theta_2_(rad)' 'Error_\theta_1_(rad)' 'Error_\theta_2_(rad)'};

% Time histories
[t,tL] = TimeLabel(dT*(0:(nSim-1)));
PlotSet( t, xPlot, 'y_label', yL, 'x_label', tL );
PlotSet( t, tqPlot, 'y_label', {'T_x','T_y'}, 'x_label', tL );
PlotSet( t, inrPlot, 'y_label', {'I_{11}','I_{22}'}, 'x_label', tL );

% Animation
DrawSCARA( 'initialize', d );
```

Figure 7-3 shows the transient response of the two joints. Both converge to their set points, but look different than the double integrator response that you saw in the previous chapter. This system is nonlinear due to the coupling between the links. For instance, in a double integrator, you would expect no overshoot of the target angle for a damping ratio of 1.0. However, you do see some in the second subplot, of θ_2, and otherwise the shape is similar to a double integrator response. You see that θ_1, in contrast, reverses direction as it reacts to the motion of the outer joint; after about 2 seconds, when the θ_2 has peaked, θ_1 also resembles a double integrator. Keep in mind that the two controllers are independent and are working at cross-purposes in some ways.

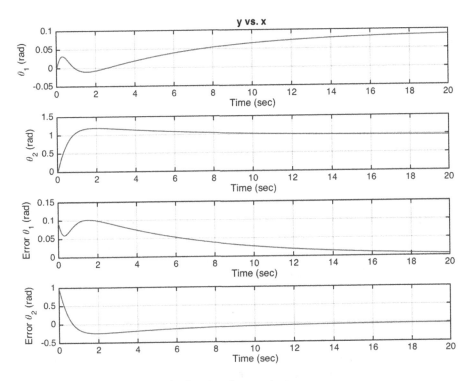

Figure 7-3. *SCARA robot angles showing the transient response*

Figure 7-4 shows the resulting inertia components. I_{11} was expected to change and I_{22} to remain constant, which is, in fact, the case.

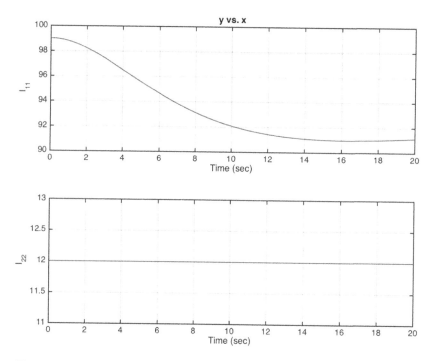

Figure 7-4. *SCARA robot inertia as the arm moves*

After the simulation is done, the script runs an animation of the arm motion. Both 2D plots and the 3D animation are needed to debug the controller and for production runs.

The same script could be extended to show a sequence of commands to the arm.

Summary

This chapter demonstrated how to write the dynamics and implement a simple control law for a two-link manipulator, the SCARA robot. You implemented coupled nonlinear equations in the right-hand side with the simple controller developed in the previous chapter. The format of the simulation was very similar to the double integrator. There are more sophisticated ways to perform this control, which would take into account the coupling between the links and which could be added to this framework. You did not implement any constraints on the motion or the control torque.

The chapter also demonstrated how to generate 3D graphics using the MATLAB graphics engine and how to make a movie. A movie is a good way to transmit your results to people and to debug your program. Table 7-1 lists the code developed in this chapter.

Table 7-1. *Chapter Code Listing*

File	Description
DrawSCARA	Draw a SCARA robot arm.
RHSSCARA	Right-hand side of the SCARA robot arm equations.
SCARADataStructure	Initialize the data structure for all SCARA functions.
SCARAIK	Generate SCARA states for the desired end effector position and angle.
SCARARobotSim	SCARA robot demo.

CHAPTER 8

■ ■ ■

Electric Motors

You will model a three-phase permanent magnet motor driven by a direct current (DC) power source. There are three coils on the stator and permanent magnets on the rotor. This type of motor is driven by a DC power source with six semiconductor switches that are connected to the three coils, known as the A, B and C coils. Two or more coils can be used to drive a brushless DC motor, but three coils are particularly easy to implement. This type of motor is used in most industrial applications today, including electric cars and robotics. It is sometimes called a *brushless DC motor* (BLDC) or a *Permanent Magnet Synchronous Motor* (PMSM).

Pulsewidth modulation is used for the switching because it is efficient; the switches are off when not needed. Coding the model for the motor and the pulsewidth modulation is relatively straightforward. In the simulation, we demonstrate using two timesteps: one for the simulation to handle the pulsewidths and one for the outer control loop. The simulation script will have multiple control flags to allow for debugging this complex system.

8-1. Modeling a Three-Phase Brushless Permanent Magnet Motor

Problem

You want to model a three-phase permanent magnet synchronous motor in a form that is suitable for control system design. A conceptual drawing is shown in Figure 8-1. The motor has three stator windings and one permanent magnet on the rotor. The magnet has two poles or one pole pair. The coordinate axes are the a, b, and c on the stator; one axis out the center of each coil following the right-hand rule, and the (d,q) coordinates fixed to the magnet in the rotating frame. In motor applications, the axes represent currents or voltages, not positions like in mechanical engineering.

Electronic supplementary material The online version of this chapter (doi:10.1007/978-1-4842-0559-4_8) contains supplementary material, which is available to authorized users.

S. Thomas and M. Paluszek, *MATLAB Recipes*, DOI 10.1007/978-1-4842-0559-4_8

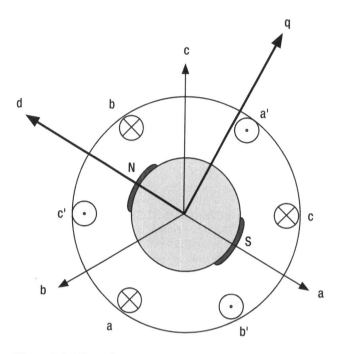

Figure 8-1. *Motor diagram showing the three phase coils a, b, and c on the stator and the two pole magnet (N,S) on the rotor. The × means the current is going into the paper, the dot means it is coming out of the paper*

Solution

The solution is to model a motor with three stator coils and permanent magnets on the rotor. You have to model the coil currents and the physical state of the rotor.

How It Works

Permanent-magnet synchronous motors use two or more windings in the stator and permanent magnets in the rotor. The rotor can have any even number of magnet poles. The phasing of the currents in the stator coils must be synchronized with the position of the rotor. Define the inductance matrix L[1]:

$$L = \frac{1}{d}\begin{bmatrix} 2L_{ss} - L_m & L_m & L_m \\ L_m & 2L_{ss} - L_m & L_m \\ L_m & L_m & 2L_{ss} - L_m \end{bmatrix} \tag{8.1}$$

---

[1]Lyshevski, S. E. *Electromechanical Systems, Electric Machines, and Applied Mechatronics*, CRC Press, 2000, pp. 589–627.

where

$$d = 2L_{ss}^2 - L_{ss}L_m - L_m^2 \qquad (8.2)$$

L_m is the mutual inductance of the phase windings and L_{ss} is the self-inductance. The phase current array, i, is

$$i = \begin{bmatrix} i_a \\ i_b \\ i_c \end{bmatrix} \qquad (8.3)$$

where i_a is the phase A stator winding current; i_b is the phase B current; and so forth. The phase voltages, u, are

$$u = \begin{bmatrix} u_a \\ u_b \\ u_c \end{bmatrix} \qquad (8.4)$$

where u_a is the phase A stator winding voltage. The dynamical equations are

$$\begin{bmatrix} \dot{i} \\ \dot{\omega}_e \\ \dot{\theta}_e \end{bmatrix} = \begin{bmatrix} -r_s L & 0 & 0 \\ 0 & -\dfrac{b}{J} & 0 \\ 0 & 1 & 0 \end{bmatrix} \begin{bmatrix} i \\ \omega_e \\ \theta_e \end{bmatrix} + \psi \begin{bmatrix} -L\omega_e \\ \dfrac{p^2 i^T}{4J} \\ 000 \end{bmatrix} \begin{bmatrix} \cos\theta_e \\ \cos\left(\theta_e + \dfrac{2\pi}{3}\right) \\ \cos\left(\theta_e - \dfrac{2\pi}{3}\right) \end{bmatrix} + \begin{bmatrix} L \\ 000 \\ 000 \end{bmatrix} u + \begin{bmatrix} 0 \\ \dfrac{p}{2J} \\ 0 \end{bmatrix} T_L \qquad (8.5)$$

where ω is the rotor angular rate and θ is the rotor angle; p is the number of rotor poles; b is the viscous damping coefficient; r_s is the stator resistance; ψ is the magnet flux; T_L is the load torque; and J is the rotor inertia. i and u are the phase winding three vectors that are shown and L is the 3 × 3 inductance matrix, also shown. Equation 8.5 is actually five equations in matrix form. The first three equations, for the current array i, are the electrical dynamics. The last two, for ω_e and θ_e, are the mechanical dynamics represented in electrical coordinates.

The driver circuitry is shown in Figure 8-2. It has six semiconductor switches. In this model, they are considered ideal, meaning they can switch instantaneously at any frequency you desire. In practice, switches have a maximum switching speed and have some transient response. Note that the motor is Y connected, meaning that the ends of the three phase windings are tied together.

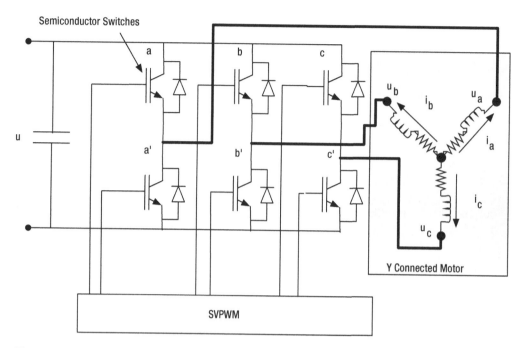

Figure 8-2. *Motor three-phase driver circuitry. The semiconductor switches shown in the diagram are IGBT (integrated gate bipolar transistors). The pulsewidth modulation block, SVPWM, is discussed in Recipe 8-3*

The right-hand-side code is shown next. The first output is the state derivative, as needed for integration. The second output is the electrical torque needed for the control. The first block of code defines the motor model data structure with the parameters needed by the dynamics equation. This structure can be retrieved by calling the function with no inputs. The remaining code implements equation 8.5. Note the suffix M used for ω and θ to reinforce that these are mechanical quantities; this distinguishes them from the electrical quantities, which are related by $p/2$, where p is the number of poles. Use of M and E subscripts is typical when writing software for motors.

```
%% RHSPMMACHINE Permanent magnet machine model in ABC coordinates.
% Assumes a 3 phase machine in a Y connection. The permanent magnet flux
% distribution is assumed sinusoidal.
%% Forms
%   d = RHSPMMachine
%   [xDot,tE] = RHSPMMachine( ˜, x, d )
%
%% Inputs
%   t   (1,1)    Time, unused
%   x   (5,1)    The state vector [iA;iB;iC;omegaE;thetaE]
%   d   (.)      Data structure
%                  .lM    (1,1)  Mutual inductance
%                  .psiM  (1,1)  Permanent magnet flux
%                  .lSS   (1,1)  Stator self inductance
%                  .rS    (1,1)  Stator resistance
%                  .p     (1,1)  Number of poles (1/2 pole pairs)
%                  .u     (3,1)  [uA;uB;uC]
```

```
%                      .tL     (1,1)   Load torque
%                      .bM     (1,1)   Viscous damping (Nm/rad/s)
%                      .j      (1,1)   Inertia
%                      .u      (3,1)   Phase voltages [uA;uB;uC]
%
%% Outputs
%   x    (5,1)    The state vector derivative
%   tE   (1,1)    Electrical torque
%
%% Reference
% Lyshevski, S. E., "Electromechanical Systems, Electric Machines, and
% Applied Mechatronics," CRC Press, 2000.

function [xDot, tE] = RHSPMMachine( ˜, x, d )

if( nargin == 0 )
  xDot = struct('lM',0.0009,'psiM',0.069, 'lSS',0.0011,'rS',0.5,'p',2,...
                'bM',0.000015,'j',0.000017,'tL',0,'u',[0;0;0]);

  return
end

% Pole pairs
pP = d.p/2;

% States
i      = x(1:3);
omegaE = x(4);
thetaE = x(5);

% Inductance matrix
denom = 2*d.lSS^2 - d.lSS*d.lM - d.lM^2;
l2    = d.lM;
l1    = 2*d.lSS - l2;
l     = [l1 l2 l2;l2 l1 l2;l2 l2 l1]/denom;

% Right hand side
tP3      = 2*pi/3;
c        = cos(thetaE + [0;-tP3;tP3]);
iDot     = l*(d.u - d.psiM*omegaE*c - d.rS*i);
tE       = pP^2*d.psiM*i'*c;
omegaDot = (tE - d.bM*omegaE - pP*d.tL)/d.j;
xDot     = [iDot;omegaDot;omegaE];
```

8-2. Controlling the Motor

Problem

You want to control the motor to produce a desired torque. Specifically, you need to compute the voltages to apply to the stator coils.

Solution

You will use *field-oriented control* (FOC) with a proportional integral controller to control the motor. FOC is a control method where the stator currents are transformed into two orthogonal components. One component defines the magnetic flux of the motor and the other defines the torque. The control voltages calculated are implemented using pulsewidth modulation of the semiconductor switches, as developed in the previous recipe.

How It Works

The motor controller is shown in Figure 8-3. This implements field-oriented control. FOC effectively turns the brushless three-phase motor into a commutated DC motor.

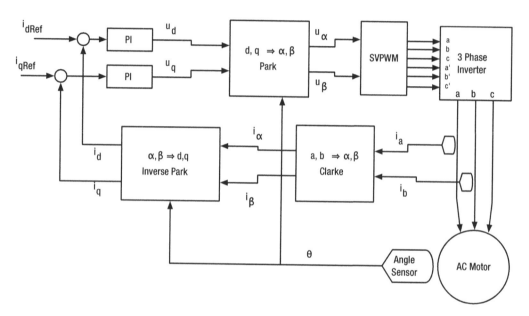

Figure 8-3. *Motor controller. PI is proportional integral controller. PWM is pulsewidth modulation. There are two current sensors measuring i_a and i_b, and one angle sensor measuring θ*

There are three electrical frames of reference in this problem. The first is the (a,b,c) frame, which is the frame of the three-phase stator shown in Figure 8-1. This is a time-varying frame. Next, you want to transform it into a two-axis time-varying frame, the (α,β) frame, and then into a two-axis time invariant frame, the (d,q) frame, which is also known as the *direct and quadrature axis*, and is fixed to the permanent magnet. In our frames, each axis is a current. With a Y connected motor, the sum of the currents is zero, so you only need to work with two currents, i_a and i_b.

$$0 = i_a + i_b + i_c \tag{8.6}$$

The (d,q) to (α,β) transformation is known as the *Forward Park transformation*:

$$\begin{bmatrix} u_\alpha \\ u_\beta \end{bmatrix} = \begin{bmatrix} \cos\theta_e & -\sin\theta_e \\ \sin\theta_e & \cos\theta_e \end{bmatrix} \begin{bmatrix} u_d \\ u_q \end{bmatrix} \tag{8.7}$$

This transforms from the stationary (d,q) frame to the rotating (α, β) frame. θ_e is in electrical axes and equals $\frac{1}{2}p\theta_M$ where p is the number of magnet poles. The *Forward Clarke transformation* for a Y connected motor is

$$\begin{bmatrix} u_\alpha \\ u_\beta \end{bmatrix} = \begin{bmatrix} 1 & 0 \\ \frac{1}{\sqrt{3}} & \frac{2}{\sqrt{3}} \end{bmatrix} \begin{bmatrix} u_a \\ u_b \end{bmatrix} \tag{8.8}$$

These two transformations are implemented in the functions ClarkeTransformationMatrix and ParkTransformationMatrix. They allow you to go from the time-varying (a,b,c) frame to the time-invariant, but rotating, (d,q) frame.

The equations for a general permanent magnet machine in the direct-quadrature frame are

$$u_q = r_s i_q + \omega_e \left(L_d i_d + \psi \right) + \frac{dL_q i_q}{dt} \tag{8.9}$$

$$u_d = r_s i_d - \omega_e L_q i_q + \frac{d\left(L_d i_d + \psi \right)}{dt} \tag{8.10}$$

where u are the voltages and i are the currents; r_s is the stator resistance; L_q and L_d are the d and q phase inductances; ω_e is the electrical angular rate; and ψ is the flux due to the permanent magnets. The electrical torque produced is

$$T_e = \frac{3}{2}p\left(\left(L_d i_d + \psi \right) i_q - L_q i_q i_d \right) \tag{8.11}$$

where p is the number of pole pairs.

The torque equation is

$$T_e = T_L + b\omega_m + J\frac{d\omega_m}{dt} \tag{8.12}$$

where b is the mechanical damping coefficient, J is the inertia, and the relationship between mechanical and electrical angular rate is

$$\omega_e = p\omega_m \tag{8.13}$$

In a magnet surface mount machine with coils in slots, $L_d = L_q \equiv L$, and ψ and the inductances are not functions of time. The equations simplify to

$$u_q = r_s i_q + \omega_e L i_d + \omega_e \psi + L \frac{di_q}{dt} \tag{8.14}$$

$$u_d = r_s i_d - \omega_e L i_q + L \frac{di_d}{dt} \tag{8.15}$$

You control direct current i_d to zero. If i_d is zero, control is linear in i_q. The torque is now

$$T_e = \frac{3}{2} p \psi i_q \tag{8.16}$$

Thus the torque is a function of the quadrature current i_q only. You can therefore control the electrical torque by controlling the quadrature current. The quadrature current is, in turn, controlled by the direct and quadrature phase voltages. The desired current i_q^s can now be computed from the torque setpoint T_e^s.

$$i_q^s = \frac{2}{3} T_e^s / (p\psi) \tag{8.17}$$

You use a proportional integral controller to compute the (d,q) voltages. The proportional part of the control drives errors to zero. However, if there is a steady disturbance, there will be an offset. The integral part can drive an error due to such a steady disturbance to zero. A proportional integral controller is of the form

$$u = K \left(1 + \frac{1}{\tau} \int \right) y \tag{8.18}$$

where u is the control, y is the measurement, τ is the integrator time constant, and K is the forward (proportional) gain. The control u will be the phase voltages and the measurement y is the current error in the (d,q) frame.

$$u_{(d,q)} = -k_F \left(i_{err} + \frac{1}{\tau} \int i_{err} \right) \tag{8.19}$$

where

$$\begin{bmatrix} i_d \\ i_q \end{bmatrix}_{err} = \begin{bmatrix} i_d \\ i_q \end{bmatrix} - \begin{bmatrix} 0 \\ i_q^s \end{bmatrix} \tag{8.20}$$

You now write a function, TorqueControl, that calculates the control voltages, $u_{(\alpha,\beta)}$, given the current state x. The state vector is the same as Recipe 8-1; that is, current i in the (a,b,c) frame plus the angle states θ and ω. You use the Park and Clarke transformations to compute the current in the (d,q) frame. You can then implement the proportional-integral controller with Euler integration. The function uses its data structure as memory—the updated structure d is passed back as an output. TorqueControl is shown next.

```
%% TORQUECONTROL Torque control of an AC machine
% Determines the quadrature current needed to produce a torque and uses a
% proportional integral controller to control the motor. We control the
% direct current to zero since we want to use just the magnet flux to react
% with the quadrature current. We could control the direct current to
% another value to implement field-weakening control but this would result
% in a nonlinear control system.
%% Forms
%   d = TorqueControl
%   [u, d, iAB] = TorqueControl( torqueSet, x, d )
%
%% Inputs
%   torqueSet  (1,1)    Set point torque
%   x          (5,1)    State [ia;ib;ic;omega;theta]
%   d          (.)      Control data structure
%                       .kF      (1,1) Forward gain
%                       .tauI    (1,1) Integral time constant
%                       .iDQInt  (2,1) Integral of current errors
%                       .dT      (1,1) Time step
%                       .psiM    (1,1) Magnetic flux
%                       .p       (1,1) Number of magnet poles
%
%%  Outputs
%   u         (2,1)     Control voltage [alpha;beta]
%   d         (.)       Control data structure
%   iAB       (2,1)     Steady state currents [alpha;beta]
%

function [u, d, iAB] = TorqueControl( torqueSet, x, d )

% Default data structure
if( nargin == 0 )
  u = struct('kF',0.003,'tauI',0.001, 'iDQInt',[0;0], 'dT', 0.01,...
             'psiM',0.0690,'p',2);

  return
end

% Clarke and Park transforms
thetaE = 0.5*d.p*x(5);
park   = ParkTransformationMatrix( thetaE );
iPark  = park';
clarke = ClarkeTransformationMatrix;
iDQ    = iPark*clarke*x(1:2);

% Set point to produce the desired torque [iD;iQ]
iDQSet = [0;(2/3)*torqueSet/(d.psiM*d.p)];

% Error
iDQErr = iDQ - iDQSet;
```

```
% Integral term
d.iDQInt = d.iDQInt + d.dT*iDQErr;

% Control
uDQ = -d.kF*(iDQErr + d.iDQInt/d.tauI);
u   = park*uDQ;

% Steady state currents
if( nargout > 2 )
  iAB = park*iDQSet;
end
```

8-3. PulseWidth Modulation of the Switches

Problem

In the previous recipe, you calculated the control voltages to apply to the stator. Now you want to take those control voltages as an input and drive the switches via pulsewidth modulation.

Solution

You will use space vector modulation to go from a rotating, two-dimensional (α, β) frame to the rotating three-dimensional (a,b,c) stator frame, which is more computationally efficient than modulating in (a,b,c) directly.

How It Works

You will use space vector modulation to drive the switches for pulsewidth modulation.[2] This goes from (α, β) coordinates to switch states (a,b,c). Each node of each phase is either connected to ground or to $+u$. These values are shown in Figure 8-4. The six spokes in the diagram, as well as the origin, correspond to the eight discrete switch states.

---

[2]*Analog Devices*, "Implementing Space Vector Modulation with the ADMCF32X," ANF32X-17, January 2000.

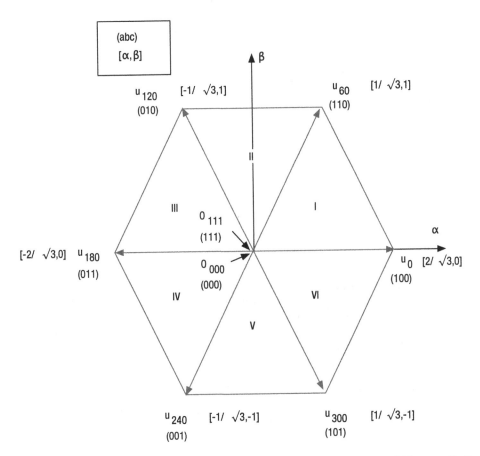

Figure 8-4. *Space vector modulation in (α, β) coordinates. You determine which sector (in Roman numerals) you are in and then pick the appropriate vectors to apply so that they, on average, attain the desired voltage. The numbers in brackets are the normalized [α, β] voltages*

Table 8-1 delineates each of these eight discrete switch states, the corresponding vector in the (α, β) coordinates, and the resulting voltages. Note that the O vectors are at the origin of the space vector modulation, while the U vectors are at 60-degree increments. The states are indexed from 0 to 7, with 0 being all open states and 7 being all closed.

Table 8-1. *Space vector modulation. In the vector names, O means open and U means a voltage is applied, while the subscripts denote the angle in the α-β plane. The switch states are a, b, c, as shown in Figure 8-2, where 1 means a switch is closed and 0 means it is open*

k	abc	Vector	u_a/u	u_b/u	u_c/u	u_{ab}/u	u_{bc}/u	u_{ac}/u
0	000	O_{000}	0	0	0	0	0	0
1	110	U_{60}	2/3	1/3	−1/3	1	0	−1
2	010	U_{120}	1/3	1/3	−2/3	0	1	−1
3	011	U_{180}	−1/3	2/3	−1/3	−1	1	0
4	001	U_{240}	−2/3	1/3	1/3	−1	0	1
5	101	U_{300}	−1/3	−1/3	2/3	0	−1	1
6	100	U_{360}	1/3	−2/3	1/3	1	−1	0
7	111	O_{111}	0	0	0	0	0	0

In order to produce the desired torque, you must use a combination of the vectors or switch states so that you achieve the desired voltage on average. You select the two vectors, O or U, bracketing the desired angle in the (α, β) plane; these are designated k and $k + 1$, where k refers to the number of the vector in Table 8-1. You must then calculate the amount of time to spend in each switch state, for each pulsewidth period. The durations of these two segments, T_k and T_{k+1}, are found from this equation,

$$\begin{bmatrix} T_k \\ T_{k+1} \end{bmatrix} = \frac{\sqrt{3}}{2} \frac{T_s}{u_d} \begin{bmatrix} \sin\dfrac{k\pi}{3} & -\cos\dfrac{k\pi}{3} \\ -\sin\dfrac{(k-1)\pi}{3} & \cos\dfrac{(k-1)\pi}{3} \end{bmatrix} \begin{bmatrix} u_\alpha \\ u_\beta \end{bmatrix} \tag{8.21}$$

The corresponding (a,b,c) switch patterns are each used for the calculated time, averaging to the designated voltage.

The time spent in each pattern, T_k or T_{k+1} is then split into two equal portions so that the total pulse pattern is symmetric. The zero time T_0, when no switching is required, is split evenly between the endpoints and the middle of the pulse T_s – so that the time in the middle pattern (O_{111}) is twice the time in each end pattern (O_{000}). This results in a total of seven segments, depicted in Figure 8-5. The total middle time is designated T_7.

$$T_0 = \frac{1}{4}\left(T_s - \left(T_k + T_{k+1}\right)\right) \tag{8.22}$$

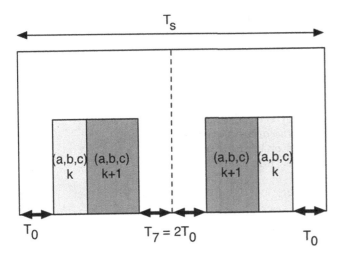

Figure 8-5. *Pulse Period Segments. Each pulse period T_s is divided into seven segments so that the two switching patterns, k and k + 1, are applied symmetrically*

The implementation of the pulse segments is slightly different for the even and odd sectors in Figure 8-4. Both are symmetric about the midpoint of the pulse as described, but you reverse the implementation of patterns k and $k + 1$. This is shown for the resulting voltages u in the following equations. You use the first in even sectors and the second in odd sectors.

$$\begin{bmatrix} u_0 & u_k & u_{k+1} & u_7 & u_{k+1} & u_k & u_0 \end{bmatrix} \tag{8.23}$$

and

$$\begin{bmatrix} u_0 & u_{k+1} & u_k & u_7 & u_k & u_{k+1} & u_0 \end{bmatrix} \tag{8.24}$$

Using the different patterns for odd and even vectors minimizes the number of commutations per cycle. You determine the sector from the angle Θ formed by the commanded voltages u_α and u_β.

$$\Theta = \operatorname{atan} \frac{u_\beta}{u_\alpha} \tag{8.25}$$

The pulsewidth modulation routine, SVPWM, does not actually compute an arctangent. Rather it looks at the unit u_α and u_β vectors and determines first their quadrant and then their sector without any need for trigonometric operations.

The first section of SVPWM implements the timing for the pulses. Just as in the previous recipe for the controller, the function uses its data structure as memory—the updated structure is passed back as an output. This is an alternative to persistent variables.

```
%% SVPWM Implement space vector pulsewidth modulation.
% Space vector pulsewidth modulation takes the alpha and beta voltage
% components and enables the switches on a 6 switch inverter to drive a
% 3 phase AC motor. The data structure serves as the function memory.
% Memory variables are marked.
%
% The modulation has seven pulse subperiods each pulse period. These
% are arrange symmetrically about the center of the pulse. A zero
% pulse is at the beginning, middle and end. The order of the active
% pulses (for the two active space vectors) is ordered differently for
% even and odd sectors in the alpha-beta plane. This minimizes switches.
%
% Type SVPWM for a demo using a sine wave input.
%
%% Forms
%   d = SVPWM
%   [s, d] = SVPWM( t, d )
%
%% Inputs
%   t    (1,1)  Time
%   d    (.)    Data structure
%               .dT          (1,1) Simulation time step (input)
%               .tLast       (1,1) Time of last pulse (memory)
%               .tUpdate     (1,1) Update period for new pulses (input)
%               .u           (2,1) Voltage vector [alpha;beta] (input) (V)
%               .uM          (1,1) Maximum voltage (parameter) (V)
%               .tP          (1,7) Time for each pulse segment (output)
%               .sP          (3,7) [a;b;c] for each pulse segment (output)
%
%% Outputs
%   s    (3,1)  Switch states (1 or 0)
%   d    (.)    Updated data structure
%
%% Reference
% Implementing Space Vector Modulation with the ADMCF32X, ANF32X-17,
% Analog Devices, January 2000.
%% See also
% SVPWM>Demo

function [s, d] = SVPWM( t, d )

% Default data structure
if( nargin < 1 && nargout == 1 )
  s = struct( 'dT',1e-6,'tLast',-0.0001,'tUpdate',0.001,'u',[0;0],...
              'uM',10,'tP',zeros(1,7),'sP',zeros(3,7));
  return;
end
```

```
% Run the demo
if( nargin < 1 )
  Demo;
  return;
end

% Update the pulsewidths at update time
if( t >= d.tLast + d.tUpdate || t == 0 )
  [d.sP, d.tP] = SVPW( d.u, d.tUpdate, d.uM );
  d.tLast = t;
end

% Time since initialization of the pulse period
dT = t - d.tLast;
s  = zeros(3,1);

for k = 1:7
  if( dT < d.tP(k) )
    s = d.sP(:,k);
    break;
  end
end
```

The pulsewidth vectors are computed in the subfunction SVPW. You first compute the quadrant and then the sector without using any trigonometric functions. This is done using simple if/else statements and a switch statement. Note that the modulation index k is simply designated k, and $k + 1$ is designated kP1. You compute the times for the two space vectors that bound the sector. You then assemble the seven subperiods.

```
%%% SVPWM>SVPW Compute the space vector pulsewidths
% [sP, tP] = SVPW( u, tS, uD )
%
%  Inputs:
%  u    (2,1)    Voltage vector
%  tS   (1,1)    Update period
%  uD   (1,1)    Maximum voltage
%
%  Outputs:
%  sP   (3,7)    Switch patterns
%  tP   (1,7)    Pulse times
function [sP, tP] = SVPW ( u, tS, uD )

% Make u easier to interpret
alpha = 1;
beta  = 2;

% Determine the quadrant
if( u(alpha) >= 0 )
  if( u(beta) > 0 )
    q = 1;
```

```
    else
        q = 4;
    end
else
    if( u(beta) > 0 )
        q = 2;
    else
        q = 3;
    end
end
sqr3 = sqrt(3);

% Find the sector. k1 and k2 define the edge vectors
switch q
    case 1 % [+,+]
        if( u(beta) < sqr3*u(alpha) )
            k       = 1;
            kP1     = 2;
            oddS    = 1;
        else
            k       = 2;
            kP1     = 3;
            oddS    = 0;
        end
    case 2 % [-,+]
        if( u(beta) < -sqr3*u(alpha) )
            k       = 3;
            kP1     = 4;
            oddS    = 1;
        else
            k       = 2;
            kP1     = 3;
            oddS    = 0;
        end
    case 3 % [-,-]
        if( u(beta) < sqr3*u(alpha) )
            k       = 5;
            kP1     = 6;
            oddS    = 1;
        else
            k       = 4;
            kP1     = 5;
            oddS    = 0;
        end
    case 4 % [+,-]
        if( u(beta) < -sqr3*u(alpha) )
            k       = 5;
            kP1     = 6;
            oddS    = 1;
```

```
    else
        k       = 6;
        kP1     = 1;
        oddS    = 0;
    end
end

% Switching sequence
piO3    = pi/3;
kPiO3   = k*pi/3;
kM1PiO3 = kPiO3-piO3;

% Space vector pulsewidths
t   = 0.5*sqr3*(tS/uD)*[ sin(kPiO3)      -cos(kPiO3);...
                        -sin(kM1PiO3)  cos(kM1PiO3)]*u;

% Total zero vector time
t0 = tS - sum(t);
t  = t/2;

% Different order for odd and even sectors
if( oddS )
    sS = [0 k kP1 7 kP1 k 0];
    tPW = [t0/4 t(1) t(2) t0/2 t(2) t(1) t0/4];
else
    sS = [0 kP1 k 7 k kP1 0];
    tPW = [t0/4 t(2) t(1) t0/2 t(1) t(2) t0/4];
end
tP = [tPW(1) zeros(1,6)];

for k = 2:7
    tP(k) = tP(k-1) + tPW(k);
end

% The switches corresponding to each voltage vector
% From 0 to 7
%               a b c
s           = [ 0 0 0;...
                1 0 0;...
                1 1 0;...
                0 1 0;...
                0 1 1;...
                0 0 1;...
                1 0 1;
                1 1 1]';
sP = zeros(3,7);

for k = 1:7
    sP(:,k) = s(:,sS(k)+1);
end
```

The built-in demo is fairly complex, so it is in a separate subfunction. You simply specify an example input, *u*, using trigonometric functions.

```
function Demo
%%% SVPWM>Demo Function demo
% Calls SVPWM with a sinusoidal input u.
% This demo will run through an array of times and create a plot of the
% resulting voltages.

d       = SVPWM;
tEnd    = 0.003;
n       = tEnd/d.dT;
a       = linspace(0,pi/4,n);
tP3     = 2*pi/3;
uABC    = 0.5*[cos(a);cos(a-tP3);cos(a+tP3)];
uAB     = ClarkeTransformationMatrix*uABC(1:2,:); % a-b to alpha-beta
tSamp = 0;
t       = 0;
tPP     = 1;
x       = zeros(4,n);
for k = 1:n
  if( t >= tSamp )
    tSamp = tSamp + d.tUpdate;
    tPP     = ~tPP;
  end
  d.u     = uAB(:,k);
  [s, d] = SVPWM( t, d );
  t       = t + d.dT;
  x(:,k) = [SwitchToVoltage(s,d.uM);tPP];
end

[t,tL] = TimeLabel( (0:(n-1))*d.dT);

PlotSet(t,[uABC;x],'x_label',tL,'plot_title','Voltages',...
    'y_label', {'u_a' 'u_b' 'u_c' 'u_{ap}' 'u_{bp}' 'u_{cp}' 'Pulse' } );
```

Figure 8-6 shows the state vector pulsewidth modulation from the built-in demo. There are three pulses in the plot, each 0.001 seconds long. Each pulse period has seven subperiods.

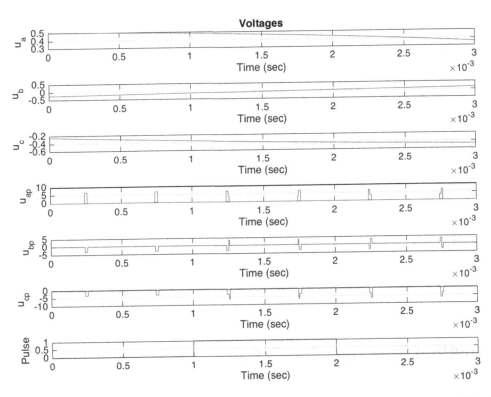

Figure 8-6. *The desired voltage vector and the space vector modulation pulses and pulsewidth. The bottom plot shows the pulse periods. Note that the pulse sequences are symmetric within each pulse period*

The function SwitchToVoltage converts switch states to voltages. It assumes instantaneous switching and no switch dynamics.

```
%% SwitchToVoltage Switch state to voltage
% Converts the switch state for a six switch inverter to a, b and c
% voltages. The switches are numbered
%
%   a  b  c
%   a' b' c'
%
%% Form
%   u = SwitchToVoltage( s, uDC )
%
%% Inputs
%   s       (3,1)   Switches
%   uDC     (1,1)   DC voltage
%
%% Outputs
%   u       (3,1)   Three phase voltages [uA;uB;uC]
%
```

```matlab
function u = SwitchToVoltage( s, uDC )

% Switch states [a;b;c]
sA     = [1 1 0 0 0 1;...
          0 1 1 1 0 0;...
          0 0 0 1 1 1];

% Array of voltages
uA     = [ 2 1 -1 -2 -1 1;...
          -1 1 2 1 -1 -2;...
          -1 -2 -1 1 2 1];

% Find the correct switch state
u      = [0;0;0];
for k = 1:6
  if( sum(sA(:,k) - s) == 0 )
    u = uA(:,k)*uDC/3;
    break;
  end
end
end
```

8-4. Simulating the Controlled Motor

Problem

You want to simulate the motor with torque control using space vector modulation.

Solution

Write a script to simulate the motor with the controller. Include options for closed-loop control and balanced three-phase voltage inputs.

How It Works

The header for the script, PMMachineDemo, is shown in the following listing. The control flags bypassPWM and torqueControlOn are described, as well as the two periods implemented—one for the simulation and a longer period for the control.

```matlab
%% Simulation of a permanent magnet AC motor
% Simulates a permanent magnet AC motor with torque control. The simulation has
% two options. The first is torqueControlOn. This turns torque control on and
% off. If it is off the phase voltages are a balanced three phase voltage set.
%
```

```
% bypassPWM allows you to feed the phase voltages directly to the motor
% bypassing the pulsewidth modulation switching function. This is useful for
% debugging your control system and other testing.
%
% There are two time constants for this simulation. One is the control period
% and the second is the simulation period. The latter is much shorter because it
% needs to simulate the pulsewidth modulation.
%
% For control testing the load torque and setpoint torque should be the same.
```

The body of the script follows. Three different data structures are initialized from their corresponding functions, as described in the previous recipes; that is, from SVPWM, TorqueControl, and RHSPMMachine. Note that we are only simulating the motor for a small fraction of a second, 0.05 seconds, and the timestep is just 1e-6 seconds. The controller timestep is set to 100 times the simulation timestep.

```
%% Initialize all data structures
dS       = SVPWM;
dC       = TorqueControl;
d        = RHSPMMachine;
dC.psiM = d.psiM;
dC.p     = d.p;
d.tL     = 1.0; % Load torque (Nm)


%% User inputs
tEnd            = 0.05;      % sec
torqueControlOn = false;
bypassPWM       = false;
torqueSet       = 1.0;      % Set point (Nm)
dC.dT           = 100*dS.dT; % 100x larger than simulation dT
dS.uM           = 1.0;      % DC Voltage at the input to the switches
magUABC         = 0.1;      % Voltage for the balanced 3 phase voltages

if (torqueControlOn && bypassPWM)
  error('The_control_requires_PWM_to_be_on.');
end

%% Run the simulation
nSim = ceil(tEnd/dS.dT);
xP   = zeros(10,nSim);
x    = zeros(5,1);

% We require two timers as the control period is larger than the simulation period
t    = 0.0; % simulation timer
tC   = 0.0; % control timer

for k = 1:nSim
  % Electrical degrees
  thetaE = x(5);
  park   = ParkTransformationMatrix( thetaE );
  clarke = ClarkeTransformationMatrix;
```

```
  % Compute the voltage control
  if( torqueControlOn && t >= tC )
    tC          = tC + dC.dT;
    [dS.u, dC] = TorqueControl( torqueSet, x, dC );
  elseif( ~torqueControlOn )
    tP3    = 2*pi/3;
    uABC = magUABC*dS.uM*[cos(thetaE);cos(thetaE-tP3);cos(thetaE+tP3)];
    if( bypassPWM )
      d.u = uABC;
    elseif( t >= tC )
      tC   = tC + dC.dT;
      dS.u = park*clarke*uABC(1:2,:);
    end
  end

  % Space Vector Pulsewidth Modulation
  if( ~bypassPWM )
    dS.u = park'*dS.u;
    [s,dS] = SVPWM( t, dS );
    d.u = SwitchToVoltage(s,dS.uM);
  end

  % Get the torque output for plotting
  [~,tE] = RHSPMMachine( 0, x, d );
  xP(:,k) = [x;d.u;torqueSet;tE];

  % Propagate one simulation step
  x = RungeKutta( @RHSPMMachine, 0, x, dS.dT, d );
  t = t + dS.dT;
end

%% Generate the time history plots
[t, tL] = TimeLabel( (0:(nSim-1))*dS.dT );

figure('name','3_Phase_Currents');
plot(t, xP(1:3,:));
grid on;
ylabel('Currents');
xlabel(tL);
legend('i_a','i_b','i_c')

PlotSet( t, xP([4 10],:), 'x_label', tL, 'y_label', {'\omega_e' 'T_e_(Nm)'}, ...
  'plot_title','Electrical', 'figure_title','Electrical');

thisTitle = 'Phase_Voltages';
if ~bypassPWM
  thisTitle = [thisTitle '_-_PWM'];
end
```

```
PlotSet( t, xP(6:8,:), 'x_label', tL, 'y_label', {'u_a' 'u_b' 'u_c'}, ...
  'plot_title',thisTitle, 'figure_title',thisTitle);

thisTitle = 'Torque/Speed';
if ~bypassPWM
  thisTitle = [thisTitle '_-_PWM'];
end
```

Turn off torque control to test the motor simulation, with the results shown in Figure 8-7. The two plots show the torque speed curves. The first is with direct three-phase excitation; that is, bypassing the pulsewidth modulation, by setting bypassPWM to false. Directly controlling the phase voltages this way, while creating the smoothest response, would require linear amplifiers, which are less efficient than switches. This would make the motor much less efficient overall and would generate unwanted heat. The second plot is with space vector pulsewidth modulation. The plots are nearly identical, indicating that the pulsewidth modulation is working.

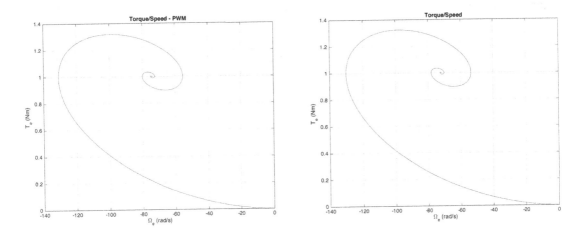

Figure 8-7. *Torque speed curves for a balanced three-phase voltage excitation and a load torque of 1.0 Nm. The left figure shows the curve for direct three-phase input and the right shows the curve for the space vector pulsewidth modulation input. They are nearly identical*

Now turn on torque control, via the torqueControlOn flag, and get the results shown in Figure 8-8. The overshoot is typical for torque control. Note that the load torque is set equal to the torque set point of 1 Nm. There is limit cycling near the endpoint.

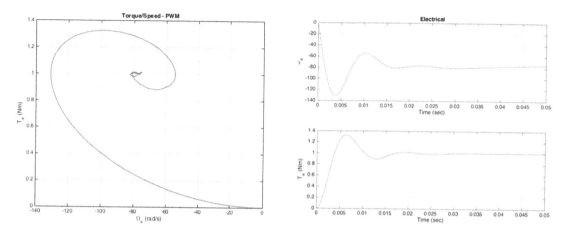

Figure 8-8. *PI torque control of the motor*

The pulsewidths and resulting coil currents are shown in Figure 8-9. A zoomed view of the end of the pulsewidth plot with shading added to alternate pulsewidths is in Figure 8-10. This makes it easier to see the segments of the pulsewidths and verify that they are symmetric.

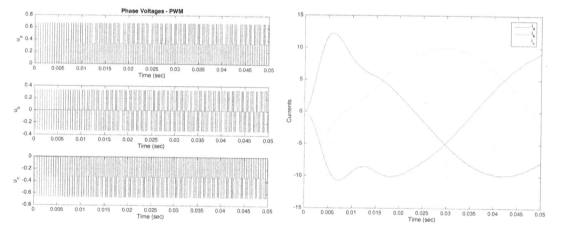

Figure 8-9. *Voltage pulsewidths and resulting currents for PI torque control*

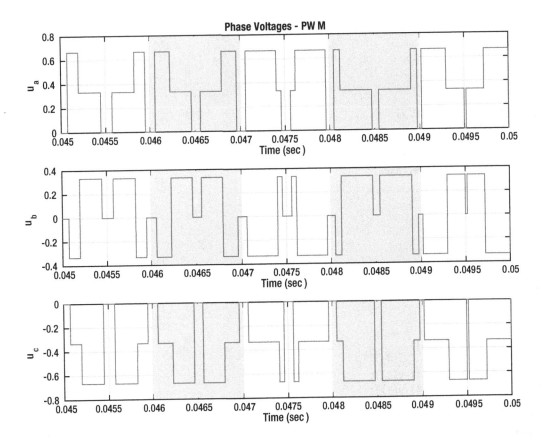

Figure 8-10. *Pulsewidths with shading*

The code that adds the shading uses `fill` with transparency via the `alpha` parameter. In this case, you hard-code the function to show the last five pulsewidths, but this could be generalized to a time window or to shade the entire plot.

We did take the time to add an input for the pulsewidth length, so that this could be changed in the main script and the function would still work. Note that the axes children were reordered as the last step to keep the shading from obscuring the plot lines.

```
%% ADDFILLTOPWM Add shading to the motor pulsewidth plot
% Adds gray shading to alternate pulsewidths for the last 5 pulses of the
% plot. The pulsewidth plot should be the current axes.
%
%% Form
%   AddFillToPWM( dT )
%
%% Input
%   dT (1,1) Pulsewidth
%% Output
%   None.
```

201

```
function AddFillToPWM( dT )

if nargin == 0
  dT = 0.001;
end

hAxes = get(gcf,'children');
nAxes = length(hAxes);

for j = 1:nAxes
  if strcmp(hAxes(j).type,'axes')
    axes(hAxes(j));
    AddFillToAxes;
  end
end

  function AddFillToAxes

  hold on;
  y = axis;
  xMin = y(2) - 5*dT;
  xMax = y(2);
  axis([xMin xMax y(3:4)])
  x0 = xMin;
  yMin = y(3) + 0.01*(y(4)-y(3));
  yMax = y(4) - 0.01*(y(4)-y(3));
  for k = [2 4]
    xMinK = x0 + (k-1)*dT;
    xMaxK = x0 + k*dT;

    fill([xMinK xMaxK xMaxK xMinK],...
         [yMin,yMin,yMax,yMax],...
         [0.8 0.8 0.8],'edgecolor','none','facealpha',0.5);
  end
  babes = get(gca,'children');
  set(gca,'children',[babes(end); babes(1:end-1)])
  hold off;

  end

end
```

Summary

This chapter demonstrated how to write the dynamics and implement a field-oriented control law for a three-phase motor. A proportional-integral controller with space vector pulsewidth modulation was used to drive the six switches. This produces a low-cost controller for a motor. Table 8-2 lists the code developed in the chapter.

Table 8-2. *Chapter Code Listing*

File	Description
AddFillToPWM	Add shading to the motor pulsewidth plot.
ClarkeTransformationMatrix	Clarke transformation matrix.
ParkTransformationMatrix	Park transformation matrix.
PMMachineDemo	Permanent magnet motor demonstration.
RHSPMMachine	Right-hand-side of a permanent magnet brushless 3-phase electrical machine.
SVPWM	Implements space vector pulsewidth modulation.
SwitchToVoltage	Converts switch states to voltages.
TorqueControl	Proportional integral torque controller.

CHAPTER 9

Fault Detection

Introduction

Fault detection is the process of detecting failures, also known as *faults*, in a dynamical system. It is an important area for systems that are supposed to operate without human supervision. There are many ways of detecting failures. The simplest is using boolean logic to check against fixed thresholds. For example, you might check an automobile's speed against a speed limit. Other methods include fuzzy logic, parameter estimation, expert systems, statistical analysis, and parity space methods. This chapter implements one type of fault detection system, a detection filter. This is based on linear filtering. The detection filter is a state estimator tuned to detect specific failures. You will design a detection filter system for an air turbine. You will also be shown how to build a graphical user interface (GUI) as a front end to the fault detection simulation.

9-1. Modeling an Air Turbine

Problem

You need to make a numerical model of an air turbine to demonstrate detection filters.

Solution

Write the equations of motion for an air turbine. You will use a linear model of the air turbine to simplify the model and the detection filter design. This will allow you to model the system with a state space model.

How It Works

Figure 9-1 shows an air turbine.[1] It has a constant pressure air supply. You can control the valve from the air supply, the pressure regulator, to control the speed of the turbine. The air flows past the turbine blades causing it to turn. The control needs to adjust the air pressure to handle variations in the load. You measure the air pressure p downstream from the valve and you also measure the rotational speed of the turbine ω with a tachometer.

---

[1]PhD thesis of Jere Schenck Meserole, "Detection Filters for Fault-Tolerant Control of Turbofan Engines," Massachusetts Institute of Technology, Department of Aeronautics and Astronautics, 1981.

Electronic supplementary material The online version of this chapter (doi:10.1007/978-1-4842-0559-4_9) contains supplementary material, which is available to authorized users.

S. Thomas and M. Paluszek, *MATLAB Recipes*, DOI 10.1007/978-1-4842-0559-4_9

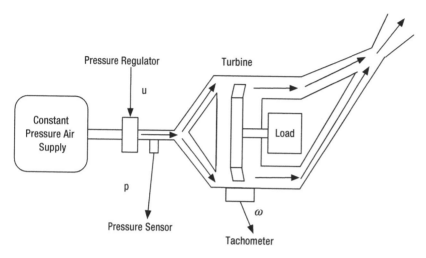

Figure 9-1. *Air turbine. The arrows show the airflow. The air flows through the turbine blade tips, causing it to turn*

The dynamical model for the air turbine is

$$\begin{bmatrix} \dot{p} \\ \dot{\omega} \end{bmatrix} = \begin{bmatrix} -\dfrac{1}{\tau_p} & 0 \\ \dfrac{K_t}{\tau_t} & -\dfrac{1}{\tau_t} \end{bmatrix} \begin{bmatrix} p \\ \omega \end{bmatrix} + \begin{bmatrix} \dfrac{K_p}{\tau_p} \\ 0 \end{bmatrix} u \tag{9.1}$$

This is a state space system

$$\dot{x} = ax + bu \tag{9.2}$$

where

$$a = \begin{bmatrix} -\dfrac{1}{\tau_p} & 0 \\ \dfrac{K_t}{\tau_t} & -\dfrac{1}{\tau_t} \end{bmatrix} \tag{9.3}$$

$$b = \begin{bmatrix} \dfrac{K_p}{\tau_p} \\ 0 \end{bmatrix} \tag{9.4}$$

The state vector is

$$\begin{bmatrix} p \\ \omega \end{bmatrix}$$

(9.5)

The pressure downstream from the regulator is equal to $K_p u$ when the system is in equilibrium. τ_p is the regulator time constant and τ_t is the turbine time constant. The turbine speed is $K_t p$ when the system is in equilibrium. The tachometer measures ω and the pressure sensor measures p. The load is folded into the time constant for the turbine.

The code for the right-hand side of the dynamical equations is shown next. Only one line of code is the right-hand side. The rest returns the default data structure. The simplicity of the model is due to its being a state space model. The number of states could be large, yet the code would not change.

```
function xDot = RHSAirTurbine( ~, x, d )

% Default data structure
if( nargin < 1 )
  kP   = 1;
  kT   = 2;
  tauP = 10;
  tauT = 40;
  c    = eye(2);
  b    = [kP/tauP;0];
  a    = [-1/tauP 0; kT/tauT -1/tauT];

  xDot = struct('a',a,'b',b,'c',c,'u',0);
  return
end

% Derivative
xDot = d.a*x + d.b*d.u;
```

The response to a step input for u is shown in Figure 9-2. The pressure settles faster than the turbine. This is due to the turbine time constant and the lag in the pressure change. The residuals are very small because there are no failures.

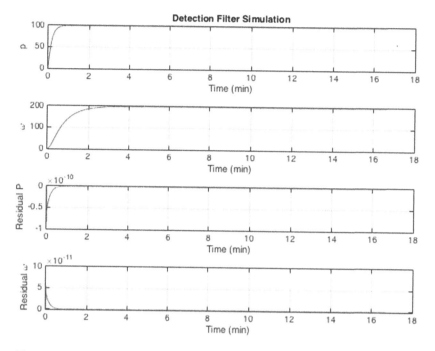

Figure 9-2. *Air turbine response to a step pressure regulator input*

9-2. Building a Detection Filter

Problem

You want to build a system to detect failures in an air turbine using the linear model developed in the previous recipe.

Solution

You will build a detection filter that detects pressure regulator failures and tachometer failures. Our plant model (continuous a, b, and c state space matrices) will be an input to the filter building function.

How It Works

The detection filter is an estimator with a specific gain matrix that multiplies the residuals.

$$
\begin{bmatrix} \dot{\hat{p}} \\ \dot{\hat{\omega}} \end{bmatrix} = \begin{bmatrix} -\dfrac{1}{\tau_p} & 0 \\ \dfrac{K_t}{\tau_t} & -\dfrac{1}{\tau_t} \end{bmatrix} \begin{bmatrix} \hat{p} \\ \hat{\omega} \end{bmatrix} + \begin{bmatrix} \dfrac{K_p}{\tau_p} \\ 0 \end{bmatrix} u + \begin{bmatrix} d_{11} & d_{12} \\ d_{21} & d_{22} \end{bmatrix} \begin{bmatrix} p - \hat{p} \\ \omega - \hat{\omega} \end{bmatrix}
\tag{9.6}
$$

where $\hat{p}$ is the estimated pressure and $\hat{\omega}$ is the estimated angular rate of the turbine. The D matrix is the matrix of detection filter gains. These feed back the residuals, the difference between the measured and estimated states, into the detection filter. The residual vector is

$$r = \begin{bmatrix} p - \hat{p} \\ \omega - \hat{\omega} \end{bmatrix}$$

(9.7)

The D matrix needs to be selected so that this vector tells you the nature of the failure. The gains should be selected so that

- The filter is stable.

- If the pressure regulator fails, the first residual, $p - \hat{p}$ is non-zero but the second remains zero.

- If the turbine fails, the second residual $\omega - \hat{\omega}$ is non-zero but the first remains zero.

The gain matrix is

$$D = a + \begin{bmatrix} \dfrac{1}{\tau_1} & 0 \\ 0 & \dfrac{1}{\tau_2} \end{bmatrix}$$

(9.8)

The time constant τ_1 is the pressure residual time constant. The time constant τ_2 is the tachometer residual time constant. In effect, you cancel out the dynamics of the plant and replace them with decoupled detection filter dynamics. These time constants should be shorter than the time constants in the dynamical model so that you detect failures quickly. However, they need to be at least twice as long as the sampling period to prevent numerical instabilities.

Write a function with three actions: an initialize case, an update case, and a reset case. varargin is used to allow the three cases to have different input lists. The function signature is

function d = DetectionFilter(action, varargin)

The header and syntax for DetectionFilter are shown next. Some LaTeX equations are used to describe the function.

```
%% DetectionFilter Builds and updates a linear detection filter.
% The detection filter gain matrix d is designed during the initialize
% action. The continuous matrices are then discretized using the internal
% function CToDZOH. The esimated state and residual vectors are initialized
% to the size dictated by a. During the update action, the residuals and
% new estimated state are calculated and stored in the data structure d.
%
% The residuals calculation is
%
% $$r = y - c\hat{x}$$
%
% The estimated state calculated with the detection filter gains is
%
```

```
% $$\hat{x}_{k+1} = a*\hat{x} + +b*u + d*r$$
%
%% Form:
%   d = DetectionFilter( 'initialize', d, tau, dT );
%   d = DetectionFilter( 'update', u, y, d );
%   d = DetectionFilter( 'reset', d );
%
%% Inputs
%   action   (1,:)  'initialize' or 'update'
%   d        (.)    Data structure
%                      .a (:,:) State space continuous a matrix
%                      .b (:,1) State space continuous b matrix
%                      .c (:,:) State space continuous c matrix
%   tau      (:,1)  Vector of time constants
%   dT       (1,1)  Time step
%   u        (:,1)  Actuation input
%   y        (:,1)  Measurement vector
%
%% Outputs
%   d        (.)    Updated data structure
%                      .a (:,:) State space discrete a matrix
%                      .b (:,1) State space discrete b matrix
%                      .c (:,:) State space discrete c matrix
%                      .d (:,:) Detection filter gain matrix
%                      .x (:,1) Estimated states
%                      .r (:,1) Residual vector
```

The filter is built and initialized in the following code in DetectionFilter. The continuous state space model of the plant, in this case our linear air turbine model, is an input. The selected time constants τ are also an input, and they are added to the plant model, as in equation 9.8. The function discretizes the plant a and b matrices and the computed detection filter gain matrix d.

```
switch lower(action)
  case 'initialize'
    d   = varargin{1};
    tau = varargin{2};
    dT  = varargin{3};

    % Design the detection filter
    d.d = d.a + diag(1./tau);

    % Discretize both
    d.d         = CToDZOH( d.d, d.b, dT );
    [d.a, d.b]  = CToDZOH( d.a, d.b, dT );

    % Initialize the state
    m   = size(d.a,1);
    d.x = zeros(m,1);
    d.r = zeros(m,1);
```

The update for the detection filter is in the same function. Note the equations are implemented as described in the header.

```
case 'update'
  u   = varargin{1};
  y   = varargin{2};
  d   = varargin{3};
  r   = y - d.c*d.x;
  d.x = d.a*d.x + +d.b*u + d.d*r;
  d.r = r;
```

Finally, create a reset action to allow you to reset the residual and state values for the filter in between simulations.

```
case 'reset'
  d   = varargin{1};
  m   = size(d.a,1);
  d.x = zeros(m,1);
  d.r = zeros(m,1);
end
```

9-3. Simulating the Fault Detection System

Problem

You want to simulate a failure in the plant and demonstrate the performance of the failure detection.

Solution

You will build a MATLAB script that designs the detection filter using the function from the previous recipe and then simulates it with a user selectable pressure regulator or tachometer failure. The failure can be total or partial.

How It Works

The script designs a detection filter using DetectionFilter from the previous recipe and implements it in a loop. Runge-Kutta integration propagates the continuous domain right-hand-side of the air turbine, RHSAirTurbine. The detection filter is discrete time.

The script has two scale factors, uF and tachF, that multiply the regulator input and the tachometer output to simulate failures. Setting a scale factor to zero is a total failure and setting it to one indicates that the device is working perfectly. If you fail one, expect the associated residual to be non-zero and the other to stay at zero.

```
%% Simulation of a detection filter
% Simulates detecting failures of an air turbine.
% An air turbine has a constant pressure air source that sends air
% through a duct that drives the turbine blades. The turbine is
% attached to a load.
%
```

```
% The air turbine model is linear. Failures are modeled by multiplying
% the regulator input and tachometer output by a constant. A constant
% of 0 is a total failure and 1 is perfect operation.

%% User inputs

% Failures. Set to any number. 0 is total failure. 1 is working.
% uF scales the actuation u. tachF scales the rate measurement.
uF    = 1;
tachF = 0;

% Time constants for failure detection
tau1 = 0.3; % sec
tau2 = 0.3; % sec

% End time
tEnd = 1000; % sec

% State space system
d = RHSAirTurbine;

%% Initialization
dT = 0.02; % sec
n  = ceil(tEnd/dT);

% Initial state
x = [0;0];

%% Detection Filter design
dF = DetectionFilter('initialize',d,[tau1;tau2],dT);

%% Run the simulation

% Control. This is the regulator input.
u = 100;

% Plotting array
xP = zeros(4,n);
t  = (0:n-1)*dT;

for k = 1:n
  % Measurement vector including measurement failure
  y       = [x(1);tachF*x(2)]; % Sensor failure
  xP(:,k) = [x;dF.r];

  % Update the detection filter
  dF = DetectionFilter('update',u,y,dF);
```

```
  % Integrate one step
  d.u = uF*u; % Actuator failure
  x   = RungeKutta( @RHSAirTurbine, t(k), x, dT, d );
end

%% Plot the states and residuals
[t,tL] = TimeLabel(t);
yL     = {'p' '\omega' 'Residual P' 'Residual_\omega' };
tTL    = 'Detection_Filter_Simulation';
PlotSet( t, xP,'x_label',tL,'y_label',yL,'plot_title',tTL,'figure_title',tTL)
```

In Figure 9-3, the regulator fails and its residual is non-zero. In Figure 9-4, the tachometer fails and its residual is non-zero. The residuals show what has failed clearly. Simple boolean logic (i.e., if end statements) are all that is needed.

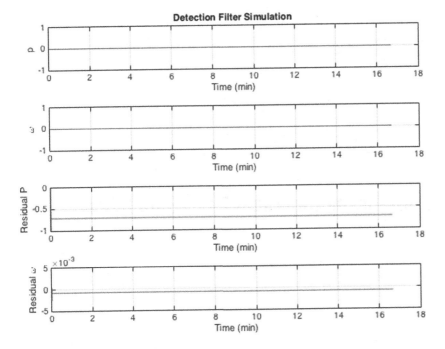

Figure 9-3. *Air turbine response to a failed regulator*

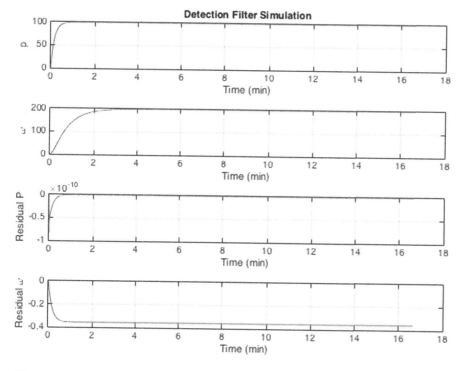

Figure 9-4. *Air turbine response to a failed tachometer*

9-4. Building a GUI for the Detection Filter Simulation

Problem

You want a GUI to provide a graphical interface to the fault detection simulation that will allow you to evaluate the filter's performance.

Solution

You will use the MATLAB GUIDE to build a GUI that allows you to

- Set the residual time constants.
- Set the end time for the simulation.
- Set the pressure regulator input.
- Introduce a pressure regulator or tachometer fault at any time.
- Display the states and residuals in a plot.

214

How It Works

The MATLAB GUI building system, GUIDE, is invoked by typing guide at the command line. There are several options for GUI templates, or a blank GUI; you will start from the GUI with uicontrols. First, let's make a list of the controls you will need from our desired features list:

- Edit boxes for the simulation duration, residual time constants τ_1 and τ_2, pressure regulator setting u

- Edit boxes for the pressure regulator and tachometer fault parameters, with buttons for sending the newly commanded values to the simulation

- Text box for displaying the calculated detection filter gains

- Run button for starting a simulation

- Plot axes

In order to change the fault parameters while the simulation is running, you will need the loop to check a variable that can be externally set by the GUI. You can do this using global variables.

The template for the GUI controls gives you a couple edit boxes with labels, a set of radio buttons, and two action buttons for Calculate and Reset. You will use the edit boxes for the first two items on the list of controls and use the space with the radio buttons for the fault parameters. Figure 9-5 shows the template GUI in GUIDE before you make any changes to it.

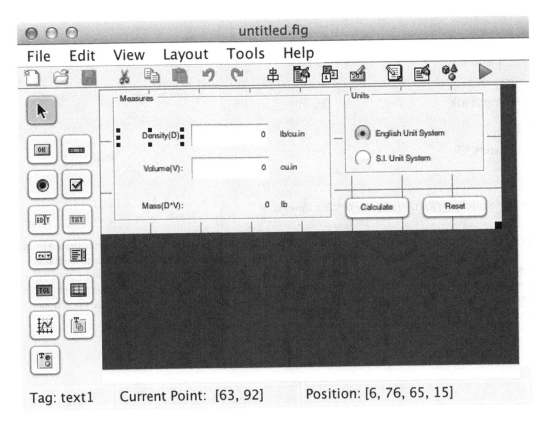

Figure 9-5. *Template of a GUI with uicontrols*

215

Simply double-click an item in the template GUI in GUIDE to open the inspector and edit the item's text and font size, and so forth. For a text item, change the String field in the item's Inspector. For a frame item, such as the Measures frame, change the Title field. For an edit box, change the Tag field. Make the following changes to the left-hand set of controls:

1. Change the String for the Density(D) label to "Duration".

2. Change the String for the Volume(V) label to "Input".

3. Increase the label font sizes to 10 pt.

4. Change the Tag for the density edit box to "duration".

5. Change the Tag for the volume edit box to "input".

6. Change the Tag for the mass text box to "gains".

7. Change the Title of the Measures frame to "Parameters".

After making these changes, click the green triangle button to save and run the GUI. MATLAB saves the .fig file with the name you specify, as well as a corresponding .m file. We choose to name our GUI DetectionFilterGUI. The resulting initial GUI is shown in Figure 9-6.

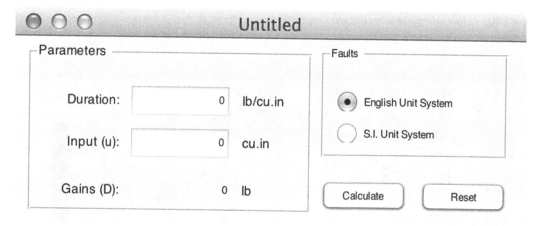

Figure 9-6. *Snapshot of the GUI after the first few changes*

At this point, you can start work on the GUI code itself. The template GUI stores its data, calculated from the data the user types into the edit boxes, in a field called metricdata. You can do a find/replace to change this field to filterdata throughout the m-file. Similarly, you can replace "density" with "duration" and "volume" with "input". Changing the Tag of the edit boxes changes the name of the callback functions (i.e., from density_Callback to duration_Callback), but not the names of the variables inside the function bodies. The find/replace step is shown in Figure 9-7.

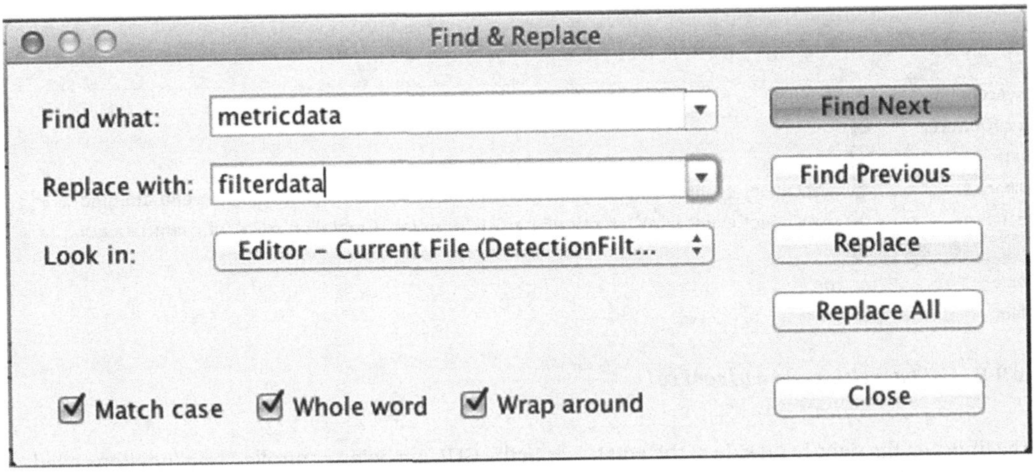

Figure 9-7. *Find/Replace of* metricdata *fieldname*

The updated duration_Callback function is shown next. You can keep the error-checking code that ensures that the input is a legitimate number. Note that MATLAB provides a nice hint on the best way to convert the contents of the graphics object from a string to a double, or how to keep it as a string. The guidata function stores the new value of the changed parameter in the figure itself using graphics handles.

```
function duration_Callback(hObject, eventdata, handles)
% hObject     handle to duration (see GCBO)
% eventdata   reserved - to be defined in a future version of MATLAB
% handles     structure with handles and user data (see GUIDATA)

% Hints: get(hObject,'String') returns contents of duration as text
%        str2double(get(hObject,'String')) returns contents of duration as a double
duration = str2double(get(hObject, 'String'));
if isnan(filterdata)
    set(hObject, 'String', 0);
    errordlg('Input_must_be_a_number','Error');
end

% Save the new duration value
handles.filterdata.duration = duration;
guidata(hObject,handles)
```

The callback strings that are stored with the uicontrols can be seen in the Inspector by double-clicking the control, as shown in Figure 9-8, for the "duration" edit box.

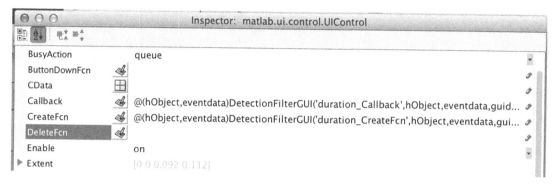

Figure 9-8. Callback strings for a uicontrol

The units, on the right-hand side of the edit boxes in the GUI, are being controlled by a function called by the units radio buttons. First, remove the entire Units panel; if you try to run the GUI now, it will throw an error due to the missing fields for the English and metric units. Next, remove the code relating to this "unitgroup" in the GUI's m-file. You can also remove the code that sets the units fields, since you can hard-code these strings; in the template, they are labelled "text4", "text5", and "text6". Remove lines in initialize_gui and the entire unitgroup_SelectionChangedFcn function.

Remove in initialize_gui():

```
set(handles.unitgroup, 'SelectedObject', handles.english);
set(handles.text4, 'String', 'lb/cu.in');
set(handles.text5, 'String', 'cu.in');
set(handles.text6, 'String', 'lb');
```

Set the initial values of the "duration" and inputs variables to the values from the simulation script:

```
handles.filterdata.duration = 1000;
handles.filterdata.input = 100;
```

Now, the GUI can run. You can change the units strings for the Duration, Input, and Gains in the Inspector now that you can removed the function that was setting them. You can give the figure a new name, Detection Filter GUI (click the figure background instead of one of the controls).

The next step is to add a new panel to the right-hand side of the GUI with edit boxes and buttons for failure parameters uF and tachF. Each items needs a Static Text uicontrol, the edit box, and a push button. The frame with these items added is shown in Figure 9-9.

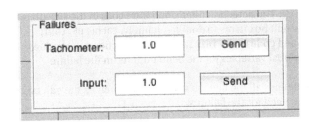

Figure 9-9. A panel with edit box and button uicontrols

Then, you can make the GUI and the panel on the right bigger; insert boxes for the time constants, τ_1 and τ_2; and add two plot axes. You have to leave a lot of room on the left-hand side of the axes for the axis labels. Change the Tag of the top axis to *states* and the bottom axis to *residuals*. The final GUI with all its uicontrols is shown in GUIDE in Figure 9-10. Note that the tags are shown on the axes.

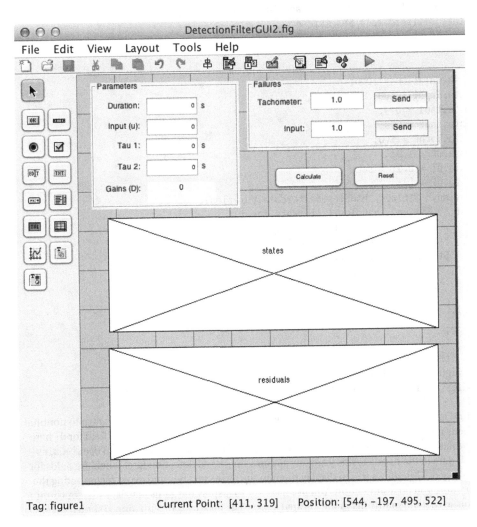

Figure 9-10. Finished GUI shown in GUIDE

Now, you have quite a bit of code to add to the GUI. The detection filter simulation goes in the Calculate callback. You have to add the code to convert the new edit box items to doubles, namely, tachF, uF, tau1, and tau2, as in the duration_Callback. You need to add code to the initialize_gui function to set values of all the fields. Finally, you need to add handling of global variables for the Send buttons on the failure parameters.

First, let's make sure that the initialize function defines all the needed variables and then fix the edit box callbacks. You define the two global variables that you need for the failures.

```
% ----------------------------------------------------------------
function initialize_gui(fig_handle, handles, isreset)

global tachFSent
global inputFSent
% If the filterdata field is present and the reset flag is false, it means
% we are we are just re-initializing a GUI by calling it from the cmd line
% while it is up. So, bail out as we dont want to reset the data.
if isfield(handles, 'filterdata') && ~isreset
    return;
end

handles.filterdata.duration = 1000;
handles.filterdata.input = 100;
handles.filterdata.tau1 = 0.3;
handles.filterdata.tau2 = 0.3;
handles.filterdata.tachF = 1.0;
handles.filterdata.uF = 1.0;
handles.filterdata.dT = 0.1; % sec
handles.filterdata.dF = [];
set(handles.duration, 'String', handles.filterdata.duration);
set(handles.input,    'String', handles.filterdata.input);
set(handles.tau1,    'String', handles.filterdata.tau1);
set(handles.tau2,    'String', handles.filterdata.tau2);
set(handles.uF,    'String', handles.filterdata.uF);
set(handles.tachF,    'String', handles.filterdata.tachF);
set(handles.gains, 'String', '[]');

tachFSent = false;
inputFSent = false;

% Update handles structure
guidata(handles.figure1, handles);
UpdateGains(handles.figure1, [], handles);
```

The reset feature is from the template GUI; you will leave it because it allows a user to return to nominal values for all the fields if they get the filter into an unstable state. Note that you are adding a field for dT here and a variable dF, which stores the detection filter data structure. You add a call to a function UpdateGains after setting the GUI data in the handles; this function updates the stored detection filter when the fields for tau1 or tau2 are changed. This allows you to display them in the gains text box and avoid recomputing the filter matrices every time you do a simulation. You use num2str to display the gains matrix, with a maximum of digits of precision so that the matrix fits in the allotted space. The UpdateGains function is shown here.

```
function UpdateGains(hObject, eventdata, handles)

tau1 = handles.filterdata.tau1;
tau2 = handles.filterdata.tau2;
dT = handles.filterdata.dT;

d = RHSAirTurbine;
dF = DetectionFilter('initialize',d,[tau1;tau2],dT);
handles.filterdata.dF = dF;
set(handles.gains, 'String', num2str(dF.d,3));
guidata(hObject,handles)
```

Now you can update the callbacks for tau1 and tau2. After setting the value in the handles, you call the new update function, just as you did in the initialize function. The function for tau1 is shown next; the same changes must be made to tau2.

```
function tau1_Callback(hObject, eventdata, handles)
% hObject     handle to tau1 (see GCBO)
% eventdata   reserved - to be defined in a future version of MATLAB
% handles     structure with handles and user data (see GUIDATA)

tau1 = str2double(get(hObject, 'String'));
if isnan(tau1)
    set(hObject, 'String', 0);
    errordlg('Input_must_be a_number','Error');
end

% Save the new duration value
handles.filterdata.tau1 = tau1;
guidata(hObject,handles)
UpdateGains(hObject,[],handles);
```

Now, you need to set the Send button callbacks to set the global variables. The Send button tags were set to sendTach and sendInput, respectively. The only code needed in the callbacks is to declare and set the global variables to true. The function for sendInput is shown next; the same changes must be made to sendTach, using the tachFSent global variable.

```
% --- Executes on button press in sendInput.
function sendInput_Callback(hObject, eventdata, handles)
% hObject     handle to sendInput (see GCBO)
% eventdata   reserved 2013 to be defined in a future version of MATLAB
% handles     structure with handles and user data (see GUIDATA)

global inputFSent
inputFSent = true;
```

Now, you are ready to add the Calculate function. It is based on the simulation script from the previous recipe. You add handling of the global variables to change the failure parameters during the simulation loop. You also add real-time plot updates to give the user immediate feedback on the residuals. The TimeLabel function is used to get the scale factor for the time labeling using the duration field, before the simulation loop starts.

You calculate a parameter, dP, for the number of steps between plotting by using floor. Basically, you update the plot 100 times during the simulation. In the loop, you plot dots for the current state, and residuals if the remainder of the current step k divided by dP is zero. Updating graphics using drawnow or by selecting axes in a loop can be very slow, so this is a simple method to limit the time spent on the graphics.

■ **Tip**   Use an inner if statement with rem for intermittent graphics updates during a loop if plotting every step is too slow.

Also note that you use the form of plot where the axes handle can be passed in to avoid making the axes current using axes. MATLAB warns you that doing so can be very slow. However, there is no reason not to do so once the loop is finished, when creating the legends.

```
% --- Executes on button press in calculate.
function calculate_Callback(hObject, eventdata, handles)
% hObject     handle to calculate (see GCBO)
% eventdata   reserved - to be defined in a future version of MATLAB
% handles     structure with handles and user data (see GUIDATA)

global inputFSent
global tachFSent

% get the data from the handles
u = handles.filterdata.input;
duration = handles.filterdata.duration;
tachF = handles.filterdata.tachF;
uF = handles.filterdata.uF;
dT = handles.filterdata.dT;

% initialize the simulation states and arrays
n  = ceil(duration/dT);
x  = [0;0];
d  = RHSAirTurbine;
dF = handles.filterdata.dF;
dF = DetectionFilter('reset',dF);
xP = zeros(4,n);
t  = (0:n-1)*dT;
dP = floor(n/100);

% prepare for plotting during the simulation
[tt,tL] = TimeLabel(duration);
tF = tt/duration;
axes(handles.states)
cla
hold on
axes(handles.residuals)
cla
hold on
xlabel(tL)
```

```
for k = 1:n
  if inputFSent
    inputFSent = false;
    data = guidata(hObject);
    uF = data.filterdata.uF;
  end
  if tachFSent
    tachFSent = false;
    data = guidata(hObject);
    tachF = data.filterdata.tachF;
  end
  y        = [x(1);tachF*x(2)]; % Sensor failure
  xP(:,k) = [x;dF.r];
  dF = DetectionFilter('update',u,y,dF);
  d.u = uF*u; % Actuator failure
  x    = RungeKutta( @RHSAirTurbine, t(k), x, dT, d );
  if rem(k,dP)==0
    plot(handles.states,tF*t(k), xP(1,k),'b.' );
    plot(handles.states,tF*t(k), xP(2,k),'r.' );
    plot(handles.residuals,tF*t(k), xP(3,k), 'b.' );
    plot(handles.residuals,tF*t(k), xP(4,k), 'r.' );
    drawnow
  end
end

% Plot the states and residuals
axes(handles.states)
plot(tF*t, xP(1:2,:) )
legend('p','\omega')
axes(handles.residuals)
plot(tF*t, xP(3:4,:) )
legend('r_p','r_{\omega}')
```

Now, you have a functioning GUI that plots the progress of the simulation and allow you to inject faults at any time. Figure 9-11 shows the result of a simulation with no faults.

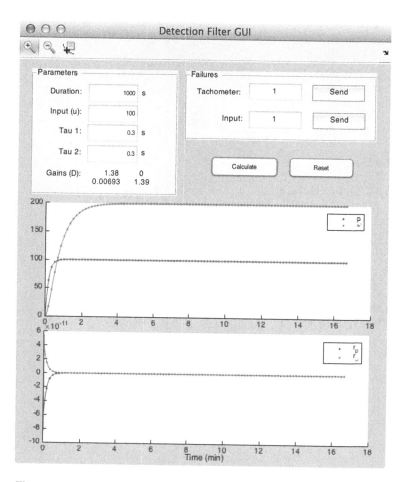

Figure 9-11. *GUI runs with no faults*

You have now built a tool that can be used to explore the parameter space of a model without generating dozens of plot windows. Note that adding a few toolbar buttons to enables the user to zoom or get data points from the plots. Additional features that could be added include menu items, such as saving and reloading particular cases, or exporting a run to the workspace, a mat-file, or a text file. Figure 9-12 shows a run with an input fault injected partway through the simulation. This affects the states as well as the residual. In order to replicate such a run, you would have to record the values of tachF and uF over time along with the initial conditions.

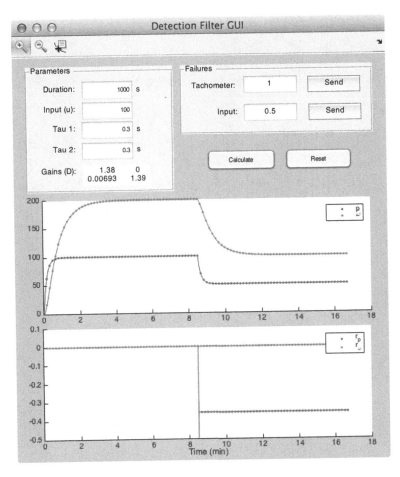

Figure 9-12. *GUI run with injected input fault*

Summary

This chapter demonstrated how to design a detection filter for detecting faults in a dynamical system. The system is demonstrated with an air turbine that can experience a pressure regulator failure and a tachometer failure. In addition, you learned to use GUIDE to design a GUI to automate filter simulations. The GUI demonstrates real-time plotting and injecting failures into an ongoing simulation loop. Table 9-1 lists the code developed in this chapter.

Table 9-1. *Chapter Code Listing*

File	Description
RHSAirTurbine	Air turbine dynamics model in continuous state-space form.
DetectionFilter	Builds and updates a linear detection filter.
DetectionFilterSim	Simulation of a detection filter.
DetectionFilterGUI	Run the detection filter simulation from a GUI.
DetectionFilterGUI.fig	Layout of the GUI for GUIDE.

CHAPTER 10

■ ■ ■

Chemical Processes

In chemical engineering, the production of chemicals needs to be modeled and the production process controlled. Our example will be a simple process in which the pH of a mixed solution needs to be controlled. This problem is interesting because the process is highly nonlinear and the sensor model does not have an explicit solution for the pH measurement. Modeling the sensor will require use of the numerical solver `fzero`.

The specific chemical process that you will study consists of an acid (HNO_3) stream, a buffer ($NaHCO_3$) stream, and a base ($NaOH$) stream that are mixed in a stirred tank.[1] This is based on a bench-scale experiment developed at the University of California, Santa Barbara (UCSB), to study chemical process control.[2] Figure 10-1 shows a diagram of the system, with three incoming streams $q1$, $q2$, and $q3$, and a valve to the output stream $q4$, where you will measure pH. The goal is to achieve a neutral pH.

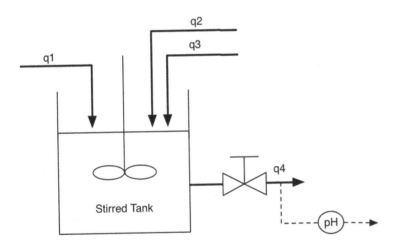

Figure 10-1. *Chemical mixing problem*

[1]Henson, M. A. and D. E. Seborg, *Nonlinear Process Control*, Prentice-Hall, 1997.
[2]Henson, M. and D. Seborg, "Adaptive Nonlinear Control of a pH Neutralization Process", *IEEE Transactions on Control Systems Technology*, vol. 2, no. 3, August 1994.

Electronic supplementary material The online version of this chapter (doi:10.1007/978-1-4842-0559-4_10) contains supplementary material, which is available to authorized users.

S. Thomas and M. Paluszek, *MATLAB Recipes*, DOI 10.1007/978-1-4842-0559-4_10

10-1. Modeling the Chemical Mixing Process

Problem

You want to model the chemical process consisting of an acid stream, a buffer stream, and a base stream that are mixed in a stirred tank.

Solution

Model the chemical equilibria by adding two reaction invariants for each inlet stream and write the dynamical equations using the invariants. These are coded in a right-hand-side function that also defines the model data structure.

How It Works

Reaction invariants are quantities whose values do not change during a reaction. Each is a combination of chemicals that do not vary. The inputs are nitric acid (HNO_3), sodium bicarbonate or baking soda ($NaHCO_3$), and sodium hydroxide or lye ($NaOH$). There is a pair of invariants for each input stream i. The two reaction invariants W_a and W_b are

$$W_{ai} = \left[H^+\right]_i - \left[OH^-\right]_i - \left[HCO_3^-\right]_i - 2\left[CO_3^=\right]_i \tag{10.1}$$

$$W_{bi} = \left[H_2CO_3\right]_i + \left[HCO_3^-\right]_i + \left[CO_3^=\right]_i \tag{10.2}$$

$I = 1$ is for the acid stream, $I = 2$ for the buffer stream, $i = 3$ for the base stream, and $i = 4$ is for the mixed effluent. The dynamical equations for the effluent invariants are derived via mass balances to be

$$\dot{W}_{a4} = \frac{1}{Ah}(W_{a1} - W_{a4})q_1 + \frac{1}{Ah}(W_{a2} - W_{a4})q_2 + \frac{1}{Ah}(W_{a3} - W_{a4})q_3 \tag{10.3}$$

$$\dot{W}_{b4} = \frac{1}{Ah}(W_{b1} - W_{b4})q_1 + \frac{1}{Ah}(W_{b2} - W_{b4})q_2 + \frac{1}{Ah}(W_{b3} - W_{b4})q_3 \tag{10.4}$$

where q_i is the volumetric flow rates for the ith stream, A is the cross-sectional area of the mixing tank, and h is the liquid level. The liquid level is governed by a differential equation

$$\dot{h} = \frac{1}{A}\left[q_1 + q_2 + q_3 - C_v(h+z)^n\right] \tag{10.5}$$

where C_v is the valve coefficient, n is the valve exponent, and z is the vertical distance between the bottom of the mixing tank and the outlet of the effluent stream. You can measure h. Normally, you need to estimate the reaction invariants, but for this problem, you will assume they are measured. These equations are all first-order and are therefore the state equations for the system. The flow rates are all multiplied by the states, meaning that their influence on the derivatives is a product of the states and the streams. The differential equations for the effluent invariants are singular when $h = 0$. This is because if the tank is empty, the flows have to be zero.

The resulting right-hand-side function, RHSpH, is shown next. It follows the format needed by the RungeKutta integrator (see Recipe 6-2)—that is, RHS(t,x,d)—with a tilde replacing the first input, because the dynamics are independent of time. Note the data structure that is defined and returned if there are no inputs. This model has quite a few parameters, which are documented in the header.

```
%% RHSpH Dynamics of a chemical mixing process.
% The process consists of an acid (HNO3) stream, buffer (NaHCO3) stream,
% and base (NaOH) stream that are mixed in a stirred tank. The mixed effluent
% exits the tank through a valve. The chemical equilibria is modeled by
% introducing two reaction invariants for each inlet stream. i = 1 for the
% acid, i = 2 for the buffer, i = 3 for the base, and i = 4 for the effluent.
%
%              +        -          -         =
%   wAi = [H ]i - [OH ]i - [HCO3 ]i - 2[CO3 ]i
%
%                         -         =
%   wBi = [H2CO3]i + [HCO3 ]i + 2[CO3 ]i
%
%% Forms
%   d = RHSpH
%   xDot = RHSpH( t, x, d )
%
%% Inputs
%   t           (1,1) Time, unused
%   x           (3,1) State [wA4;wB4;h]
%   d           (.)   Structure
%                     .wA1      (1,1) Acid invariant A, (M)
%                     .wA2      (1,1) Buffer invariant A, (M)
%                     .wA3      (1,1) Base invariant A, (M)
%                     .wB1      (1,1) Acid invariant B, (M)
%                     .wB2      (1,1) Buffer invariant B, (M)
%                     .wB3      (1,1) Base invariant B, (M)
%                     .a        (1,1) Cross-sectional area of mixing tank (cm2)
%                     .cV       (1,1) Valve coefficient
%                     .n        (1,1) Valve exponent
%                     .z        (1,1) Vertical distance between bottom of
%                                     tank and outlet of effluent (cm)
%                     .q1       (1,1) Volumetric flow of HNO3 (ml/s)
%                     .q2       (1,1) Volumetric flow of NaHCO3 (ml/s)
%                     .q3       (1,1) Volumetric flow of NaOH (ml/s)
%
%% Outputs
%   xDot        (3,1) State derivative
%
%% Reference
% Henson, M. A. and D. E. Seborg. (1997.) Nonlinear Process
% Control, Prentice-Hall. pp. 207-210.
```

```
function xDot = RHSpH( ~, x, d )

if( nargin < 1 )
  % Note: Cv was omitted in the reference; we calculated it assuming a constant
  % liquid level in the tank of 14 cm.
  d = struct('wA1',0.003,'wA2',-0.03,'wA3',-3.05e-3,...
             'wB1',0.0, 'wB2', 0.03,'wB3', 5.0e-5,...
             'a',207,'cV',4.5860777,'n',0.607,'z',11.5,...
             'q1',16.6,'q2',0.55,'q3',15.6);
  xDot = d;
  return;
end

wA4 = x(1);
wB4 = x(2);
h   = x(3);

hA   =  1/(h*d.a);

xDot  = [hA*( (d.wA1 - wA4)*d.q1 + (d.wA2 - wA4)*d.q2 + (d.wA3 - wA4)*d.q3 );...
         hA*( (d.wB1 - wB4)*d.q1 + (d.wB2 - wB4)*d.q2 + (d.wB3 - wB4)*d.q3 );...
         d.q1 + d.q2 + d.q3 - d.cV*(h + d.z)^d.n];
```

The default values in the data structure are drawn from the data in the reference, with the exception of C_v; this was neglected by the reference, so we calculated a value for an equilibrium tank level.

```
ans =

  wA1: 0.003
  wA2: -0.03
  wA3: -0.00305
  wB1: 0
  wB2: 0.03
  wB3: 5e - 05
    a: 207
   cV: 4.5861
    n: 0.607
    z: 11.5
   q1: 16.6
   q2: 0.55
   q3: 15.6
```

The goal of this chapter is to design an equilibrium point controller. We could rewrite the equations as linear equations in which each state and input is replaced with, for example,

$$q_3 = q_{30} + \delta q_3 \tag{10.6}$$

$$h = h_0 + \delta h \tag{10.7}$$

where δq_3 is small. We could then formally derive the linear control system. However, we will leave that for the interested reader and just go ahead and implement a linear control system.

10-2. Sensing the pH of the Chemical Process

Problem

The pH sensor is modeled by a nonlinear equation that cannot be solved explicitly for pH.

Solution

Use the MATLAB fzero function to solve for pH.

How It Works

The equation for pH is

$$0 = W_{a4} + 10^{(\text{pH}-14)} - 10^{-\text{pH}} + W_{b4}\frac{1+2\times10^{(\text{pH}-pK_2)}}{1+10^{(pK_1-\text{pH})}+10^{(\text{pH}-pK_2)}} \tag{10.8}$$

Recall that W_{a4} and W_{b4} are the reaction invariants for the mixed effluent as defined in Recipe 10-1. pK_1 and pK_2 are the base-10 logarithms of the H_2CO_3 and HCO_3^- disassociation constants.

$$pK_a = -\log_{10} K_a$$

The function that generates the measurement is PHSensor.

```
%% PHSensor Model pH measurement of a mixing process
% Compute pH as a function of wA4 and wB4 and also the slope of pH with
% respect to those states. Requires the use of fzero.
%
%%  Forms
%    pH = PHSensor( x, d )
%    d = PHSensor('struct')
%
%%  Inputs
%    x   (2,:) State [wA4;wB4]
%    d   (.)   Data structure
%              .pK1      (1,1) Base 10 log of a disassociation constant (H2CO3)
%              .pK2      (1,1) Base 10 log of a disassociation constant (HCO3-)
%
%% Outputs
%    pH (:,:) pH of the solution
%
%% Reference
% Henson, M. A. and D. E. Seborg. Nonlinear Process control, Prentice-Hall,
% 1997. pp. 207-210.
```

The body of PHSensor calls fzero to compute the pH. This requires an objective function that will be searched for a zero near the input point. Use a neutral pH of 7.0 as the initial condition for the optimization. The function is vectorized for multiple input states, computing a square matrix of pH with the combinations of W_{a4} and W_{b4}.

```
% Compute the pH starting from neutral
n    = size(x,2);
pH   = zeros(n,n);
pH0  = 7.0;
for  k = 1:n
  for j = 1:n
    d.wA4 = x(1,k);
    d.wB4 = x(2,j);
    pH(k,j) = fzero( @Fun, pH0, [], d );
  end
end
```

■ **Tip** Use fzero to solve for the zero point for complex single equations. Use fminzero for sets of equations with multiple values to be found that minimize the function.

Notice that as per our usual pattern, we have defined a data structure d for passing data to the sensor model. Our two parameters are pK_1 and pK_2.

```
if( ischar(x) )
  pH = struct('pK1',-log10(4.47e-7),'pK2',-log10(5.62e-11));
  return
end
```

Equation 10.8 is embodied in the subfunction Fun, which is passed to fzero.

```
function y = Fun( pH, d )
%%% PHSensor>Fun Function to be zeroed via fzero
%  y = Fun( pH, d )

y  = d.wA4 + 10^(Ph - 14) - 10^(-pH) ...
        + d.wB4*(1 + 2*10^(pH - d.pK2))/(1 + 10^(d.pK1 - pH) + 10^(pH - d.pK2));
```

A demo is included in the function, as suggested in the best practices described in the style recipes. The demo specifies a range of values for the states-the invariants—based on the numbers in the reference.

```
% Demo
if( nargin < 1 )
  x(1,:) = linspace(-9e-4,0);
  x(2,:) = linspace(0,1e-3);
  d      = PHSensor('struct');
  PHSensor( x, d );
  return
end
```

The results are plotted at the end of the main function.

```
if( nargout == 0 )
  h = figure;
  set(h,'Name','PH_Sensor');
  mesh(pH)
  xlabel('WB4');
  ylabel('WA4');
  zlabel('pH')
  grid on
  rotate3d on

  clear pH
end
```

The plotting uses the mesh function. It is important to remember that the rows of p correspond to W_{a4} and the columns to W_{b4}. Columns are x and rows are y in the mesh plot. Figure 10-2 shows the mesh plot and also the alternative surf plot (with 'edgecolor' set to 'none'). Note the two MATLAB commands:

grid on
rotate3d on

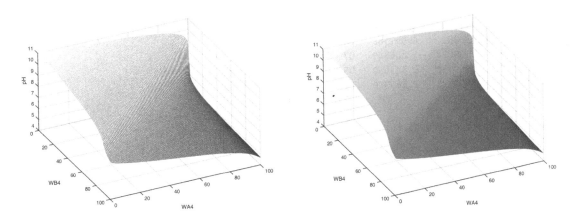

Figure 10-2. surf *and* mesh *plots of the pH sensor output*

Always use the on to be certain that the commands are executed rather than toggled; otherwise, you can get unexpected results if you have just run another script or function with those commands.

Notice that the relationship between the pH and the reaction invariants is highly nonlinear. You would ideally like a relationship

$$pH = c \begin{bmatrix} W_{a4} \\ W_{b4} \end{bmatrix} \tag{10.9}$$

where c is a 2 × 2 matrix with constant coefficients. This might be true in the flat regions, but it is not true in the "waterfall" region.

When using this function in a simulation, you need it to run as fast as possible, without any diagnostics installed for fzero. During debugging, however, you may need addition information. fzero can display information on each iteration by setting the Display option. For instance, with the 'iter' setting it will print information for each iteration. The updated fzero call is

```
pH(k,j) = fzero( @Fun, pH0, optimset('Display','iter'), d );
```

and the results for a single state are

```
>> d = PHSensor('struct')
d =
    pK1: 6.3497
    pK2: 10.25

>> pH = PHSensor( [-4.32e - 4;5.28e - 4], d )

Search for an interval around 7 containing a sign change:
Func-count      a          f(a)             b          f(b)           Procedure
    1                 7  -2.39821e - 07          7  -2.39821e - 07    initial interval
    3           6.80201  -4.16536e - 05    7.19799   3.09792e - 05    search

Search for a zero in the interval [6.80201, 7.19799]:
Func-count     x          f(x)                Procedure.
    3        7.19799    3.09792e - 05         initial
    4        7.0291     4.96758e - 06         interpolation
    5        7.00028   -1.88684e - 07         interpolation
    6        7.00133    3.84365e - 09         interpolation
    7        7.00131    2.86799e - 12         interpolation
    8        7.00131           0 ˙            interpolation

Zero found in the interval [6.80201, 7.19799]

pH =

      7.0013
```

This was a very rapid solution, as it is very near the starting point of 7.0. Note that fzero first found an interval containing a sign change, and then searched for the zero. fzero can also output diagnostic information when complete, instead of printing it during operation. For instance, if the call is

```
[pH(k,j),fval,exitflag,output] = fzero( @Fun, pH0, [], d );
```

then the output structure is available, such as

```
output =

    intervaliterations: 1
             iterations: 5
              funcCount: 8
              algorithm: 'bisection,_interpolation'
                message: 'Zero_found_in_the_interval_[6.80201,_7.19799]'
```

Note that the algorithm used, bisection, is listed along with the total number of iterations and function evaluations. Consider a slight variation of the input state, lowering W_{b4} to $4e^{-4}$ M. The number of iterations jumps significantly.

```
>> pH = PHSensor( [-4.32e-4;4e-4], d )
output =

    intervaliterations: 8
            iterations: 7
             funcCount: 24
             algorithm: 'bisection,_interpolation'
               message: 'Zero_found_in_the_interval_[4.76,_9.24]'
pH =
        9.022
```

In particular, note that viewing the diagnostic information for your problem can help confirm if your tolerances are suitable. Consider the final iterations of the previous case.

```
Search for a zero in the interval [4.76, 9.24]:
 Func-count      x          f(x)            Procedure
    17          9.24    2.04571e - 05       initial
    18       9.04068    1.42294e - 06       interpolation
    19       9.02583    2.87604e - 07       interpolation
    20       9.02207    5.59178e - 09       interpolation
    21       9.02199    2.25694e - 11       interpolation
    22       9.02199     1.7808e - 15       interpolation
    23       9.02199    5.42101e - 20       interpolation
    24       9.02199    5.42101e - 20       interpolation
```

The search pushed the function value all the way down to 5.4e – 20, which may be more restrictive than needed. The default tolerances can be viewed by getting the default options structure using optimset.

```
>> options = optimset('fzero')

options =

        Display: 'notify'
     MaxFunEvals: []
         MaxIter: []
          TolFun: []
            TolX: 2.2204e - 16
     FunValCheck: 'off'
       OutputFcn: []
        PlotFcns: []
```

The default tolerance on the function value, TolX, is 2.2204e-16. Note that you passed in the name of the selected optimization routine, fzero, to optimiset. The same can be done with fminbnd and fminsearch.

■ **Tip** Use optimset with the name of the optimization function to get the default options structure.

Now consider that you want to evaluate how fzero performs over a range of inputs. Assume that you create a separate function for Fun and make a script to record extra data from output during a run. Figure 10-3 shows a plot using pcolor. of the resulting recorded function evaluations. You can see the rapid changes due to the nonlinearities of the model. The maximum number of function evaluations does not exceed 35.

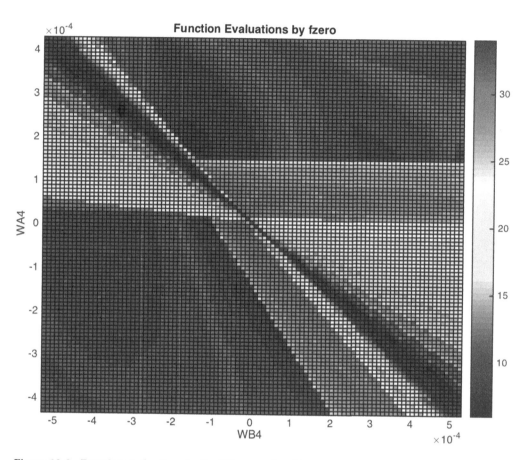

Figure 10-3. *Function evaluations for the PHSensor algorithm*

The following is the augmented code creating the plot.

```
%% Script for debugging PHSensor algorithm

% Nominal operating conditions from the reference
x10 = -4.32e - 4;
x20 = 5.28e - 4;

x       = [];
x(1,:) = linspace(2*x10,0);
x(2,:) = linspace(0,2*x20);
d       = PHSensor('struct');
```

```
% Compute the pH starting from neutral
n     = size(x,2);
pH    = zeros(n,n);
fEvals = zeros(n,n);
pH0 = 7.0;
for k = 1:n
  for j = 1:n
    d.wA4 = x(1,k);
    d.wB4 = x(2,j);
    % Options: TolX, Display, FunValCheck
    % ('TolX',1e - 10);
    % ('Display','iter')
    % ('FunValCheck','on') % no errors found for demo
    options = optimset('FunValCheck','on');
    [pH(k,j),fval,exitflag,output] = fzero( @Fun, pH0, options, d );
    fEvals(k,j) = output.funcCount;
  end
end

figure('Name','PH_Sensor');
surf(pH,'edgecolor','none')
xlabel('WB4');
ylabel('WA4');
zlabel('pH')
grid on
rotate3d on

figure('Name','Evaluations')
s = pcolor(x(2,:),x(1,:),fEvals);
set(s,'edgecolor','none')
xlabel('WB4');
ylabel('WA4');
colormap jet
title('Function_Evaluations_by_fzero')
```

10-3. Controlling the Effluent pH

Problem

You want to control the pH level in the mixing tank when the flow of acid or base varies.

Solution

You will vary the base stream, $i = 3$, to maintain the pH. This means changing the value of q_3 using a proportional integral controller. This allows you to handle step disturbances.

How It Works

A proportional integral controller is of the form

$$u = K\left(1 + \frac{1}{\tau}\int\right) y \tag{10.10}$$

where u is the control, y is the measurement, τ is the integrator time constant, and K is the forward (proportional) gain. The control is $u = q_3$ and the measurement is $y = $ pH. There is one control, q_3, and one output, pH. This makes this a single-input/single-output process. However, the connection between q_3 and pH involves three dynamical states: h, W_{a4}, and W_{b4}. The relationship between the states and pH is nonlinear. Another issue is that q_3 cannot be negative; that is, you cannot extract the base from the tank. This should not pose a problem if the equilibrium q_3 is high enough.

Despite these potential problems, this very simple controller works for this problem for a fairly wide range of disturbances. The equilibrium value is input with a perturbation that has an proportional and integral term. The integral term uses simpler Euler integration. The full script is described in the next recipe; here, attention is called to the lines implementing the control.

The control variables are defined next. The pH setpoint is neutral; that is, a pH of 7. kF is the forward gain and tau is the time constant from equation 10.10, set to 2 and 60 seconds, respectively. q3Set is the nominal setpoint for the base flow rate, taken from the reference.

```
%% Control design
pHSet   = 7.0;
tau     = 60.0; % (sec)
kF      = 2.0;  % forward gain
q3Set   = 15.6; % (ml/s)
```

The following code snippet shows the implementation that takes place in a loop. The error is calculated as the difference between the modeled pH measurement and the pH setpoint. Note the Euler integration, where intErr is updated using simply the timestep times the error. Note also that there is a flag, controlIsOn, which allows you to run the script in open loop, without the control being applied.

```
% Proportional-integral Control
err = pH - pHSet;
if controlIsOn
  d.q3   = q3Set - kF*(err + intErr/tau);
  intErr = intErr + dT*err;
else
  d.q3 = q3Set;
end
```

To rigorously determine the forward gain and time constant for this problem, you would need to linearize the right-hand side for the simulation at the operating point and do a rigorous single-input/single-output control design that involves Bode plots, Root-Locus, and other techniques. This is beyond the scope of this book. For now, simply select values that produce a reasonable response.

10-4. Simulating the Controlled pH Process

Problem

You want to simulate the stirred tank, mixing three streams—acid, buffer, and base—to demonstrate control of the pH level. The base stream is the control variable in response to perturbations in the buffer and acid streams.

Solution

Write a script PHProcessSim with the controller, starting at an equilibrium state. Use the proportional-integral controller as derived in the previous recipe. The script will be structured to allow you to insert pulses in either or both the acid and buffer streams.

How It Works

The disturbances d are deviations in q_1 and q_2,

$$d = \begin{bmatrix} q_1 \\ q_2 \end{bmatrix} \qquad (10.11)$$

which are the acid and buffer streams. The base stream is q_3 and the reaction invariants for the mixed effluent are W_{a4} and W_{b4}.

Specify the user inputs to the script first. You are putting it into an equilibrium state and will investigate small disturbances from steady-state. There is a flag, controlIsOn, for turning the control system on or off. The timestep and duration are determined by iterating over a few values.

```
%% User inputs

% Time (sec)
tEnd = 60*60;
dT = 1.0;

% States
wA4 = -4.32e-4; % Reaction invariant A for effluent stream (M)
wB4 = 5.28e-4; % Reaction invariant B for effluent stream (M)
h   = 14.0; % liquid level (cm)

% Closed or open loop
controlIsOn = true;
```

The disturbances are modeled as pulses to d.q1 and d.q2. The user parameters are the size and the start/stop times of the pulses. This setup allows you to run cases similar to the reference.

```
% Disturbances
% The pulses will be applied according to the start and end times of tPulse:
%    q1 = q10 + deltaQ1; and q2 = q20 + deltaQ2;
% Small pulse: 0.65 ml/s in q2
% Large pulses: 2.0 ml/s
```

```
% Very large pulses: 8.0 ml/s
deltaQ1 = 8.0; % +/- 1.5
deltaQ2 = 0.0; % 0.65 1.45 0.45 - 0.55 % values from reference
tPulse1 = [5 15]*60;
```

In the remainder of the script, you obtain the data structures defined in the previous recipes, specify the control parameters, and create the simulation loop. The measurements of the invariants are assumed to be exact; in practice, they need to be estimated. However, you should always test the controller under ideal conditions first to understand its behavior without complications. The pH measurement is modeled using PHSensor from Recipe 10-2. The right-hand side for the process is defined in Recipe 10-1. Integration is performed using the RungeKutta defined in Chapter 6.

```
%% Data format
dSensor = PHSensor('struct');
d       = RHSpH;

%% Control design
pHSet = 7.0;
tau   = 60.0; % (sec)
kF    = 2.0; % forward gain
q3Set = 15.6; % (ml/s)
q10   = d.q1;
q20   = d.q2;

%% Run the simulation

% Number of sim steps
n = ceil(tEnd/dT);

% Plotting arrays
xP = zeros(7,n);
t  = (0:n - 1)*dT;

% Initial states
x       = [wA4;wB4;h];
intErr = 0;

for k = 1:n
  % Measurement
  dSensor.wA4 = x(1);
  dSensor.wB4 = x(2);
  pH          = PHSensor( x, dSensor );

  % Proportional-integral Control
  err = pH - pHSet;
  if controlIsOn
    d.q3 = q3Set - kF*(err + intErr/tau);
    intErr = intErr + dT*err;
  else
    d.q3 = q3Set;
  end
```

```
% Disturbance
if( t(k) > tPulse1(1) && t(k) < tPulse1(2) )
   d.q1 = q10 + deltaQ1;
else
   d.q1 = q10;
end

if( t(k) > tPulse2(1) && t(k) < tPulse2(2) )
   d.q2 = q20 + deltaQ2;
else
   d.q2 = q20;
end

% Store data for plotting
xP(:,k) = [x;pH;d.q1;d.q2;d.q3];

% Integrate one step
x = RungeKutta( @RHSpH, 0, x, dT, d );
end

%% Plot
[t,tL] = TimeLabel(t);
yL     = {'W_{a4}' 'W_{b4}' 'h' 'pH' 'q_1' 'q_2' 'q_3'};
tTL    = 'PH_Process_Control';
if ~controlIsOn
   tTL = [tTL '_-_Open_Loop'];
end
PlotSet( t, xP,'x_label',tL,'y_label',yL,'plot_title',tTL,'figure_title',tTL)
PlotSet( t, xP([4 7],:),'x_label',tL,'y_label',yL([4 7]),'plot_title',tTL,
         'figure_title',tTL)
```

Now, you give results for running this script with some different pulses. The nominal plot gives all three states: the measured pH, the flow rates for the acid, base, and the buffer streams. A more compact plot shows just the pH and the commanded value of q_3. We added a line in the plotting code to amend the plot title for an open-loop response, so that if you run the script repeatedly, you can more easily identify the plots.

■ **Tip**   Use your control flags and string variables to customize the names of your plots.

Figure 10-4 shows the closed response with no disturbances at all, run for 30 simulated minutes. You can see that the values from the reference have not produced an exact equilibrium, but that the values achieved are quite close. Reaction invariant W_{b4} changes by less than 0.005×10^{-4}; the liquid level h by less than 0.1 cm; and the base flow rate q_3 by about 0.05 ml/s. This is equivalent to a very small step response. Note the settling time is about 5 minutes. These results give you confidence that you have coded the problem correctly. You see this initial response in the following simulations, before the perturbations are applied.

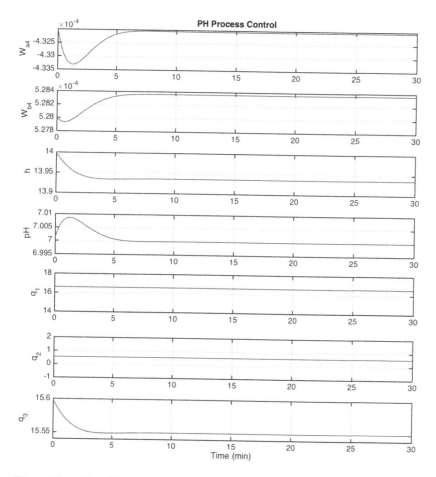

Figure 10-4. *Closed-loop response with no perturbations*

Next, Figure 10-5 shows the open-loop response with a pulse of 0.65 ml/s in the buffer stream, starting at 20 minutes and ending at 40 minutes. Note that the pH rises to nearly 7.4 and q_3 does in fact stay constant at the setpoint. Figure 10-6 shows the closed-loop transients in the pH and base flow q_3. The pH rise is limited to less than 7.2 and the pH and base flow rate are reach equilibrium within about 10 minutes of the start and end of the pulse. This compares favorably with the plots in the reference, which compare adaptive and nonadaptive nonlinear control schemes.

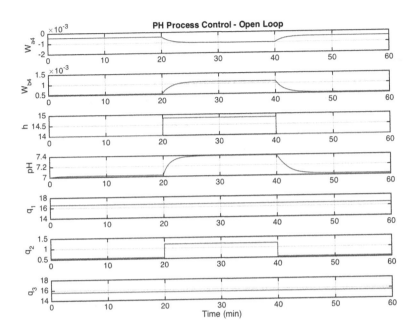

Figure 10-5. *Open-loop response with a 0.65 ml/s pulse in q_2*

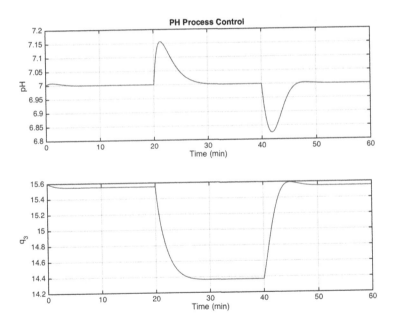

Figure 10-6. *Performance of the controller with a 0.65 ml/s pulse in q_2*

Figure 10-7 shows the transients with larger, offset perturbations of 2 ml/s in both q_1 and q_2. The pulse in q_1 is applied from 5 to 15 minutes and the pulse in q_2 from 25 to 40 minutes. Figure 10-8 has plots of just the pH and control flow q_3.

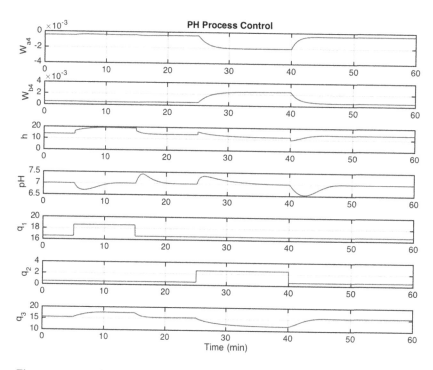

Figure 10-7. *Performance of the controller with large perturbations of 2 ml/s in q1 and q2*

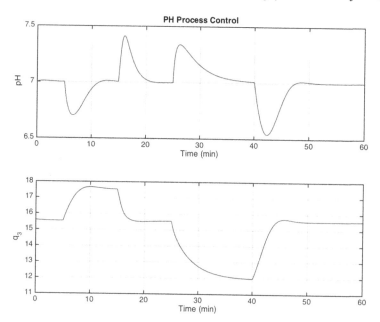

Figure 10-8. *Larger plots of the q1 /q2 perturbation results*

Figure 10-9 shows the transients with a very large perturbation in q_2 of 8 ml/s from 5 to 35 minutes. The controller no longer works very well, with a much longer settling time than the previous examples and the base flow rate q_3 still dropping at the end of the pulse. A pulse value of 10 ml/s causes the simulation to "blow up," or produce imaginary values. It is always necessary to see the limits of the control performance in a nonlinear system.

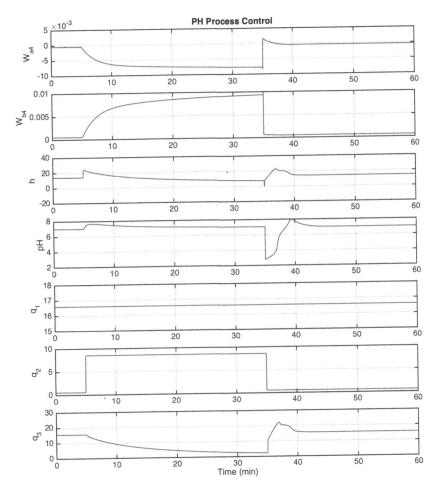

Figure 10-9. *Performance of the controller with a very large perturbation (8 ml/s) in q_2*

Finally, since you are using a numerical optimization routine, it is instructive to profile the simulation to determine the proportion of execution time spent on fzero. The Profiler can be accessed from the Command Window button called Run and Time. The summary from running the pH simulation is shown in Figure 10-10. Out of nearly 19 seconds spent in the simulation, fully 12.6 seconds are spent inside fzero itself. Only 4.4 seconds were spent integrating, of which 3.4 seconds were spent in the right-hand side. The summary has hyperlinks to the individual functions, which are timed line by line. Figure 10-11 shows the time spent inside fzero, with percentages calculated in addition to absolute times. The objective function, PHSensor > Fun, was called 56,131 times, taking only 1.27 seconds (10% of the execution time). Significant chunks of time were spent in sprintf and optimget.

■ **Tip** Always do a run with the Profiler when you are implementing a numerical search or optimization routine. This gives you insight into the number of iterations used and any unsuspected bugs in your code.

In this case, there is not much optimization that can be done, as most of the time is spent in fzero itself and not in the objective function, but you wouldn't have known that without running the analysis. Whenever you are using numerical tools and have a script or function taking more than a second or two to run, analysis with Profiler is merited.

Profile Summary
Generated 22-Jun-2015 10:46:05 using cpu time.

Function Name	Calls	Total Time	Self Time*	Total Time Plot (dark band = self time)
PHProcessSim	1	18.839 s	0.734 s	
PHSensor	7201	13.402 s	0.754 s	
fzero	7200	12.648 s	8.363 s	
RungeKutta	7200	4.405 s	0.962 s	
RHSpH	28801	3.442 s	3.442 s	
optimget	36000	2.192 s	1.012 s	
PHSensor>Fun	56131	1.270 s	1.270 s	
optimget>optimgetfast	36000	1.181 s	1.181 s	
fcnchk	7200	0.823 s	0.823 s	
PlotSet	2	0.288 s	0.089 s	
graph2d/...e/subplotHGUsingMATLABClasses	9	0.069 s	0.060 s	
subplot	9	0.069 s	0.000 s	

Figure 10-10. *Profiler summary from the simulation*

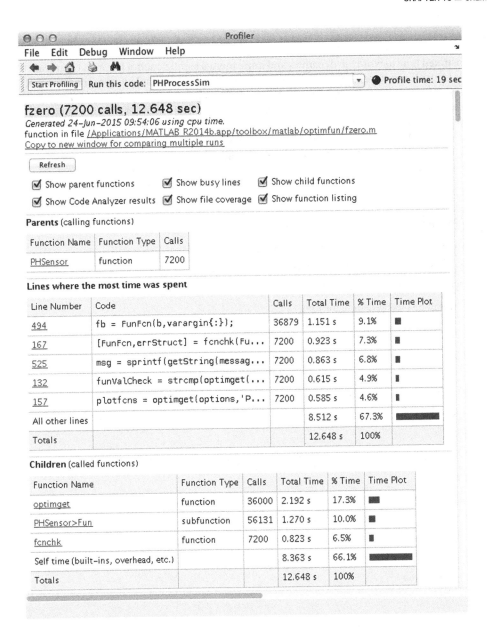

Figure 10-11. Profiler results for fzero

Summary

This chapter demonstrated how to write the dynamics and implement a simple control law for a chemical process. The process is highly nonlinear, but you can control the process with a simple proportional integral controller. The pH sensor does not have a closed form solution and you need the MATLAB `fzero` function to find pH from the invariants. The use of MATLAB plotting functions `mesh` and `surf` for showing three-dimensional data were demonstrated. You used a simulation script to evaluate the performance of the controller for a variety of conditions and to run the script in the Profiler to analyze the time spent on the numerical routines. Table 10-1 lists the code developed in this chapter.

Table 10-1. *Chapter Code Listing*

File	Description
PHSensor	Model pH measurement of a mixing process.
PHProcessSim	Simulation of a pH neutralization process.
RHSpH	Dynamics of a chemical mixing process.
SensorTest	Script to test the sensor algorithm.

CHAPTER 11

Aircraft

Our aircraft model is a three-dimensional point mass. This models only the translational dynamics in three dimensions. Translation is motion in the x, y, and z directions. An aircraft controls its motion by changing its orientation with respect to the wind (banking and angle of attack) and by changing the thrust its engine produces. In our model we assume that our airplane can instantaneously change its orientation and thrust for control purposes. This simplifies our model but at the same time allows us to simulate most aircraft operations, such as takeoff, level flight and landing. We also assume that the mass of the aircraft does not vary with time.

11-1. Creating a Dynamic Model of an Aircraft

Problem

You need a numerical model to simulate the three-dimensional trajectory of an aircraft in the atmosphere. The model should allow you to demonstrate control of the aircraft from takeoff to landing.

Solution

You will build a six-state model using flight path coordinates. The controls will be roll angle, angle of attack, and thrust. You will not simulate the attitude dynamics of the aircraft. The attitude dynamics are necessary if you want to simulate how long it takes for the aircraft to change angle of attack and roll angle. In our model, you assume the aircraft can instantaneously change angle of attack, roll angle, and thrust.

How It Works

Our aircraft will have six states, needed to simulate velocity and position in three dimensions, and three controls. The controls are roll angle, ϕ; angle of attack, α; and thrust, T. You aren't going to use Cartesian coordinates and their time derivatives (i.e., velocities) as states; instead, you will use flight path coordinates. Flight path coordinates are shown in two dimensions in Figure 11-1. Roll, ϕ, is about the x axis and heading ψ is out of the page. Drag, D, is opposite the velocity vector.

Electronic supplementary material The online version of this chapter (doi:10.1007/978-1-4842-0559-4_11) contains supplementary material, which is available to authorized users.

S. Thomas and M. Paluszek, *MATLAB Recipes*, DOI 10.1007/978-1-4842-0559-4_11

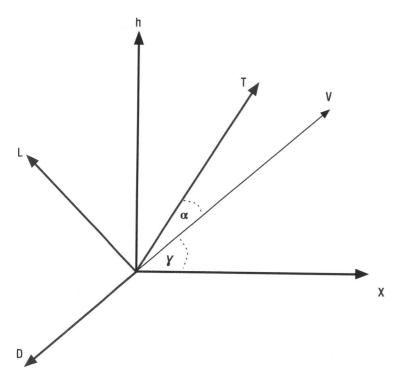

Figure 11-1. *Flight path coordinates in two dimensions*

The angle of attack, α, is adjusted to change the lift, L, and drag. The thrust vector, T, is aligned with the body x axis. The flight path angle, γ, is the angle between the x axis and the velocity vector, V. The state vector, s, is

$$s = \begin{bmatrix} v \\ \dot{\gamma} \\ \psi \\ x \\ y \\ h \end{bmatrix} \tag{11.1}$$

v is the velocity magnitude; γ is the flight path angle in the xz plane; ψ is the angle in the xy plane; x,y,h are the Cartesian coordinates. h is altitude, or the z coordinate. The dynamical equations are

$$
\begin{bmatrix} \dot{v} \\ \dot{\gamma} \\ \dot{\psi} \\ \dot{x} \\ \dot{y} \\ \dot{h} \end{bmatrix} = \begin{bmatrix} \dfrac{T\cos\alpha - D}{m} - g\cos\gamma \\ \dfrac{(L+T\sin\alpha)\cos\phi - mg\cos\gamma}{mv} \\ \dfrac{(L+T\sin\alpha)\sin\phi}{mv\cos\gamma} \\ v\cos\gamma\cos\psi \\ v\cos\gamma\sin\psi \\ v\sin\gamma \end{bmatrix}
\tag{11.2}
$$

g is the gravitational acceleration, m is mass, D is drag force, and L is lift force. Define the dynamic pressure as

$$
q = \frac{1}{2}\rho v^2
\tag{11.3}
$$

where ρ is the atmospheric density. Our simple lift and drag model is

$$
D = qs\left(C_{D_0} + kC_L^2\right)
\tag{11.4}
$$

$$
L = qsC_L
\tag{11.5}
$$

$$
C_L = C_{L_\alpha}\alpha
\tag{11.6}
$$

The first equation is called the drag polar. C_{D_0} is the drag at zero lift. k is the drag from lift coupling coefficient. s is the wetted area. This lift model is only valid for small angles of attack α, as it does not account for stall, which is when the airflow becomes detached from the wing and lift goes to zero rapidly.

Our RHS function that implements these equations is RHSAircraft. Notice that the equations are singular when $v = 0$ in equation 11.2. The header provides a warning about this singularity.

```
%% RHSAIRCRAFT Six DOF point mass aircraft model.
%% Form:
%   d                   = RHSAircraft;
%   [sDot, D, LStar] = RHSAircraft( t, s, d )
%% Description
% Computes the right hand side for a point mass aircraft. If you call it
% without any arguments, it will return the default data structure.
% sDot(2) and sDot(3) will be infinite when v = 0. The default atmosphere
% model is AtmosphericDensity which uses an exponential atmosphere.
%
%% Inputs
%   t    (1,1)    Time (unused)
%   s    (6,1)    State vector [v;gamma;psi;x;y;h]
%   d    (.)      Data structure
%                 .m              (1,1) Aircraft mass
%                 .g              (1,1) Gravitational acceleration
%                 .thrust         (1,1) Thrust
```

```
%                      .alpha              (1,1) Angle of attack
%                      .phi                (1,1) Roll angle
%                      .s                  (1,1) Surface area
%                      .cD0                (1,1) Zero lift drag
%                      .k                  (1,1) Lift drag coupling term
%                      .cLAlpha            (1,1) Lift coefficient
%                      .density            (1,1) Pointer to the atmospheric
%                                                density function
%
%% Outputs
%   sDot  (6,1)  State vector derivative d[v;gamma;psi;x;y;h]/dt
%   D     (1,1)  Drag
%   LStar (1,1)  Lift/angle of attack
```

The function body is shown next. Assemble the state derivative, sDot, as one array since the terms are simple. Each element is on a separate line for readability. Return D and LStar as auxiliary outputs for use by the equilibrium calculation.

```matlab
function [sDot, D, LStar] = RHSAircraft( ˜, s, d )

% Default data structure
if( nargin == 0 )
  sDot = struct('m',5000, 'g', 9.806, 'thrust',0,'alpha',0, 'phi',0,...
                'cLAlpha',2*pi,'cD0',0.006,'k',0.06,'s',20,'density',
                     @AtmosphericDensity);
  return
end

% Save as local variables
V     = s(1);
gamma = s(2);
psi   = s(3);
h     = s(6);

% Trig functions
cG    = cos(gamma);
sG    = sin(gamma);
cPsi  = cos(psi);
sPsi  = sin(psi);
cB    = cos(d.phi);
sB    = sin(d.phi);

% Exponential atmosphere
rho   = feval(d.density,h);

% Lift and Drag
qS    = 0.5*rho*d.s*v^2;   % dynamic pressure
cL    = d.cLAlpha*d.alpha;
cD    = d.cD0 + d.k*cL^2;
LStar = qS*d.cLAlpha;
L     = qS*cL;
D     = qS*cD;
```

```
% Velocity derivative
% sDot is d[v;gamma;psi;x;y;h]/dt
lT   = L + d.thrust*sin(d.alpha);
sDot = [ (d.thrust*cos(d.alpha) - D)/d.m - d.g*sG;...
          (lT*cB - d.m*d.g*cG)/(d.m*v);...
          lT*sB/(d.m*v*cG);...
          v*cPsi*cG;...
          v*sPsi*cG;...
          v*sG];
```

A more sophisticated right-hand side would pass function handles for the drag and lift calculations so that the user could use their own model. We passed a function handle for the atmospheric density calculation to allow the user to select their density function. We could have done the same for the aerodynamics model. This would make RHSAircraft more flexible.

Notice that we had to write an atmospheric density model, AtmosphericDensity, to provide as a default for the RHS function. This model uses an exponential equation for the density, which is the simplest possible representation. The function has a demo of the model, which uses a log scale for the plot.

```
%% AtmosphericDensity Atmospheric density from an exponential model.
% Computes the atmospheric density at the given altitude using an
% exponential model. Produces a demo plot up to an altitude of 100 km.
%% Form:
%    rho = AtmosphericDensity( h )
%
%%   Inputs
%    h      (1,:)    Altitude (m)
%
%% Outputs
%    rho    (1,:) Density (kg/m^3)

function rho = AtmosphericDensity( h )

% Demo
if( nargin < 1 )
  h = linspace(0,100000);
  AtmosphericDensity( h );
  return
end

% Density
rho = 1.225*exp(-2.9e - 05*h.^1.15);

% Plot if no outputs are requested
if( nargout < 1 )
  PlotSet(h,rho,'x_label','h_(m)','y_label','Density_(kg/m^3)',...
          'figure_title','Exponential_Atmosphere',...
          'plot_title','Exponential Atmosphere',...
          'plot_type','y_log');
  clear rho
end
```

11-2. Finding the Equilibrium Controls for an Aircraft Using Numerical Search

Problem

You want to find roll angles, thrusts and angles of attack that cause the velocity, flight path angle, and bank angle state (roll angle) derivatives to be zero. This is a point of equilibrium.

Solution

You will use Downhill Simplex, via the MATLAB function fminsearch, to find the equilibrium angles.

How It Works

The first step is to find the controls that produce a desired equilibrium state, known as the set point. Define the set point as the vector

$$\begin{bmatrix} v_s \\ \gamma_s \\ \psi_s \end{bmatrix} \tag{11.7}$$

with set values for the velocity, v_s; heading, ψ_s; and flight path angle, γ_s. Substitute these into the first three dynamical equations from equation 11.2 and set the left-hand side to zero.

$$0 = \begin{bmatrix} T\cos\alpha - D(v_s,\alpha) - mg\cos\gamma_s \\ (L(v_s,\alpha) + T\sin\alpha)\cos\phi - mg\cos\gamma_s \\ (L(v_s,\alpha) + T\sin\alpha)\sin\phi \end{bmatrix} \tag{11.8}$$

The controls are angle of attack, α; roll angle, ϕ; and thrust, T. Since there are three equations in three unknowns, you can get a single solution. The easiest way to solve for the equilibrium controls is to use fminsearch. This routine finds the three controls that zero the three equations.

The function, EquilibriumControl.m, uses fminsearch in a loop to handle multiple states. Within the loop, you compute an initial guess of the control. The thrust needs to balance drag so you compute this at zero angle of attack. The lift must balance gravity so you compute the angle of attack from that relationship. Without a reasonable initial guess, the algorithm may not converge or may converge to a local minimum. The cost function is nested within the control function.

```
function [u, c] = EquilibriumControl( x, d, tol )
n   = size(x,2);
u   = zeros(3,n);
c   = zeros(1,n);
p   = optimset('TolFun',tol);
% additional options during testing:
%'PlotFcns',{@optimplotfval,@PlotIteration},'Display','iter','MaxIter',50);
for k = 1:n
  [~,D,LStar] = RHSAircraft(0,x(:,k),d);
  alpha       = d.m*d.g/LStar;
  u0          = [D;alpha;0];
```

```
[umin,cval,exitflag,output] = fminsearch( @Cost, u0, p, x(:,k), d );
u(:,k)          = umin;
c(k)            = Cost( u(:,k), x(:,k), d );
end
```

The default output is to plot the results.

```
% Plot if no outputs are specified
if( nargout == 0 )
  yL = {'T (N)', '\alpha_(rad)', '\phi_(rad)' 'Cost'};
  s = 'Equilibrium_Control:Controls';
  PlotSet(1:n,[u;c],'x_label','set','y_label',yL, ...
          'plot_title',s, 'figure_title',s);

  yL = {'v' '\gamma' '\psi' 'h'};
  s = 'Equilibrium Control:States';
  PlotSet(1:n,x([1:3 6],:),'x_label','set','y_label',yL, ...
          'plot_title',s,'figure_title',s);
  clear u
end
```

The cost function is shown next. Use a quadratic cost that is the unweighted sum of the squares of the state derivatives.

```
%% Find the cost of a given control
function c = Cost( u, x, d )

d.thrust  = u(1);
d.alpha   = u(2);
d.phi     = u(3);

xDot      = RHSAircraft(0,x,d);
y         = xDot(1:3);
c         = sqrt(y'*y);
```

The function has a built-in demo that looks at thrust and angle of attack at a constant velocity but increasing altitude, from 0 to 10 km.

```
if( nargin < 1 )
  x = [200*ones(1,101);...
       zeros(4,101);...
       linspace(0,10000,101)];
  d = RHSAircraft;
  EquilibriumControl( x, d )
  return;
end
```

Figure 11-2 shows the states for which the controls are calculated in the built-in demo. Figure 11-3 shows the resulting controls. As expected, the angle of attack goes up with altitude, but the thrust goes down. The decreasing air density reduces drag and lift, so you need to decrease thrust but increase angle of attack to generate more lift. The roll angle is nearly zero.

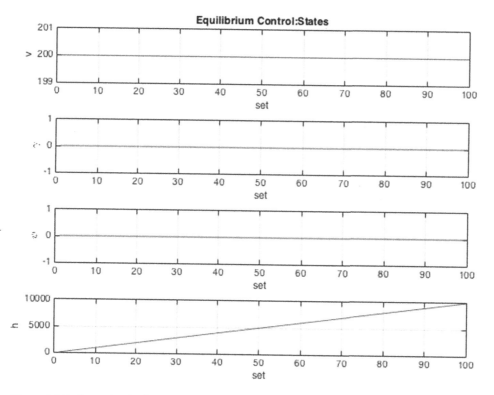

Figure 11-2. *States for the demo. Only altitude (h) is changing*

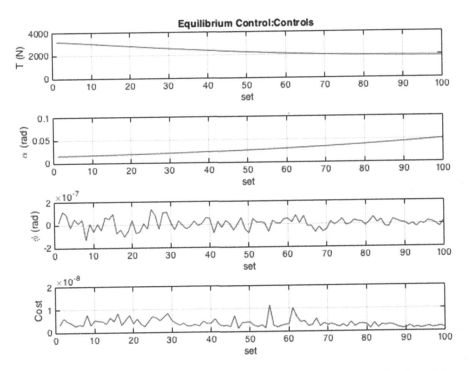

Figure 11-3. *Controls for the demo. Thrust decreases with altitude and angle of attack increases*

Figure 11-3 also plots the cost. The cost should be nearly zero if the function is working as desired.

During debugging, while writing a function requiring optimization, it may be helpful to have additional insight into the numerical search process. While you only need umin, consider the additional outputs available from fminsearch in this version of the function call.

```
[umin,cval,exitflag,output] = fminsearch( @Cost, u0, p, x(:,k), d )
```

The output structure includes the number of iterations and the exit flag indicates the exit condition of the function: whether the tolerance was reached (1), the maximum number of allowed iterations was exceeded (0), or if a user-supplied output function terminated the search (–1). We put a breakpoint in the script to check these outputs. For a state of $v = 200$ and $h = 300$ at $k = 4$, the output will be

```
>> u0
u0 =

          2880.4
          0.016255
                 0

>> [umin,cval,exitflag,output] = fminsearch( @Cost, u0, p, x(:,k), d );
umin =
          3180.7
          0.016237
          3.459e-08
```

```
cval =

  3.2473e-09

exitflag =
    1

output =
  iterations: 141
   funcCount: 260
   algorithm: 'Nelder-Mead_simplex_direct_search'
     message: 'Optimization_terminated:_the_current_x_satisfies_the_termination
              criteria_usin...'
```

So you can see that the search required 141 iterations and that the thrust increased to 3180 N from our initial guess of 2880 N. The resulting cost is 3e⁻⁹. Another alternative for more information is to set the Display option of fminsearch to iter or final, with the default being notify. In this case, the options look like

```
p = optimset('TolFun',tol,'Display','iter');
```

and the following type of output is printed to the Command Window:

```
>> d = RHSAircraft;
>> x = [200;0;0.5;0;0;5000];
>> EquilibriumControl( x, d )
```

Iteration	Func-count	min f(x)	Procedure
0	1	0.0991747	
1	4	0.0817065	initial simplex
2	6	0.0630496	expand
3	7	0.0630496	reflect
4	9	0.0133862	expand
5	10	0.0133862	reflect
6	11	0.0133862	reflect
7	13	0.0133862	contract outside
8	15	0.0133862	contract inside
...			
49	87	2.1869e-05	contract inside
50	89	2.1869e-05	contract outside

```
Exiting: Maximum number of iterations has been exceeded
         - increase MaxIter option.
         Current function value: 0.000022
```

For additional insight, you can add a plot function to be called at every iteration. MATLAB provides some default plot functions; for example, optimplotfval plots the cost function value at every iteration. You have to actually open optimplotfval in an editor to learn the necessary syntax. We add the function to the optimization options like this

```
p = optimset('TolFun',tol,'PlotFcns',@optimplotfval);
```

Figure 11-4 is generated from the first iteration of the demo.

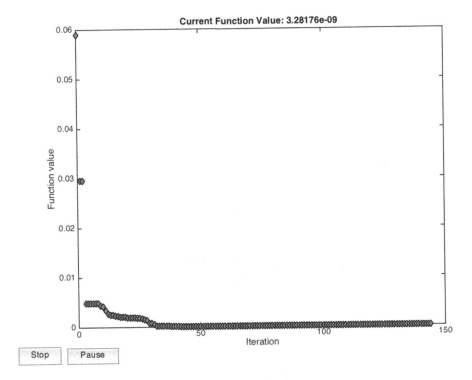

Figure 11-4. *Function value plot using* **optimplotfval**

You can see that the cost value was nearly constant on this plot, for the final 100 iterations. You can add additional plots using a cell array for PlotFcns, and each plot will be given its own subplot axis automatically by MATLAB. For tough numerical problems, you might want to generate a surface and trace the iterations of the optimization. For our problem, we add our custom plot function PlotIteration, and the results look like Figure 11-5.

```
p = optimset('TolFun',tol,'PlotFcns',{@optimplotfval,@PlotIteration});
```

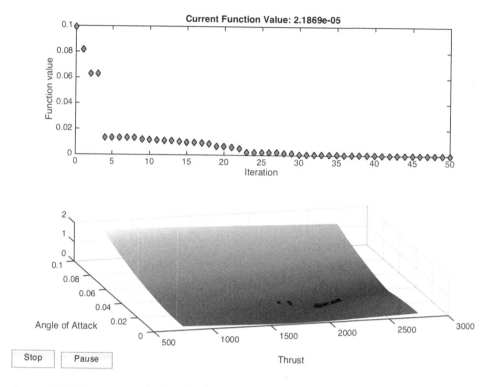

Figure 11-5. *Custom optimization plot function using a surface*

We wrote two functions: one to generate the surface and a second to plot the iteration step. MATLAB sets the iteration value to zero during initialization, so in that case, you generate the surface from the given initial state. For all other iteration values, you plot the cost on the surface using an asterisk.

```
% Plot an iteration of the numerical search
function stop = PlotIteration (u0,optimValues,state,varargin)

stop = false;
x0 = varargin{1};
d = varargin{2};
switch state
    case 'iter'
        if optimValues.iteration == 0
          a = PlotSurf( x0, u0, d );
        end
        plot3(u0(1),u0(2),optimValues.fval,'k*');
end

% Plot a surface using the given initial state for a range of controls.
% MATLAB will already have an empty axis available for plotting.
function a = PlotSurf( x0, u0, d )
```

```
u1 = linspace(max(u0(1)-1000,0),u0(1)+1000);
u2 = linspace(0,max(2*u0(2),0.1));
u3 = u0(3);
cvals = zeros(100,100);

for m = 1:100
  for l = 1:100
    cvals(l,m) = Cost( [u1(m);u2(l);u3], x0, d );
  end
end

s = surf(u1,u2,cvals);
set(s,'edgecolor','none');
a = gca;
set(a,'Tag','equilibriumcontrol');
hold on;
xlabel('Thrust')
ylabel('Angle_of_Attack')
```

Finally, note that to see the default set of options that MATLAB uses for fminsearch, call optimiset with the name of the optimization function.

```
>> options = optimset('fminsearch')

options =
          Display: 'notify'
       MaxFunEvals: '200*numberofvariables'
          MaxIter: '200*numberofvariables'
           TolFun: 0.0001
             TolX: 0.0001
       FunValCheck: 'off'
         OutputFcn: []
          PlotFcns: []
```

You see that the default tolerances are equal, at 0.0001, and the number of function evaluations and iterations is dependent on the number of variables in the input state x.

11-3. Designing a Control System for an Aircraft

Problem

You want to design a control system for an aircraft that will control the trajectory and allow for three-dimensional motion.

Solution

You will use dynamic plant inversion to feedforward the desired controls for the aircraft. Proportional controllers will be used for thrust, angle of attack, and roll angle to adjust the nominal controls to account for disturbances such as wind gusts. You will not use feedback control of the roll angle to control the heading, ψ. This is left as an exercise for you.

How It Works

Recall from the dynamic model in Recipe 11-1 that our aircraft state is

$$\begin{bmatrix} v & \gamma & \psi & x & y & h \end{bmatrix}^T \tag{11.9}$$

where v is the velocity, γ is the flight path angle, ψ is the heading, x and y are the coordinate in the flight plane, and h is the altitude. The control variables are the roll angle, ϕ; angle of attack, α; and thrust, T.

The controller is of the form

$$T = T_s + k_T \left(v_s - v \right) \tag{11.10}$$

$$\alpha = \alpha_s + k_a \left(\gamma_s - \gamma \right) \tag{11.11}$$

If the state is at s, then the controls should be at the values T_s, α_s, ϕ_s, which are the equilibrium controls. The gains k_T and k_a push the states in the right direction. The gains are a function of the flight condition. You need to expand the first two dynamical equations from equation 11.2.

$$\begin{bmatrix} \dot{v} \\ \dot{\gamma} \end{bmatrix} = \begin{bmatrix} \dfrac{T\cos\alpha - q\left(C_{D_0} + k\left(C_{L_\alpha}\alpha\right)^2\right)}{m} - g\cos\gamma \\ \dfrac{\left(qC_{L_\alpha}\alpha + T\sin\alpha\right)\cos\phi - mg\cos\gamma}{mv} \end{bmatrix} \tag{11.12}$$

Linearize and drop the terms not involving the controls.

$$\begin{bmatrix} \dot{v} \\ \dot{\gamma} \end{bmatrix} = \begin{bmatrix} \dfrac{T}{m} \\ \dfrac{q\cos\phi C_{L_\alpha}\alpha}{mv} \end{bmatrix} \tag{11.13}$$

You want the time constants τ_γ and τ_v so that the equations become

$$\begin{bmatrix} \dot{v} \\ \dot{\gamma} \end{bmatrix} = \begin{bmatrix} -\dfrac{v}{\tau_v} \\ -\dfrac{\gamma}{\tau_\gamma} \end{bmatrix} \tag{11.14}$$

Therefore

$$k_T = \frac{m}{\tau_v} \tag{11.15}$$

$$k_\alpha = \frac{mv}{q\cos\phi C_{L_\alpha}\tau_\gamma} \tag{11.16}$$

The control system is implemented in the function `AircraftControl`.

```
function [T, alpha] = AircraftControl( s, d, tauGamma, tauV, vSet, gammaSet )

u        = EquilibriumControl( s, d );
v        = s(1);
gamma    = s(2);
h        = s(6);
rho      = feval(d.density,h);
qS       = 0.5*d.s*rho*v^2;
kV       = d.m/tauV;
kGamma   = (d.m*v)/(qS*cos(d.phi)*d.cLAlpha*tauGamma);
T        = u(1) + kV *(vSet - v);
alpha    = u(2) + kGamma*(gammaSet - gamma);
```

The performance of the control system is shown in the simulation recipe (11-5). The function requires information about the flight conditions, including the atmospheric density. It first uses `EquilibriumControl` to find the controls that are needed at the current state s. The aircraft data structure is required. Additional inputs are the time constants for the controllers and the set points. You compute the atmospheric density in the function using `feval` and the input function handle. This should be the same computation as is done in `RHSAircraft`.

11-4. Plotting a 3D Trajectory for an Aircraft

Problem

You want to plot the trajectory of the aircraft in three dimensions and show the aircraft axes and times along the trajectory.

Solution

You use the MATLAB `plot3` function with custom code to draw the aircraft axes and times at select points on the trajectory. The resulting figure is shown in Figure 11-6.

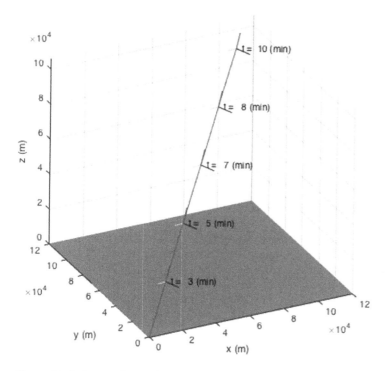

Figure 11-6. *Demo of aircraft trajectory function*

How It Works

You use plot3 to draw the 3D display. The function Plot3DTrajectory.m allows for argument pairs via varargin.

```
%% PLOT3DTRAJECTORY Plot the trajectory of an aircraft in 3D.
%% Form:
%   Plot3DTrajectory( x, varargin )
%% Description
%   Plot a 3D trajectory of an aircraft with times and local axes.
%
%% Inputs
%   x        (6,:) State vector [v;gamma;phi;x;y;h]
%   varargin {:} Parameters
%
```

We skip the demo code for now and show the drawing code next. There are similarities with our 2D plotting function, PlotSet. We use text to insert time labels and a patch object to draw the ground.

```
% Draw the figure
h = figure;
set(h,'Name',figTitle);
plot3(x(4,:),x(5,:),x(6,:));
xlabel(xLabel);
ylabel(yLabel);
zlabel(zLabel);

% Draw time and axes
if( ~isempty(t) && ~isempty(tIndex) )
    [t,~,tL] = TimeLabel(t);
    for k = 1:length(t)
        s = sprintf('_t_=_%3.0f_(%s)',t(k), tL);
        i = tIndex(k);
        text(x(4,i),x(5,i),x(6,i),s);
        DrawAxes(x(:,i),alpha(1,i),phi(1,i));
    end
end

% Add the ground
xL = get(gca,'xlim');
yL = get(gca,'ylim');
v = [xL(1) yL(1) 0;...
     xL(2) yL(1) 0;...
     xL(2) yL(2) 0;...
     xL(1) yL(2) 0];

patch('vertices',v,'faces',[1 2 3 4],'facecolor',[0.65 0.5 0.0],'edgecolor',[0.65 0.5 0.0]);
grid on
rotate3d on
axis image
zL      = get(gca,'zlim');
set(gca,'zlim',[0 zL(2)],'ZLimMode','manual');
```

The plot commands are straightforward. If a time array is entered, it draws the times along the track using sprintf and text. We use TimeLabel to get reasonable units. It also draws the aircraft axes using the nested function DrawAxes.

```
%%% Plot3DTrajectory>DrawAxes subfunction
%% DrawAxes
function DrawAxes( x, alpha, phi )

gamma = x(2);
psi = x(3);
% Aircraft frame is x forward, y out the right wing and z down
u0      = [1 0 0;0 1 0;0 0 -1];

cG      = cos(gamma+alpha);
sG      = sin(gamma+alpha);
cP      = cos(psi);
```

265

```
sP    = sin(psi);
cR    = cos(phi);
sR    = sin(phi);

u     = [cP -sP 0;sP cP 0; 0 0 1]...
        *[cG 0 -sG; 0 1 0;sG 0 cG]...
        *[1 0 0;0 cR sR; 0 -sR cR]*u0;

% Find a length for scaling of the axes
xL    = get(gca,'xlim');
yL    = get(gca,'ylim');
zL    = get(gca,'zlim');

l     = sqrt((xL(2)-xL(1))^2 + (yL(2)-yL(1))^2 + (zL(2)-zL(1))^2)/20;

x0    = x(4:6);
for k = 1:3
  x1    = x0 + u(:,k)*l;
  c     = [0 0 0];
  c(k)  = 1;
  line([x0(1);x1(1)],[x0(2);x1(2)],[x0(3);x1(3)],'color',c);
end
```

This function draws an axis system for the aircraft, *x* out the nose, *y* out the right wing, and *z* down. It uses the state vector, so needs to convert from γ and ψ to rotation matrices. The axis system is in wind axes.

The function takes parameter pairs to allow the user to customize the plot. The parameter pairs are processed here:

```
xLabel = 'x_(m)';
yLabel = 'y_(m)';
zLabel = 'z_(m)';
figTitle = 'Trajectory';
t = [];
tIndex = [];
alpha = 0.02*ones(1,size(x,2));
phi = 0.25*pi*ones(1,size(x,2));

for k = 1:2:length(varargin)
  switch lower(varargin{k})
    case 'x_label'
      xLabel = varargin{k+1};
    case 'y_label'
      yLabel = varargin{k+1};
    case 'z_label'
      zLabel = varargin{k+1};
    case 'figure_title'
      figTitle = varargin{k+1};
    case 'time'
      t = varargin{k+1};
    case 'time index'
      tIndex = varargin{k+1};
```

```
  case 'alpha'
    alpha = varargin{k+1};
  case 'phi'
    phi = varargin{k+1};
  otherwise
    error('%s_is_not_a_valid_parameter',varargin{k});
  end
end
```

We use lower in the switch statement to allow the user to input capital letters and not have to worry about case issues. Most of the parameters are straightforward. The time input could have been done in many ways. We chose to allow the user to enter specific times for the time labels. As part of this, the user must enter the indices to the state vector.

The function includes a demo. You can type Plot3DTrajectory and get the example trajectory shown in Figure 11-6. In the case of a graphics function, the demo literally shows the user what the graphics should look like and provides examples about how to use the function.

```
% Demo
if( nargin < 1 )
  l = linspace(0,1e5);
  x = [200*ones(1,100);...
       (pi/4)*ones(1,100);...
       (pi/4)*ones(1,100);1;1;1];
  t = [200 300 400 500 600];
  k = [20 40 60 80 100];
  Plot3DTrajectory( x, 'time', t, 'time_index', k, 'alpha',0.01*ones(1,100) )
  return;
end
```

11-5. Simulating the Controlled Aircraft

Problem

You want to simulate the motion of the aircraft with the trajectory controls.

Solution

You will create a script with the control system and flight dynamics. The dynamics will be propagated by RungeKutta. This is a fourth-order method, meaning the truncation errors go as the fourth power of the timestep. Given the typical sample time for a flight control system, fourth-order is sufficiently accurate for flight simulations. We will display the results using our 3D plotting function Plot3DTrajectory described in the previous recipe.

How It Works

The simulation script, AircraftSim.m, reads the data structure from RHSAircraft and changes values to match an F-35 fighter. The model only involves the thrust and drag, and even these are very simple models. The initial flight path angle and velocity are set. We turn on the control and establish the set points and time constants for the velocity and flight path angle states. For output, we plot the states, control, and a 3D trajectory.

```
%% A trajectory control simulation of an F-35 aircraft.
% The dynamics of a point mass aircraft is simulated.
%% See also
% RungeKutta, RHSAircraft, PDControl, EquilibriumControl
```

The script begins with obtaining our default data structure from the RHS function.

```
%% Data structure for the right hand side
d               = RHSAircraft;

%% User initialization
d.m             = 13300.00; % kg
d.s             = 204.00; % m^2
v               = 200; % m/sec
fPA             = pi/6; % rad

% Initialize duration and delta time
tEnd            = 40;
dT              = 0.1;

% Controller
controlIsOn = true;
tauV            = 1;
tauGamma        = 1;
d.phi           = 0;
vSet            = 220;
gammaSet        = pi/8;

%% Simulation
% State vector
x               = [v;fPA;0;0;0;0];

% Plotting and number of steps
n               = ceil(tEnd/dT);
xP              = zeros(length(x)+2,n);

% Find non-feedback settings
[~,D,LStar] = RHSAircraft(0,x,d);
thrust0         = D;
alpha0          = d.m*d.g/LStar;

% Run the simulation
for k = 1:n
  if( controlIsOn )
    [d.thrust, d.alpha] = AircraftControl( x, d, tauGamma, tauV, vSet, gammaSet );
  else
    d.thrust = thrust0;
    d.alpha = alpha0;
  end

  % Plot storage
  xP(:,k) = [x;d.thrust;d.alpha];
```

```
  % Right hand side
  x = RungeKutta(@RHSAircraft,0,x,dT,d);
end

%% Plotting
[t,tL] = TimeLabel((0:(n-1))*dT);

yL = {'T_(N)', '\alpha (rad)'};
s = 'Aircraft_Sim:Controls';
PlotSet(t,xP(7:8,:),'x_label',tL,'y_label',yL,'plot_title',s, 'figure_title',s);

yL = {'v' '\gamma' '\psi' 'x' 'y' 'h'};
s = 'Aircraft_Sim:States';
PlotSet(t,xP(1:6,:),'x_label',tL,'y_label',yL,'plot_title',s,'figure_title',s);

k = floor(linspace(2,n,8));
t = t(k);
Plot3DTrajectory( xP, 'time', t, 'time_index', k, 'alpha', xP(8,:) );
```

If the control is off, set the thrust and angle of attack to constant values to balance drag and gravity. The set points for velocity and flight path angle are slightly different than the initial conditions. This allows you to demonstrate the transient response of the controller.

The states are shown in Figure 11-7. The velocity and flight path angle converge to their set points.

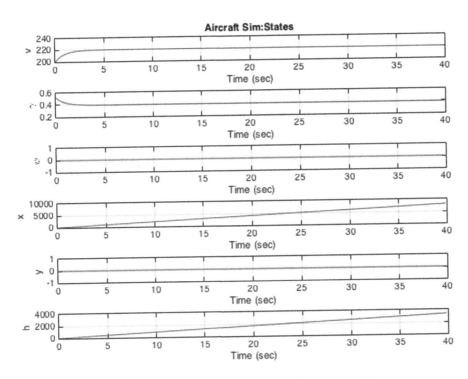

Figure 11-7. *Velocity and flight path angle converge to their desired values*

The controls are shown in Figure 11-8. The controls reach their steady values. Thrust and angle of attack change as the plane climbs. Thrust drops because the drag drops and angle of attack increases to maintain the lift/gravity balance.

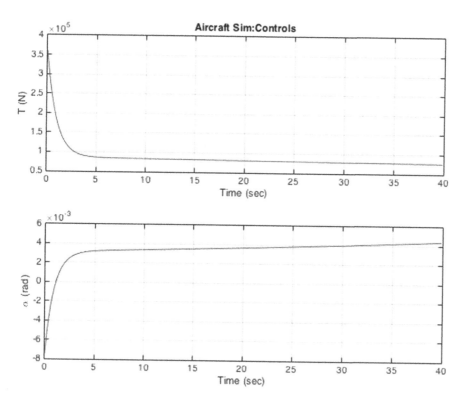

Figure 11-8. *The controls converge to the steady-state values and then change slowly to accommodate the decrease in atmospheric density as the aircraft climbs*

The 3D trajectory is shown in Figure 11-9. As expected, it climbs at a nearly constant angle at a constant velocity.

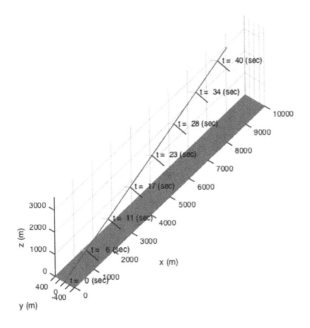

Figure 11-9. *The trajectory*

Summary

This chapter demonstrated how to write the dynamics for a point mass aircraft. You learned how to find the equilibrium control state using a search algorithm. This includes utilizing the debug output available from MATLAB for its optimization algorithms and adding custom plotting for each search iteration. You learned how to design a control system to maintain a desired velocity, bank angle and flight path angle. You learned how to make 3D plots with annotations of both text and other drawing objects. You also learned how to pass function handles to other functions to make functions more versatile. Table 11-1 lists the code developed in the chapter.

Table 11-1. *Chapter Code Listing*

File	Description
RHSAircraft	Six degree of freedom RHS for a point mass aircraft.
AtmosphericDensity	Atmospheric density as a function of altitude from an exponential model.
EquilibriumControl	Find the equilibrium control for a point mass aircraft.
AircraftControl	Computes the angle of attack and thrust for a 3D point mass aircraft.
Plot3DTrajectory	Plot a 3D trajectory of an aircraft with times and local axes.
AircraftSim	A trajectory control simulation of an aircraft.

CHAPTER 12

Spacecraft

Spacecraft pointing control is an essential technology for all robotic and manned spacecraft. A control system consists of sensing, actuation, and the dynamics of the spacecraft itself. Spacecraft control systems are of many types, but this chapter is only concerned with three-axis pointing. Reaction wheels are used for actuation.

Reaction wheels are used for control through the conservation of angular momentum. The torque on the reaction wheel causes it to spin one way and the spacecraft to spin in the opposite direction. Momentum removed from the spacecraft is absorbed in the wheel. Reaction wheels are classified as *momentum exchange devices*. You can reorient the spacecraft using wheels and without any external torques. Before reaction wheels were introduced, thrusters were often used for orientation control. This would consume propellant, which is undesirable since when you run out of propellant, the spacecraft can no longer be used.

The spacecraft is modeled as a rigid body except for the presence of three reaction wheels that rotate about orthogonal (perpendicular) axes. The shaft of the motor attached to the rotor of the wheel is attached to the spacecraft. Torque applied between the wheel and spacecraft cause the wheel and spacecraft to move in opposite angular directions. We will assume that we have attitude sensors that measure the orientation of the spacecraft. We will also assume that our wheels are ideal with just viscous damping friction.

12-1. Creating a Dynamic Model of the Spacecraft

Problem

The spacecraft is a rigid body with three wheels. Each wheel is connected to the spacecraft, as shown in Figure 12-1.

Electronic supplementary material The online version of this chapter (doi:10.1007/978-1-4842-0559-4_12) contains supplementary material, which is available to authorized users.

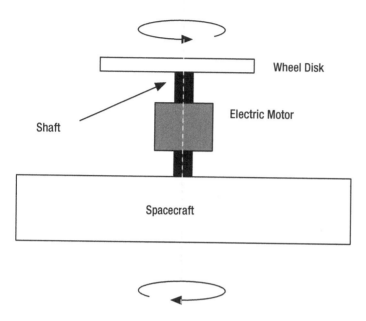

Figure 12-1. *A reaction wheel. The reaction wheel platter spins in one direction and the spacecraft spins in the opposite direction*

Solution

The equations of motion are written using angular momentum conservation. This produces a dynamical model known as the Euler equations with the addition of the spinning wheels. This is sometimes known as a *gyrostat model*.

How It Works

The spacecraft model can be partitioned into dynamics, including the dynamics of the reaction wheels, and the kinematics of the spacecraft. If you assume that the wheels are perfectly symmetric, are aligned with the three body axes, and have a diagonal inertia matrix, you can model the spacecraft dynamics with the following coupled first-order differential equations.

$$I\dot{\omega} + \omega^{\times}\left(I\omega + I_{w}\left(\omega_{w} + \omega\right)\right) + I_{w}\left(\dot{\omega}_{w} + \dot{\omega}\right) = T \tag{12.1}$$

$$I_{w}\left(\dot{\omega}_{w} + \dot{\omega}\right) = T_{w} \tag{12.2}$$

I is the 3 × 3 inertia matrix; it does not include the inertia of the wheels.

$$I = \begin{bmatrix} I_{xx} & I_{xy} & I_{xz} \\ I_{yx} & I_{yy} & I_{yz} \\ I_{zx} & I_{zy} & I_{zz} \end{bmatrix} \tag{12.3}$$

The matrix is symmetric, so $I_{xy} = I_{yx}, I_{xz} = I_{zx}, I_{zy} = I_{yz}$. ω is the angular rate vector for the spacecraft seen in the spacecraft frame.

$$\omega = \begin{bmatrix} \omega_x \\ \omega_y \\ \omega_z \end{bmatrix} \tag{12.4}$$

ω_w is the angular rate of the reaction wheels for wheels 1, 2 and 3.

$$\omega_w = \begin{bmatrix} \omega_1 \\ \omega_2 \\ \omega_3 \end{bmatrix} \tag{12.5}$$

1 is aligned with x, 2 with y, and 3 with z. In this way, the reaction wheels form an orthogonal set and can be used for three-axis control. T is the external torque on the spacecraft, which can include external disturbances such as solar pressure or aerodynamic drag, and thruster or magnetic torquer coil torques. T_w is the internal torque on the wheels. I_w is the scalar inertia of the wheels (we assume that they all have the same inertia). You can substitute the second equation into the first to simplify the equations.

$$I\dot{\omega} + \omega^\times \left(I\omega + I_w \left(\omega_w + \omega \right) \right) + T_w = T \tag{12.6}$$

$$I_w \left(\dot{\omega}_w + \dot{\omega} \right) = T_w \tag{12.7}$$

This term

$$T_e = \omega^\times \left(I\omega + I_w \left(\omega_w + \omega \right) \right) \equiv \omega \times h \tag{12.8}$$

is known as the Euler torque. If the angular rates are small, you can set this term to zero and the equations simplify to

$$I\dot{\omega} + T_w = T \tag{12.9}$$

$$I_w \left(\dot{\omega}_w + \dot{\omega} \right) = T_w \tag{12.10}$$

For kinematics, we use quaternions. A quaternion is a four-parameter representation of the orientation of the spacecraft with respect to the inertial frame. We could use angles since we really only need three states to specify the orientation. The problem with angles is that they have singularities—that is, certain orientations where an angle is undefined, and therefore, are not suitable for simulations. The derivative of the quaternion from the inertial frame to the body frame is

$$\dot{q} = \frac{1}{2} \begin{bmatrix} 0 & \omega^T \\ -\omega & \omega^\times \end{bmatrix} \tag{12.11}$$

The term $\omega^\times$ is the skew symmetric matrix that is the equivalent of the cross product and is

$$\omega^\times = \begin{bmatrix} 0 & -\omega_z & \omega_y \\ \omega_z & 0 & -\omega_x \\ -\omega_y & \omega_x & 0 \end{bmatrix} \tag{12.12}$$

The wheel torque is a combination of friction torque and control torque. Reaction wheels are usually driven by DC motors in which the back electromotive force is cancelled by current feedback within the motor electronics. The total reaction wheel torque is therefore

$$T_w = T_c + T_f \tag{12.13}$$

where T_c is the commanded reaction wheel torque and T_f is the friction torque. A simple friction model is

$$T_f = -k_d\omega_k \tag{12.14}$$

k_d is the damping coefficient and ω_k is the angular rate of the kth wheel. If k_d is large, you may have to feedforward it to the controller. This requires careful calibration of the wheel to determine the damping coefficient.

First, you define the data structure for the model that is returned by the dynamics right-hand-side function if there are no inputs. The name of the function is RHSSpacecraftWithRWA.m. Use RWA to mean Reaction Wheel Assembly. We say "assembly" because the reaction wheel is assembled from bearings, wheel, shaft, support structure, and power electronics. Spacecraft are built of assemblies.

The default unit vectors for the wheel are along orthogonal axes, such as x, y, and z. The default inertia matrix is the identity matrix, making the spacecraft a sphere. The default reaction wheel inertias are 0.001. All of the non-spinning parts of the wheels are lumped in with the inertia matrix.

```
% Default data structure
if( nargin == 0 )
    xDot = struct('inr',eye(3), 'torque',[0;0;0],'inrRWA', 0.001*[1;1;1],...
                  'torqueRWA',[0;0;0],'uRWA',eye(3), 'damping',[0;0;0]);
    return
end
```

The dynamical equations for the spacecraft are given in the following lines of code. You need to compute the total wheel torque because it is applied both to the spacecraft and the wheels. We use the backslash operator to multiply the equations by the inverse of the inertia matrix. The inertia matrix is positive definite symmetric, so specialized routines can be used to speed computation. It is a good idea to avoid computing inverses, as they can be ill-conditioned—meaning that small errors in the matrix can result in large errors in the inverse.

Save the elements of the state vector as local variables with meaningful names to make reading the code easier. This also eliminates unnecessary multiple extraction of submatrices.

You will notice that the omegaRWA variable reads from element 8 to the end of the vector using the end keyword. This allows the code to handle any number of reaction wheels. You might just want to control one axis with a wheel or have more than three wheels for redundancy. Be sure that the inputs in d match the number of wheels. Since we also input unit vectors, the wheels do not have to be aligned with x, y, and z. Note the use of the backslash operator to solve the set of linear equations for $\dot{\omega}$, omegaDotCore.

```
% Save as local variables
q        = x(1:4);
omega    = x(5:7);
omegaRWA = x(8:end);

% Total body fixed angular momentum
h = d.inr*omega + d.uRWA*(d.inrRWA.*(omegaRWA + d.uRWA'*omega));

% Total wheel torque
tRWA = d.torqueRWA - d.damping.*omegaRWA;

% Core angular acceleration
omegaDotCore = d.inr\(d.torque - d.uRWA*tRWA - Cross(omega,h));
```

Note that uRWA is an array of the reaction wheel unit vectors; that is, the spin vectors. In computing h, you have to transform ω into the wheel frame using the transform of uRWA, and then transform back before adding the wheel component to the core component, $I\omega$. The wheel dynamics are given in these lines.

```
% Wheel angular acceleration
omegaDotWheel     = tRWA./d.inrRWA - d.uRWA'*omegaDotCore;
```

The total state derivative is in these lines:

```
% State derivative
sW   = [       0 -omega(3) omega(2);...
         omega(3)        0 -omega(1);...
-omega(2) omega(1) 0]; % skew symmetric matrix qD = 0.5*[0, omega';-omega,-sW];
xDot = [qD*q;omegaDotCore;omegaDotWheel];
```

The total inertial angular momentum is an auxiliary output. In the absence of external torques, it should be conserved so it is a good test of the dynamics. A simple way to test angular momentum conservation is to run a simulation with angular rates for all the states, and then rerun it with a smaller timestep. The change in angular momentum should decrease as the timestep is decreased.

```
% Output the inertial angular momentum
if ( nargout > 1 )
   hECI = QTForm( q, h );
end
```

12-2. Computing Angle Errors from Quaternions

Problem

You want to point the spacecraft to a new target attitude (orientation) with the three reaction wheels or maintain the attitude given an external torque on the spacecraft.

Solution

Make 3 PD controllers, one for each axis. You need a function to take two quaternions and compute the small angles between them as input to these controllers.

How It Works

If you are pointing at an inertial target and wish to control about that orientation, you can simplify the rate equations by approximating ω as $\dot{\theta}$, which is valid for small angles when the order of rotation doesn't matter and the Euler angles can be treated as a vector.

$$\dot{\theta} = \omega \tag{12.15}$$

You will also multiply both sides of the Euler equation (equation 12.9) by I^{-1} to solve for the derivatives. Note that T_w, the torque from the wheels, is equivalent to Ia_w, where a is acceleration. Our system equations now become

$$\ddot{\theta} + a_w = a \tag{12.16}$$
$$I_w\left(\dot{\omega}_w + \dot{\omega}\right) = -T_w \tag{12.17}$$

The first equation is now three decoupled second-order equations, just as in Chapter 6. You can stabilize this system with our standard PD controller.

You need attitude angles as input to the PD controllers to compute the control torques. Our examples will only be for small angular displacements from the nominal attitude. You can pass the control code a target quaternion and it will compute Δ angles or you can impose a small disturbance torque.

In these cases, the attitude can be treated as a vector where the order of the rotations doesn't matter. A quaternion derived from small angles is

$$q_\Delta \approx \begin{bmatrix} 1 \\ \theta_1/2 \\ \theta_2/2 \\ \theta_3/2 \end{bmatrix} \tag{12.18}$$

You find the required error quaternion, q_Δ, by multiplying the target quaternion, q_T, with the transpose of the current quaternion

$$q_\Delta = q^T q_T \tag{12.19}$$

This algorithm to compute the angles is implemented in the following code. The quaternion multiplication is made a subfunction. This makes the code cleaner and easier to see how it relates to the algorithm. QMult is written to handle multiple quaternions at once, so the function is easy to vectorize. QPose finds the transpose of the quaternion. Both of these functions would normally be separate functions, but in this chapter they are only associated with the error computation code, so they are in the same file.

```
function deltaAngle = ErrorFromQuaternion( q, qTarget )

deltaQ          = QMult( QPose(q), qTarget );
deltaAngle      = -2.0*deltaQ(2:4);

%% Multiply two quaternions.
% Q2 transforms from A to B and Q1 transforms from B to C
```

```
% so Q3 transforms from A to C.
function Q3 = QMult( Q2,Q1 )

Q3 = [Q1(1,:).*Q2(1,:) - Q1(2,:).*Q2(2,:) - Q1(3,:).*Q2(3,:) - Q1(4,:).*Q2(4,:);...
      Q1(2,:).*Q2(1,:) + Q1(1,:).*Q2(2,:) - Q1(4,:).*Q2(3,:) + Q1(3,:).*Q2(4,:);...
      Q1(3,:).*Q2(1,:) + Q1(4,:).*Q2(2,:) + Q1(1,:).*Q2(3,:) - Q1(2,:).*Q2(4,:);...
      Q1(4,:).*Q2(1,:) - Q1(3,:).*Q2(2,:) + Q1(2,:).*Q2(3,:) + Q1(1,:).*Q2(4,:)];

%% Transpose of a quaternion
% The transpose requires changing the sign of the angle terms.
function q = QPose(q)

q(2:4,:) = -q(2:4,:);
```

The control system is implemented in the simulation loop with the following code.

```
% Find the angle error
angleError = ErrorFromQuaternion( x(1:4), qTarget );
if (controlIsOn )
    u = [0;0;0];
    for j = 1:3
        [u(j), dC(j)] = PDControl('update',angleError(j),dC(j));
    end
else
    u = [0;0;0];
end
```

12-3. Simulating the Controlled Spacecraft

Problem

You want to test the attitude controller and see how it performs.

Solution

The solution is to build a MATLAB script in which you design the PD controller matrices, and then simulate the controller in a loop, applying the calculated torques until the desired quaternion is attained or until the disturbance torque is cancelled.

How It Works

Build a simulation script for the controller, SpacecraftSim. The first thing to do with the script is check angular momentum conservation by running the simulation for 300 seconds at timesteps of 0.1 and 1 second, and comparing the magnitude of the angular momentum in the two test cases. The control is turned off by setting the controlIsOn flag to false. In the absence of external torques, if our equations are programmed correctly, the momentum should be constant. You will, however, see growth in the momentum due to error in the numerical integration. The growth should be much lower in the first case than the second case, as the smaller timestep makes the integration more exact. Note that we give the spacecraft random initial rates in both omega and omegaRWA and a nonspherical inertia, to help catch any bugs in the dynamics code.

```
tEnd                    = 300;
dT                      = 0.1;
controlIsOn             = false;
qECIToBody              = [1;0;0;0];
omega                   = [0.01;0.02;-0.03]; % rad/sec
omegaRWA                = [5;-3;2]; % rad/sec
d.inr                   = [3 0 0;0 10 0;0 0 5]; % kg-m^2
```

Figure 12-2 shows the results of the tests. Momentum growth is four orders of magnitude lower in the test with a 0.1-second timestep indicating that the dynamical equations conserve angular momentum, as they should. The shape of the growth does not change and will depend on the relative magnitudes of the various angular rates.

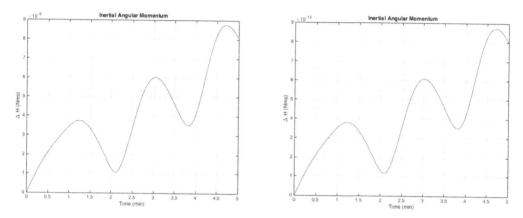

Figure 12-2. *Angular momentum conservation for 1 second and 0.1 second time steps. The growth is four orders of magnitude lower in the 0.1 second test, to le^{-13} from le^{-9}*

You initialize the script by using the data structure feature of the RHS function. This is shown next with parameters for a run with the control system on. The rates are now initialized to zero and you use the timestep of 1 second, which showed sufficiently small momentum growth in the previous test.

```
%% Data structure for the right hand side
d               = RHSSpacecraftWithRWA;
%% User initialization
% Initialize duration, delta time states and inertia
tEnd            = 600;
dT              = 1;
controlIsOn     = true;
qECIToBody      = [1;0;0;0];
omega           = [0;0;0]; % rad/sec
omegaRWA        = [0;0;0]; % rad/sec
d.inr           = [3 0 0;0 10 0;0 0 5]; % kg-m^2
qTarget         = QUnit([1;0.004;0.0;0]); % Normalize
d.torque        = [0;0;0]; % Disturbance torque
```

The control system is designed here. Note the small value of wN and the unit damping ratio. The frequency of the disturbances on a spacecraft are quite low, and the wheels have torque limits, leading to a wN much smaller than the robotics example. All three controllers are identical.

```
%% Control design
% Design a PD controller
dC             = PDControl( 'struct' );
dC(1).zeta     = 1;
dC(1).wN       = 0.02;
dC(1).wD       = 5*dC(1).wN;
dC(1).tSamp    = dT;
dC(1)          = PDControl( 'initialize', dC(1) );

% Make all 3 axis controllers identical
dC(2)          = dC(1);
dC(3)          = dC(1);
```

The simulation loop follows. As always, initialize the plotting array with zeros. The first step in the loop is finding the angular error between the current state and the target attitude. Next, the control acceleration is calculated or set to zero, depending on the value of the control flag. The control torque is calculated by multiplying the control acceleration by the spacecraft inertia. Compute the momentum for plotting purposes, and finally, integrate one timestep.

```
%% Simulation
% State vector
x = [qECIToBody;omega;omegaRWA];

% Plotting and number of steps
n  = ceil(tEnd/dT);
xP = zeros(length(x)+7,n);

% Find the initial angular momentum
[~,hECIO] = RHSSpacecraftWithRWA(0,x,d);

% Run the simulation
for k = 1:n
    % Find the angle error
    angleError = ErrorFromQuaternion( x(1:4), qTarget );
    if (controlIsOn )
        u = [0;0;0];
        for j = 1:3
            [u(j), dC(j)] = PDControl('update',angleError(j),dC(j));
        end
    else
        u = [0;0;0];
    end

    % Wheel torque is on the left hand side
    d.torqueRWA = d.inr*u;
```

```
% Get the delta angular momentum
[~,hECI]    = RHSSpacecraftWithRWA(0,x,d);
dHECI       = hECI - hECIO;
hMag        = sqrt(dHECI'*dHECI);

% Plot storage
xP(:,k)     = [x;d.torqueRWA;hMag;angleError];

% Right hand side
x           = RungeKutta(@RHSSpacecraftWithRWA,0,x,dT,d);

end
```

The output is entirely two-dimensional plots. We break them up into pages with one to three plots per page. This makes them easily readable on most computer displays.

```
%% Plotting
[t,tL] = TimeLabl((0:(n-1))*dT);

yL      = {'q_s', 'q_x', 'q_y', 'q_z'};
PlotSet( t, xP(1:4,:), 'x_label', tL, 'y_label', yL,...
  'plot_title', 'Attitude', 'figure_title', 'Attitude');

yL      = {'\omega_x', '\omega_y', '\omega_z'};
PlotSet(t, xP(5:7,:), 'x_label', tL, 'y_label', yL,...
  'plot_title', 'Body_Rates', 'figure_title', 'Body_Rates');

yL      = {'\omega_1', '\omega_2', '\omega_3'};
PlotSet( t, xP(8:10,:), 'x_label', tL, 'y_label', yL,...
  'plot_title', 'RWA_Rates', 'figure_title', 'RWA_Rates');

yL      = {'T_x_(Nm)', 'T_y_(Nm)', 'T_z_(Nm)'};
PlotSet( t, xP(11:13,:), 'x_label', tL, 'y_label', yL,...
  'plot_title', 'Control_Torque', 'figure_title', 'Control_Torque');

yL      = {'\Delta_H_(Nms)'};
PlotSet( t, xP(14,:), 'x_label', tL, 'y_label', yL,...
  'plot_title', 'Inertial_Angular_Momentum', 'figure_title', 'Inertial_Angular_Momentum');

yL      = {'\theta_x_(rad)', '\theta_y_(rad)', '\theta_z_(rad)'};
PlotSet( t, xP(15:17,:), 'x_label', tL, 'y_label', yL,...
  'plot_title', 'Angular_Errors', 'figure_title', 'Angular_Errors');
```

Note how PlotSet makes plotting much easier to set up and its code easier to read than using MATLAB's built-in plot and supporting functions. You do lose some flexibility. The y-axis labels use LaTeX notation. This provides limited LaTeX syntax. You can set the plotting to full LaTeX mode to get access to all LaTeX commands.

Note that we compute the angle error directly from the target and true quaternion. This represents our attitude sensor. In a real spacecraft, attitude estimation is quite complicated. Multiple sensors, such as combinations of magnetometers, GPS, and earth and sun sensors are used, and often rate-integrating gyros are employed to smooth the measurements. Star cameras or trackers are popular for three-axis sensing and require converting images in a camera to attitude estimates. You can't use gyros by themselves because they do not provide an initial orientation with respect to the inertial frame.

Run two tests. The first shows that our controllers can compensate for a body fixed disturbance torque. The second is to show that the controller can reorient the spacecraft.

The following is the initialization code for the disturbance torque test. The initial and target attitudes are the same, a unit quaternion, but there is a small disturbance torque in d.torque.

```
% Initialize duration, delta time states and inertia
tEnd        = 600;
dT          = 1;
controlIsOn = true;
qECIToBody  = [1;0;0;0];
omega       = [0;0;0]; % rad/sec
omegaRWA    = [0;0;0]; % rad/sec
d.inr       = [3 0 0;0 10 0;0 0 5]; % kg-m^2
qTarget     = QUnit([1;0;0.0;0]);
d.torque    = [0;0.0001;0]; % Disturbance torque (N)
```

We are running the simulations to 600 seconds to see the transients settle out. The disturbance torque is very small, which is typical for spacecraft. We make the torque single-axis to make the responses clearer. Figure 12-3 shows the complete set of output plots.

The disturbance causes a change in attitude around the y axis. This offset is expected with a PD controller. The control torque eventually matches the disturbance and the angular error reaches its maximum.

The y wheel rate grows linearly, as it has to absorb all the momentum produced by the torque. We don't limit the maximum wheel rate. In a real spacecraft, the wheel would soon saturate, reaching its maximum allowed speed. Our control system would need to have other actuators to desaturate the wheel. The inertial angular momentum also grows linearly as is expected with a constant external torque.

We now do an attitude correction around the x axis. The following is the initialization code.

```
% Initialize duration, delta time states and inertia
tEnd        = 600;
dT          = 1;
controlIsOn = true;
qECIToBody  = [1;0;0;0];
omega       = [0;0;0]; % rad/sec
omegaRWA    = [0;0;0]; % rad/sec
d.inr       = [3 0 0;0 10 0;0 0 5]; % kg-m^2
qTarget     = QUnit([1;0.004;0.0;0]); % Normalize
d.torque    = [0;0;0]; % Disturbance torque
```

We command a small attitude offset around the x axis, which is done by changing the second element in the quaternion. We unitize the quaternion to prevent numerical issues. Figure 12-4 shows the output plots.

In this case, the angular error around the x axis is reduced to zero. The inertial angular momentum remains "constant," although it jumps around a bit due to truncation error in the numerical integration. This is expected and it is good to keep checking the angular momentum with the control system running. If it doesn't remain nearly constant, the simulation has issues. Internal torques do not change the inertial angular momentum. This is why reaction wheels are called *momentum exchange devices*. They exchange momentum with the spacecraft body, but aren't added to the inertial angular momentum total.

The attitude rates remain small in both cases so that the Euler coupling torques are small. This justifies our earlier decision to treat the spacecraft as three double integrators. It also justifies our quaternion error to small angle approximation.

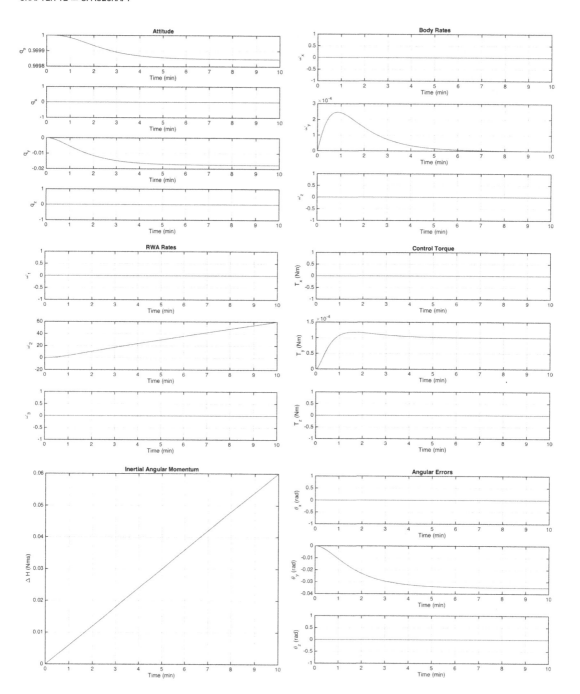

Figure 12-3. *Controlling a suddenly applied external torque*

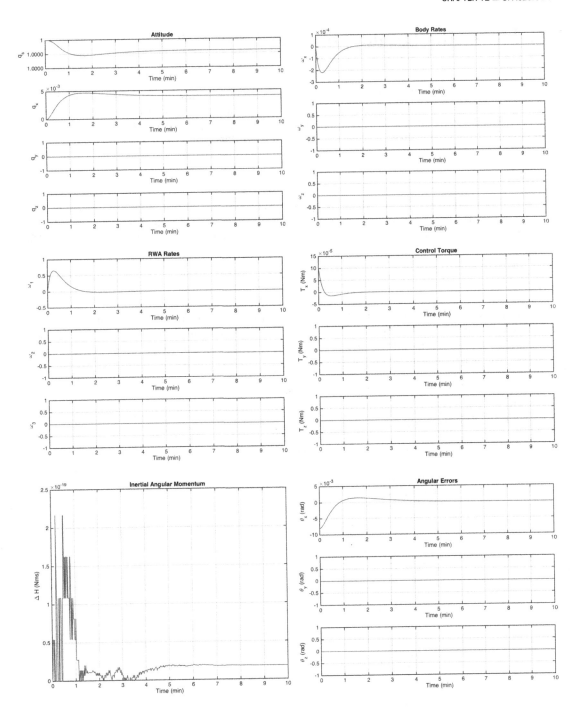

Figure 12-4. *Commanding a small attitude offset about the x-axis*

12-4. Performing Batch Runs of a Simulation

Problem

You've used the simulation script to verify momentum conservation and test the controller, but note how you have to change lines at the top by hand for each case. This is fine for development, but can make it very difficult to reproduce results; you don't know the initial conditions that generated any particular plot. You may want to run the simulation for a whole set of inputs and do Monte Carlo analysis.

Solution

Create a new function based on the script with inputs for the critical parameters. A new data structure will store both the inputs and the outputs, so you can save individual runs to mat-files. This makes it possible to replot the results of any run in the future, or redo runs from the stored inputs; for example, if you find and fix a bug in the controller.

How It Works

Start from the simulation script copied into a new file. Add a function signature. Replace the initialization variables with an input structure. Perform the simulation, and then save the input structure along with your generated output. The resulting function header is shown next. The input structure includes the RHS data, controller data, and simulation timing data.

```
%% SpacecraftSimFunction Spacecraft reaction wheel simulation function
% Perform a simulation of a spacecraft with reaction wheels given a
% particular initial state.
%% Form
% d = SpacecraftSimFunction( x0, qTarget, input )
%% Inputs
% x0         (7+n,1) Initial state
% qTarget (4,1) Target quaternion
% input       (.) Data structure
%                    .rhs (.) RHS data
%                    .pd (:) Controllers
%                    .dT (1,1) Timestep
%                    .tEnd (1,1) Duration
%                    .controlIsOn Flag
%% Outputs
%     d        (.) Data structure
%                    .input
%                    .x0
%                    .qTarget
%                    .xPlot
%                    .dPlot
%                    .tPlot
%                    .yLabel
%                    .dLabel
%                    .tLabel
```

Now, you can write a script that calls the simulation function in a loop. The possibilities are endless: you can test different targets, vary the initial conditions for a Monte Carlo simulation, or apply different disturbance torques. You can perform statistical analysis on your results, or identify and plot individual runs based on some criteria. In this example, you will find the maximum control torque applied in each run.

```
%% Multiple runs of spacecraft simulation
% Perform runs of SpacecraftSimBatch in a loop with varying initial
% conditions. Find the max control torque applied for each case.
%% See also
% SpacecraftSimFunction

sim = struct;
%% Control design
% Design a PD controller
dC            = PDControl( 'struct' );
dC(1).zeta    = 1;
dC(1).wN      = 0.02;
dC(1).wD      = 5*dC(1).wN;
dC(1).tSamp   = dT;
dC(1)         = PDControl( 'initialize', dC(1) );

% Make all 3 axis controllers identical
dC(2)         = dC(1);
dC(3)         = dC(1);

sim.pd = dC;

%% Spacecraft model
% Make the spacecraft nonspherical; no disturbances
rhs       = RHSSpacecraftWithRWA;
rhs.inr      = [3 0 0;0 10 0;0 0 5]; % kg-m^2
rhs.torque   = [0;0;0]; % Disturbance torque
sim.rhs = rhs;

%% Initialization
% Initialize duration, delta time states and inertia
sim.tEnd      = 600;
sim.dT        = 1;
sim.controlIsOn = true;

% Spacecraft state
qECIToBody  = [1;0;0;0];
omega       = [0;0;0]; % rad/sec
omegaRWA    = [0;0;0]; % rad/sec
x0 = [qECIToBody;omega;omegaRWA];

% Target quaternions
qTarget       = QUnit([1;0.004;0.0;0]); % Normalize
```

```
%% Simulation loop
clear d;
for k = 1:10;
  % change something in your initial conditions and simulate
  x0(5)    = 1e-3*k;
  thisD   = SpacecraftSimFunction( x0, qTarget, sim );

  % save the run results as a mat-file
  thisDir = fileparts(mfilename('fullpath'));
  fileName = fullfile(thisDir,'Output',sprintf('Run%d',k));
  save(fileName,'-struct','thisD');

  % store the run output
  d(k) = thisD;
end

%% Perform statistical analysis on results
% ... as you wish
for k = 1:length(d)
  tMax(k) = max(max(d(k).dPlot(2:4,:)));
end
figure;
plot (1:length(d),tMax);
xlabel ('Run')
ylabel ('Torque_(Nm)')
title ('Maximum_Control_Torque');

% Plot a single case
kPlot = 4;
PlotSpacecraftSim( d(4) );
```

Figure 12-5 shows the maximum torque results.

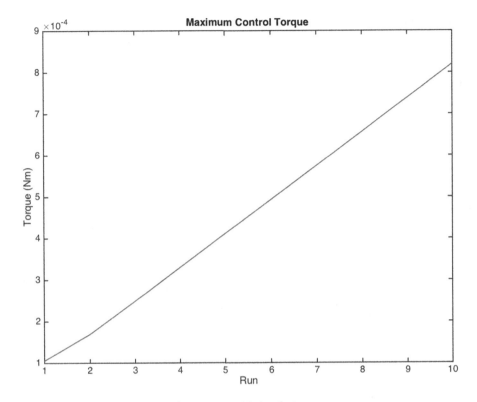

Figure 12-5. *Maximum control torque over 10 simulation runs*

An individual run's output is shown here.

```
>> d(1)
ans =

        input:   [1x1 struct]
        x0:      [10x1 double]
        qTarget: [4x1 double]
        xPlot:   [10x600 double]
        dPlot:   [7x600 double]
        tPlot:   [1x600 double]
        tLabel:  'Time (min)'
        yLabel:  {1x10 cell}
        dLabel:  {1x7 cell}
```

As another interesting example, you can give the spacecraft a higher initial rate and see how the controller responds. From the command line, change the initial rate around the *x* axis to 0.2 rad/sec and call the simulation function with no outputs, so that it generates the full suite of plots. You see that the response takes a long time, over 20 minutes, but the rate does eventually damp out.

The full simulation function is shown next. The built-in demo performs an open-loop simulation of the default spacecraft model with no control, as with the momentum conservation test performed in the previous recipe (Figure 12-2).

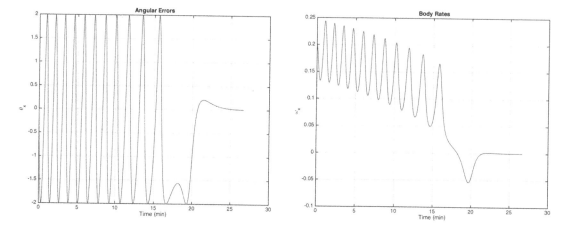

Figure 12-6. *Control response to a large rate in x. The rate does damp out, eventually!*

```
function d = SpacecraftSimFunction( x0, qTarget, input )

%% Handle inputs
if nargin == 0
    % perform an open loop simulation
    input = struct;
    input.rhs = RHSSpacecraftWithRWA;
    input.pd = [];
    input.dT = 1; % sec
    input.tEnd = 600; % sec
    input.controlIsOn = false;
    x0 = [1;0;0;0;1e-3*randn(6,1)];
    SpacecraftSimFunction( x0, [], input );
    return;
end

if isempty(x0)
    qECIToBody = [1;0;0;0];
    omega = [0;0;0]; % rad/sec
    omegaRWA = [0;0;0]; % rad/sec
    x0 = [qECIToBody;omega;omegaRWA];
end

if isempty(qTarget)
    qTarget = x0(1:4);
end

%% Simulation
% State vector
x = x0;
nWheels = length(x0)-7;
```

290

```matlab
% Plotting and number of steps
n = ceil(input.tEnd/input.dT);
xP = zeros(length(x),n);
dP = zeros(7,n);

% Find the initial angular momentum
d = input.rhs;
[~,hECIO] = RHSSpacecraftWithRWA(0,x,d);

% Run the simulation
for k = 1:n
  % Control
  u = [0;0;0];
  angleError = [0;0;0];
  if( input.controlIsOn )
     % Find the angle error
     angleError = ErrorFromQuaternion( x(1:4), qTarget );
     % Update the controllers individually
     for j = 1:nWheels
       [u(j), input.pd(j)] = PDControl('update',angleError(j),input.pd(j));
     end
  end

  % Wheel torque
  d.torqueRWA = d.inr*u;

  % Get the delta angular momentum
  [~,hECI] = RHSSpacecraftWithRWA(0,x,d);
  dHECI = hECI - hECIO;
  hMag = sqrt(dHECI'*dHECI);

  % Plot storage
  xP(:,k) = x;
  dP(:,k) = [hMag;d.torqueRWA;angleError];

  % Right hand side
  x = RungeKutta(@RHSSpacecraftWithRWA,0,x,input.dT,d);
end

[t,tL] = TimeLabl((0:(n-1))*input.dT);

%% Store data
% Record initial conditions
d = struct;
d.input = input;
d.x0 = x0;
d.qTarget = qTarget;
d.xPlot = xP;
d.dPlot = dP;
d.tPlot = t;
d.tLabel = tL;
```

291

```
y = cell(1,nWheels);
for k = 1:nWheels
    y{k} = sprintf('\\omega_%d',k);
end
d.yLabel = {'q_s','q_x','q_y','q_z','\omega_x','\omega_y','\omega_z',y{:}};
d.dLabel = {'\Delta_H_(Nms)','T_x_(Nm)', 'T_y_(Nm)', 'T_z_(Nm)', ...
    '\theta_x_(rad)', '\theta_y_(rad)', '\theta_z_(rad)'};

if nargout == 0
    PlotSpacecraftSim( d );
end
```

The plotting code is put into a separate function that accepts the output data structure. Create and save the plot labels in the simulation function. This allows you to replot any saved output. Add a statement to check for non-zero angle errors before creating the control and angle errors plots, since they are not needed for open-loop simulations.

Tip   Use the fields in your structure for plotting without renaming the variables locally, so you can copy/paste individual plots to the command line after doing a run of your simulation.

```
%% PlotSpacecraftSim Plot the spacecraft simulation output
%% Form
% PlotSpacecraftSim( d )
%% Inputs
% d (.) Simulation data structure

%% Copyright
% Copyright (c) 2015 Princeton Satellite Systems, Inc.
% All rights reserved.

function PlotSpacecraftSim( d )

t = d.tPlot;

yL = d.yLabel(1:4);
PlotSet( d.tPlot, d.xPlot(1:4,:), 'x_label', d.tLabel, 'y_label', yL,...
    'plot_title', 'Attitude', 'figure_title', 'Attitude');

yL = d.yLabel(5:7);
PlotSet(d.tPlot, d.xPlot(5:7,:), 'x_label', d.tLabel, 'y_label', yL,...
    'plot_title', 'Body_Rates', 'figure_title', 'Body_Rates');

yL = d.yLabel(8:end);
PlotSet( t, d.xPlot(8:end,:), 'x_label', d.tLabel, 'y_label', yL,...
    'plot_title', 'RWA_Rates', 'figure_title', 'RWA_Rates');
```

```
yL = d.dLabel(1);
PlotSet( d.tPlot, d.dPlot(1,:), 'x_label', d.tLabel, 'y_label', yL,...
  'plot_title', 'Inertial_Angular_Momentum',...
  'figure_title', 'Inertial_Angular_Momentum');

if any(d.dPlot(5:end,:)~=0)
  yL = d.dLabel(2:4);
  PlotSet( d.tPlot, d.dPlot(2:4,:), 'x_label', d.tLabel, 'y_label', yL,...
    'plot_title', 'Control_Torque', 'figure_title', 'Control_Torque');
  yL = d.dLabel(5:end);
  PlotSet( d.tPlot, d.dPlot(5:end,:), 'x_label', d.tLabel, 'y_label', yL,...
    'plot_title', 'Angular_Errors', 'figure_title', 'Angular_Errors');
end
```

An interesting exercise for you would be to replace the fixed disturbance input, d.torque, with a function handle that calls a disturbance function. This forms the basis of spacecraft simulation in our Spacecraft Control Toolbox, where the disturbances are calculated from the spacecraft geometry and space environment as it rotates and moves along its orbit.

Summary

This chapter demonstrated how to write the dynamics and implement a simple control law for a spacecraft with reaction wheels. Our control system is only valid for small angle changes and will not work well if the angular rates on the spacecraft get large. In addition, we do not consider the torque or momentum limits on the reaction wheels. You also learned about quaternions and how to implement kinematics of rigid body with quaternions. We showed you how to get angle errors from two quaternions. Table 12-1 lists the code developed in this chapter.

Table 12-1. *Chapter Code Listing*

File	Description
RHSSpacecraftWithRWA	RHS for spacecraft with reaction wheels.
ErrorFromQuaternion	Spacecraft simulation script.
SpacecraftSim	Spacecraft simulation script.
SpacecraftSimBatch	Spacecraft simulation function.
BatchSimRuns	Multiple runs of the spacecraft simulation.
PlotSpacecraftSim	Plot the simulation results.
QTForm	Transform a vector opposite the direction of the quaternion.
QUnit	Normalize a quaternion.

Index

A

Aircraft
    3D trajectory, 263
    control system, 261
    dynamic model, 249
    numerical search, 254
    simulation, 267
Animation
    GUIDE editor
        blank GUI, 107
        BoxAnimationGUI, 109
        button, 108
        CloseRequestFcn, 110
        edit box, 108–109
        MATLAB, 109
        questdlg, 113
        text label, 108
    line objects, 98
    MATLAB app, 114
    store and playback, 97
    TimeDisplayGUI, 104
    uicontrol button, 102

B

Brushless DC motor (BLDC), 177

C

Chemical mixing process
    disturbances, 239
    modelling, 228
    PHProcessSim
        closed-loop transients, 242
        numerical optimization
          routine, 245
        open-loop response, 242
        profiler, 246
        user inputs, 239
    pH sensor, 231
    proportional integral controller, 237

D

Double integrator
    digital control, 148
    fixed-step numerical integration
        mathematical modeling, 140
        MATLAB code, 142
    multiple subplots, 154
    proportional-derivative controller
        CToDZOH function, 148
        default values, 148
        differential equation, 143
        engineering function, 147
        initialize mode, 148
        pole-placement, 144
        undamped natural frequency, 144
        update function, 148
    time units, 153
    writing equations, 139
Dynamic field names, 9
Dynamic graphics functions
    animation
        execution times, 96
        keyboard command, 95
        patch objects, 93
        pause commands, 95

E

Electric motors
    field-oriented control, 181
    pulse-width modulation, 186
    simulation, 196
        data structures, 197
        PI torque control, 200
        pulse width, 201
    three-phase permanent magnet
        synchronous motor, 177
        space vector modulation, 186
        SVPWM, 189
        SwitchToVoltage function, 195
        total pulse pattern, 188

© Stephanie Thomas and Michael Paluszek 2015
S. Thomas and M. Paluszek, *MATLAB Recipes*, DOI 10.1007/978-1-4842-0559-4

Printed in the United States
By Bookmasters